D0071102

MUSICAL PERCEPT[

DATE DUE

MAR 2 7 2003	JAN 0 7 2013	
MAR 2 9 2006		
NOV 27 2012		
JAN 08		

W/D

GAYLORD PRINTED IN U.S.A.

MMB

MMB MUSIC, INC.

CONTEMPORARY ARTS BUILDING
3526 WASHINGTON AVENUE
SAINT LOUIS, MISSOURI 63103-1019 USA
314 531-9635; 800 543-3771 (USA/Canada); Fax 314 531-8384
http://www.mmbmusic.com

MUSICAL
PERCEPTIONS

---

edited by

RITA AIELLO

with

JOHN A. SLOBODA

New York   *Oxford*

OXFORD UNIVERSITY PRESS

1994

Oxford University Press

Oxford   New York   Toronto
Delhi   Bombay   Calcutta   Madras   Karachi
Kuala Lumpur   Singapore   Hong Kong   Tokyo
Nairobi   Dar es Salaam   Cape Town
Melbourne   Auckland   Madrid

and associated companies in
Berlin   Ibadan

Copyright © 1994 by Oxford University Press, Inc.

Published by Oxford University Press, Inc.,
198 Madison Avenue, New York, New York 10016

Oxford is a registered trademark of Oxford University Press

All rights reserved. No part of this publication may be reproduced,
stored in a retrieval system, or transmitted, in any form or by any means,
electronic, mechanical, photocopying, recording, or otherwise,
without the prior permission of Oxford University Press.

Library of Congress Cataloging-in-Publication Data
Musical perceptions / edited by Rita Aiello with John A. Sloboda.
p. cm.   Includes bibilographical references and index.
ISBN 0-19-506475-5
ISBN 0-19-506476-3 (pbk.)
1. Music—Psychology.
2. Auditory perception.
3. Music—Philosophy and aesthetics.
I. Aiello, Rita.
II. Sloboda, John A.
ML3830.M983   1994   781'.11—dc20
93-28888

5   7   9   8   6   4

Printed in the United States of America
on acid-free paper

To my daughter Daniela Caterina

PREFACE

Musical Perceptions is an introduction to the perception and cognition of music for readers in music and psychology. It presents a spectrum of the current research, and describes some of the many developments that have occurred in the perception and cognition of music over the last decades. This book includes twelve contributed chapters that discuss musical meaning, philosophical perspectives of music, comparisons beween music and language, the importance of music theory in perceptual research, research in musical development and music performance, the perception of melodies, tonality and rhythm, and the application of neural network models in music perception. The contributors' chapters give a detailed description of their research. I have prefaced each chapter with an introduction to provide a general background in which to place the significance of the contributor's research (John Sloboda contributed the introduction to his own chapter).

Because *Musical Perceptions* aims to foster a closer interaction between the artistic, the pedagogical, and the scientific aspects of music perception research, it includes contributions from both musicians and psychologists. Undoubtedly, the question "How do we perceive music?" is the main theme of this book. But there is also a second question, more difficult to answer, that underlines its intent: "How does music perception give rise to musical meaning?" Although the material discussed here offers only a small glimpse into the current vast literature on music perception and cognition, the reader will find the many references useful for more in-depth study.

I have tested the chapters that follow in my classes because they reflect the topics I teach in my perception of music courses at the Juilliard School, the Manhattan School of Music, and in the department of psychology at New York University. I am very grateful to my students for their comments and suggestions. In addition to being used in psychology of music courses (be they offered in music or in psychology departments), this volume could also be used in courses in the philosophy and the aesthetics of music, music education, and music theory.

The book opens with three chapters that address the perception of music from a philosophical perspective. Chapter 1 by Leonard Meyer, reprinted from *Emotion and Meaning in Music*, is of historical significance, and Meyer's ideas are still at the heart of the psychology of music today. Meyer explains how a listener may listen to music from several philosophical positions. Furthermore, Meyer shows how the melodic, rhythmic, and harmonic organization of music gives rise to musical meaning.

In Chapter 2, I describe comparisons between the perception of music and the perception of language at the phonetic, syntactic, and semantic levels. My intent is not to underline the obvious similarities between the two, but to use the comparisons to point out what is intrinsically unique to music. Nicholas Cook's contribution (Chapter 3) offers a music theorist's view on music perception research, and his criticisms are thought-provoking. Cook argues that many studies in music perception are experiments in ear training strategies that do not reflect what music listeners actually do when they listen to music.

Chapters 4, 5, and 6 focus on musical development and music performance. Lyle Davidson (Chapter 4) traces the development of songsinging from the young child to the adult, and discusses the perceptual changes in tonal relationship that a student in music school undergoes. Davidson proposes that we do not yet have a comprehensive view of musical development because we fail to learn from the uncoordinated data we already have at hand. For Jeanne Bamberger (Chapter 5), listening to music in a new way enriches one's understanding of music. She elegantly describes how music students acquire new ways of listening to a piece when sharing with each other their descriptions of the piece.

In Chapter 6, John Sloboda brings new insights to research on music performance. Specifically, Sloboda examines recent studies that evaluate the ability to play notated solo compositions expressively, and the musical intentions of the performers. In addition, Sloboda discusses musical talent, practicing, and other factors that may be considered biographical precursors of musical excellence.

Aspects of the perception of melody and tonality are addressed in Chapters 7, 8, and 9. Jay Dowling (Chapter 7) defines the features that make a melody perceptually relevant. Drawing from his extensive research in this area, Dowling explains the perceptual strategies that we engage in when listening to tonal, atonal, and transposed melodies. Butler and Brown (Chapter 9) propose that the perception of tonality is influenced by the temporal organization of the pitches and not by the pitches themselves. They show experimentally that the frequency with which certain musical intervals are heard within a piece is what conveys information about the tonality of that piece.

In Chapter 9, Jamshed Bharucha demonstrates the relationship between tonality and expectation. Specifically, he explains the cognitive processes that underlie tonal expectation and their acquisition, and differentiates between the musical expectations that are related to the general style of a piece and those that are related to an actual composition. Moreover, Bharucha illustrates how musical expectations may be investigated with the application of neural networks.

Both Chapters 10 and 11 address the perception of rhythm and timing, but from different perspectives. While Sternberg and Knoll (Chapter 10) report on the ability of musicians to perceive, produce, and imitate microrhythmic patterns in the context of a laboratory setting, Shaffer and Todd (Chapter 11) describe the ways in which pianists reproduce rhythms while playing actual performances at the piano. In chapter 12, I address the importance of developing more studies in the perception of music that use as stimuli compositions from the musical repertoire rather than aesthetically impoverished laboratory sounds. Ultimately, research in the perception of music should help us understand the meaning and the aesthetics of music.

R. A.

New York
April 1993

ACKNOWLEDGMENTS

My students are a very important part of my life. It is with them that I share my love for music and my interest in understanding how music is perceived. Their questions and comments have given me insights in the meanings of music, and have presented me with new perspectives. I thank all of them. It was a milestone for me to read the transcript of Leonard Bernstein's lectures *The Unanswered Question: Six Talks at Harvard*. As a musician and as a teacher, I thank the late maestro for what I learned.

Many colleagues have helped me with various aspects of this book. I acknowledge with deep gratitude the late Louis Gerstman, professor of psychology at the City College and the Graduate Center of the City University of New York, and a musician at heart. His enthusiasm and expert advice helped me envision how my lectures on the perception of music could become the book now at hand. In addition, I thank John Lewers, a dear friend, for the exchanges of ideas we have had since our student days; Edgar (Ted) Coons for his guidance and friendship; and Thomas Bever for introducing me to the literature in the perception of music. My thanks also to John Sloboda, David Butler, Leonard Meyer, David Burrows, Kendall Durell Briggs, Jerry Kerlin, Michael Palij, Valerie Bernhardt, Joan Bossert, and Paul Schlotthauer. Jane Gottlieb, the chief librarian at the Juilliard School, was very gracious in answering all my questions and in discussing many references at length.

Above all, I am grateful to my mother and to my husband, John G. J. Ritter, for their support.

CONTENTS

CONTRIBUTORS

RITA AIELLO
The Juilliard School and
Department of Psychology
New York University and
The Manhattan School of Music
New York, New York

JEANNE BAMBERGER
Department of Music
Massachusetts Institute of Technology
Cambridge, Massachusetts

JAMSHED J. BHARUCHA
Department of Psychology
Dartmouth College
Hanover, New Hampshire

HELEN BROWN
Division of Music
Purdue University
West Lafayette, Indiana

DAVID BUTLER
School of Music
The Ohio State University
Columbus, Ohio

NICHOLAS COOK
Department of Music
University of Southampton
Highfield, Southampton
England

LYLE DAVIDSON
Project Zero
Harvard University
Cambridge, Massachusetts and
The New England Conservatory
Boston, Massachusetts

W. JAY DOWLING
Program in Applied Cognition
and Neuroscience
University of Texas, Dallas
Richardson, Texas

RONALD L. KNOLL
Bell Laboratories
Murray Hill, New Jersey

LEONARD B. MEYER
Department of Music
University of Pennsylvania
Philadelphia, Pennsylvania

L. H. SHAFFER
Department of Psychology
University of Exeter
Exeter, England

JOHN A. SLOBODA
Department of Psychology
University of Keele
Keele, Staffordshire
England

SAUL STERNBERG
Department of Psychology
University of Pennsylvania
Philadelphia, Pennsylvania

NEIL P. McANGUS TODD
Department of Psychology
University of Exeter
Exeter, England and
Department of Music
City University
London, England

Philosophical Perspectives

1

Emotion and Meaning
in Music

LEONARD B. MEYER

Introduction

Leonard B. Meyer, one of the most important figures in the field of music aesthetics, has been pivotal in the growth of the psychology of music for almost four decades. The historical importance of his first book, *Emotion and Meaning in Music,* 1956, is evident in the frequency with which it is quoted, and in the impact that the theories it set forth have had on the psychology of music as a whole. *Emotion and Meaning in Music* focuses primarily on the moment-to-moment processes that take place in listening to total compositions and argues that the central meaning of music is to be found in the structural interplay of its elements and forms, rather than in associations to nonmusical events. Specifically, Meyer considers what kind of patterning underlies music, what implications are suggested by its melodic, rhythmic, and harmonic organization, and how these implications are realized or not realized in the ongoing sequence of events.

Meyer's writings address musical meaning from a psychological perspective. His theories are grounded in Gestalt psychology and information theory. The laws of Gestalt psychology (e.g., good continuation, similarity, common fate) relate to patterns in any modality, be it visual, auditory, or tactile, and provide explanations for the fact that some patterns seem particularly "good" or "complete" (the reader may wish to consult Rudolph Arnheim's *Art and Visual Perception,* 1969, for an in-depth discussion of Gestalt psychology; see also the introduction to Dowling's chapter 7 in this volume). The principles of information theory offer parameters for understanding how much information

Reprinted from L. B. Meyer, *Emotion and Meaning in Music.* Chicago: University of Chicago Press, 1956. Used by permission.

the listener can possibly derive when listening to music. (The works of Moles, 1966, Kraehenbuehl and Coons, 1959, Coons and Kraehenbuehl, 1958, and Youngblood, 1958, provide a background in information theory and music). In this vein, a style is a system of probabilities; the music, as it unfolds, sets the probabilities for what will happen next. The listener who is aware of the style may successfully predict what will follow, thus deriving a satisfactory meaning from the music. Deviations from the musical norms violate the listener's expectations and create patterns of tension and resolution.

Meyer's theories of meaning in music (1956) *preceded* a great deal of psychological research in meaning and emotional responses (see Gaver & Mandler, 1987; Mandler, 1984; Schachter & Singer, 1962). Psychologists (Mandler, 1984; Schachter & Singer, 1962) have shown that a subject's knowledge of a stimulus is of paramount importance in determining his or her emotional reactions to that stimulus. Meyer's theories of expectation and resolution in music have been found to be empirically valid (Schmuckler, 1989).

The first chapter of *Emotion and Meaning in Music* addresses music from a philosophical point of view. Music can have an intrinsic "absolute" meaning or can have an extrinsic "referential" meaning. Furthermore, the meaning of music may be interpreted from the viewpoint of the "formalist" (i.e., the listener who values the abstract patterning of music in and of itself) or from the viewpoint of the "expressionist" (i.e., the listener who views music as a means to express emotions). Meyer claims that a philosophy of music may legitimately endorse either of the opposing positions on each dimension. For example, an absolute expressionist (Meyer himself is an absolute expressionist) is a listener who believes that musical meaning is intrinsic in the music, and who derives an emotional meaning from understanding the interplay of the musical relationships.

We reprint the first chapter of *Emotion and Meaning in Music* not only because of its historical importance but to bring into focus the importance of having a philosophical perspective in addressing questions about the perception of music and to emphasize the historical importance of the book. Like Meyer, we believe that the philosophical positions of listeners may influence their perception of music. Research in the psychology of music asks what people perceive, but seldom have the subjects' philosophical views been taken into account. Studying what subjects report when hearing music should go hand in hand with asking questions about their philosophical perspective of music.

Meyer's latest book, *Style and Music: Theory, History, and Ideology,* 1989, further develops his belief that a musical style is a result of human choices that develop because of psychological, cultural, and musical constraints.

REFERENCES

Arnheim, R. (1969). *Art and visual perception.* Berkeley: University of California Press.

Coons, E., & Kraehenbuehl, D. (1958). Information as a measure of structure in music. *Journal of Music Theory, 2,* 127–61.

Gaver, W. W., & Mandler, G. (1987). Play it again, Sam: On liking music. *Cognition and Emotion, 1*(3), 259–82.

Kraehenbuehl, D., & Coons, E. (1959). Information as a measure of experience in music. *Journal of Aesthetics and Art Criticism, XVII,* 510–22.

Mandler, G. (1984). *Mind and body: Psychology of emotion and stress.* New York: Norton.

Meyer, L. B. (1956). *Emotion and meaning in music.* University of Chicago Press.

Meyer, L. B. (1957). Meaning in music and information theory. *Journal of Aesthetics and Art Criticism, XV*(4), 412–24.

Meyer, L. B. (1961). On rehearing music. *Journal of the American Musicological Society, XIV*(2), 257–73.

Meyer, L. B. (1967). *Music, the arts and ideas: Patterns and predictions in twentieth-century music.* Chicago: University of Chicago Press.

Meyer, L. B. (1973). *Explaining music: Essays and explorations.* Chicago: University of Chicago Press.

Meyer, L. B. (1974). Concerning the sciences, the arts—AND the humanities. *Critical Inquiry, 1*(1), 163–217.

Meyer, L. B. (1975). Grammatical simplicity and relational richness: The trio of Mozart's G minor symphony. *Critical Inquiry, 2*(4), 693–761.

Meyer, L. B. (1980). Exploiting limits: Creation, archetypes, and style change. *Daedalus, 109*(2), 177–205.

Meyer, L. B. (1982). Process and morphology in the music of Mozart. *The Journal of Musicology, 1*(1), 317–41.

Meyer, L. B. (1989). *Style and music: Theory, history, and ideology.* Philadelphia: University of Pennsylvania Press.

Moles, A. (1966). *Information theory and esthetic perception.* Translated by J. E. Cohen. Urbana: University of Illinois Press.

Schachter, S., & Singer, J. (1962). Cognitive, social and physiological determinants of emotional state. *Psychological Review, 69,* 379–99.

Schmuckler, M. A. (1989). Expectation in music: Investigation of melodic and harmonic processes. *Music Perception, 7*(2), 109–50.

Youngblood, J. E. (1958). Style as information. *Journal of Music Theory, 2,* 24–35.

Past Positions as to the Nature of Musical Experience

Composers and performers of all cultures, theorists of diverse schools and styles, aestheticians, and critics of many different persuasions are all agreed that music has meaning and that this meaning is somehow communicated to both partici- pants and listeners. This much, as least, we may take for granted. But what constitutes musical meaning and by what processes it is communicated has been the subject of numerous and often heated debates.

The first main difference of opinion exists between those who insist that musical meaning lies exclusively within the context of the work itself, in the perception of the relationship set forth within the musical work of art, and those who contend that, in addition to these abstract, intellectual meanings, music also communicates meanings which in some way refer to the extramusical world of concepts, actions, emotional states, and character. Let us call the former group the "absolutists" and the latter group the "referentialists."

In spite of the persistent wrangling of these two groups, it seems obvious that absolute meanings and referential meanings are not mutually exclusive: that they can and do coexist in one and the same piece of music, just as they do in a poem or a painting. In short, the arguments are the result of a tendency toward philosophical monism rather than a product of any logical opposition between types of meaning.

Because this study deals primarily with those meanings which lie within the closed context of the musical work itself, it is necessary to emphasize that the prominence given to this aspect of musical meaning does not imply that other kinds of meaning do not exist or are not important.

On the contrary, the musical theory and practice of many different cultures in many different epochs indicates that music can and does convey referential meaning. The musical cosmologies of the Orient in which tempi, pitches, rhythms, and modes are linked to and express concepts, emotions, and moral qualities; the musical symbolisms depicting actions, character, and emotion, utilized by many Western composers since the Middle Ages; and evidence fur- nished by testing listeners who have learned to understand Western music—all these indicate that music can communicate referential meanings.

Some of those who have doubted that referential meanings are "real" have based their skepticism upon the fact that such meanings are not "natural" and universal. Of course, such meanings depend upon learning. But so, too, do purely musical meanings—a fact that will become very clear in the course of this study.

Others have found the fact that referential meanings are not specific in their denotation a great difficulty in granting status to such meanings. Yet such preci- sion is not a characteristic of the nonmusical arts either. The many levels of connotation play a vital role in our understanding of the meanings communicated by the literary and plastic arts.

Let us now make a second point clear, namely, that the distinction just drawn between absolute and referential meanings is not the same as the distinction between the aesthetic positions which are commonly called "formalist" and "expressionist." Both the formalist and the expressionist may be absolutists; that is, both may see the meaning of music as being essentially intramusical (non-referential); but the formalist would contend that the meaning of music lies in the perception and understanding of the musical relationships set forth in the work of art and that meaning in music is primarily intellectual, while the expressionist would argue that these same relationships are in some sense capable of exciting feelings and emotions in the listener.

This point is important because the expressionist position has often been confused with that of the referentialist. For although almost all referentialists are expressionists, believing that music communicates emotional meanings, not all expressionists are referentialists. Thus when formalists, such as Hanslick or Stravinsky, reacting against what they feel to be an overemphasis upon referential meaning, have denied the possibility or relevance of any emotional response to music, they have adopted an untenable position partly because they have confused expressionism and referentialism.

One might, in other words, divide expressionists into two groups: absolute expressionists and referential expressionists. The former group believe that expressive emotional meanings arise in response to music and that these exist without reference to the extramusical world of concepts, actions, and human emotional states, while the latter group would assert that emotional expression is dependent upon an understanding of the referential content of music.

The Present Position and Criticism of Past Assumptions

The present study is concerned with an examination and analysis of those aspects of meaning which result from the understanding of and response to relationships inherent in the musical progress rather than with any relationships between the musical organization and the extramusical world of concepts, actions, characters, and situations. The position adopted admits both formalist and absolute expressionist viewpoints. For though the referential expressionists and the formalists are concerned with genuinely different aspects of musical experience, the absolute expressionists and the formalists are actually considering the same musical processes and similar human experiences from different, but not incompatible, viewpoints.

Broadly speaking, then, the present investigation seeks to present an analysis of musical meaning and experience in which both the expressionist and the formalist positions will be accounted for and in which the relationship between them will become clear.

Past accounts given by the proponents of each of these positions have suffered from certain important weaknesses. The chief difficulty of those who have adopted the absolutist expressionist position is that they have been unable to account for the processes by which perceived sound patterns become experienced as feelings and emotions. In fact, strange as it may seem, they have generally avoided any discussion of emotional responses whatsoever. These shortcomings have led to a general lack of precision both in their account of musical experience and in their discussions of musical perception.

But, at least, the expressionists have recognized the existence of problems in their position. The formalists, on the other hand, have either found no problems to recognize or have simply turned the other way, seeking to divert attention from their difficulties by attacking referentialism whenever possible. Yet the formalists are faced with a problem very similar to that confronting the expressionists: namely, the difficulty and necessity of explaining the manner in which an abstract, nonreferential succession of tones becomes meaningful. In failing to explain in what sense such musical patterns can be said to have meaning, they have also found themselves unable to show the relation of musical meaning to meaning in general.

Finally, this failure to explain the processes by which feelings are aroused and meanings communicated has prevented both groups from seeing that their positions should make them allies rather than opponents. For the same musical processes and similar psychological behavior give rise to both types of meaning; and both must be analyzed if the variety made possible by this aspect of musical experience is to be understood.

Readers familiar with past studies in the aesthetics and psychology of music will perhaps note that much of the earlier work in these fields is not discussed in this study and that many traditional problems are ignored. This neglect stems from the conviction that the assumptions and orientation of this literature have proved sterile and are today untenable. Since this literature has been explicitly and cogently criticized by such writers as Cazden,[1] Farnsworth,[2] and Langer,[3] only a brief comment on these earlier assumptions seems necessary here, in the hope that the position of this book will thereby be clarified.

The psychology of music has, since its beginnings, been plagued by three interrelated errors: hedonism, atomism, and universalism. Hedonism is the confusion of aesthetic experience with the sensuously pleasing. As Susanne Langer writes:

> Helmholtz, Wundt, Stumpf, and other psychologists . . . based their inquiries on the assumption that music was a form of *pleasurable sensation*. . . . This gave rise to an aesthetic based on liking and disliking, a hunt for a sensationist definition of beauty. . . . But beyond a description of tested pleasure-displeasure reactions to simple sounds or elementary sound complexes . . . this approach has not taken us. . . .[4]

The attempt to explain and understand music as a succession of separable, discrete sounds and sound complexes is the error of atomism. Even the meager achievement which Mrs. Langer allows to studies of this kind must be still further depreciated. For the tested pleasure-displeasure reactions are not what most of the psychologists tacitly assumed them to be: they are not universals (good for all times and all places) but products of learning and experience.

This is the third error, the error of universalism: the belief that the responses obtained by experiment or otherwise are universal, natural, and necessary. This universalist approach is also related to the time-honored search for a physical, quasi-acoustical explanation of musical experience—the attempt, that is, to account for musical communication in terms of vibrations, ratios of intervals, and the like.

These same errors have also plagued music theory. Attempts to explain the effect of the minor mode of Western music, to cite but one example, in terms of consonance and dissonance or in terms of the harmonic series have resulted in uncontrolled speculations and untenable theories. Even those not thus haunted by the ghost of Pythagoras have contributed little to our understanding of musical meaning and its communication. For, on the whole, music theorists have concerned themselves with the grammar and syntax of music rather than with its meaning or the affective experiences to which it gives rise.

Today we are, I think, able to take a somewhat more enlightened view of these matters. The easy access which almost all individuals have to great music makes it quite apparent that a Beethoven symphony is not a kind of musical banana split, a matter of purely sensuous enjoyment. The work of the Gestalt psychologists has shown beyond a doubt that understanding is not a matter of perceiving single stimuli, or simple sound combinations in isolation, but is rather a matter of grouping stimuli into patterns and relating these patterns to one another. And finally, the studies of comparative musicologists, bringing to our attention the music of other cultures, have made us increasingly aware that the particular organization developed in Western music is not universal, natural, or God-given.

Evidence as to the Nature and Existence
of the Emotional Response to Music

Any discussion of the emotional response to music is faced at the very outset with the fact that very little is known about this response and its relation to the stimulus. Evidence that it exists at all is based largely upon the introspective reports of listeners and the testimony of composers, performers, and critics. Other evidence of the existence of emotional responses to music is based upon the behavior of performers and audiences and upon the physiological changes that accompany musical perception. Although the volume and intercultural character of this evidence compel us to believe that an emotional response to music does take place, it tells us almost nothing about the nature of the response or about the causal connection between the musical stimulus and the affective response it evokes in listeners.

Subjective Evidence

From Plato down to the most recent discussions of aesthetics and the meaning of music, philosophers and critics have, with few exceptions, affirmed their belief in the ability of music to evoke emotional responses in listeners. Most of the treatises on musical composition and performance stress the importance of the communication of feeling and emotion. Composers have demonstrated in their writings and by the expression marks used in their musical scores their faith in the affective power of music. And finally, listeners, past and present, have reported with remarkable consistency that music does arouse feelings and emotions in them.

The first difficulty with this evidence is that, taken at its face value, without benefit of a general theory of emotions as a basis for interpretation, it yields no precise knowledge of the stimulus which created the emotional response. Because music flows through time, listeners and critics have generally been unable to pinpoint the particular musical process which evoked the affective response which they describe. They have been prone, therefore, to characterize a whole passage, section, or composition. In such cases the response must have been made to those elements of the musical organization which tend to be constant, e.g., tempo, general range, dynamic level, instrumentation, and texture. What these elements characterize are those aspects of mental life which are also relatively stable and persistent, namely, moods and associations, rather than the changing and developing affective response with which this study is concerned.

Much confusion has resulted from the failure to distinguish between emotion felt (or affect) and mood. Few psychologists dealing with music have been as accurate on this point as Weld, who notes that: "The emotional experiences which our observers reported are to be characterized rather as moods than as emotions in the ordinary sense of the term. . . . The emotion is temporary and evanescent; the mood is relatively permanent and stable."[5] As a matter of fact, most of the supposed studies of emotion in music are actually concerned with mood and association.

Taken at face value the introspective data under consideration not only fail to provide accurate knowledge of the stimulus (music) but they cannot even furnish clear and unequivocal information about the responses reported. For several reasons the verbalizations of emotions, particularly those evoked by music, are usually deceptive and misleading.

Emotions are named and distinguished from one another largely in terms of the external circumstances in which the response takes place. Since, aside from the often fortuitous associations which may be aroused, music presents no external circumstances, descriptions of emotions felt while listening to music are usually apocryphal and misleading. If they are to be used at all, they must be analyzed and considered in the light of a general theory of the relation of musical stimuli to emotional responses.

Second, a clear distinction must be maintained between the emotions felt by the composer, listener, or critic—the emotional response itself—and the emotional states denoted by different aspects of the musical stimulus. The depiction of musical moods in conjunction with conventional melodic or harmonic formulas, perhaps specified by the presence of a text, can become signs which designate human emotional states. Motives of grief or joy, anger or despair, found in the works of baroque composers or the affective and moral qualities attributed to special modes or *rāgas* in Arabian or Indian music are examples of such conventional denotative signs. And it may well be that when a listener reports that he felt this or that emotion, he is describing the emotion which he believes the passage is supposed to indicate, not anything which he himself has experienced.

Finally, even where the report given is of a genuine emotional experience, it is liable to become garbled and perverted in the process of verbalization. For emotional states are much more subtle and varied than are the few crude and standardized words which we use to denote them.

In this connection it would seem that many of the introspections supplied by subjects in the studies made by Vernon Lee, C. S. Myers, Max Schoen, and others contain a large amount of what psychiatrists call "distortion." For example, when a subject in an experiment by Myers reports that while listening to a particular musical selection she had "a restful feeling throughout . . . like one of going downstream while swimming,"[6] she is obviously translating unspeakable feelings into symbolic form. The interpretation of such symbols is the task of the psychiatrist, not the music critic. To the music critic such introspections show only that some response, not necessarily a specifically musical one, was present. For it is always possible that the thoughts and reveries thus revealed are without any relation to musical experience. The musical stimuli may have functioned merely as a kind of catalytic agent, enabling the response to take place but playing no controlling part in shaping or determining the experience and figuring nowhere in the end result, except perhaps negatively.

Objective Evidence: Behavior

The responses of listeners can also be observed and studied objectively. Two general categories of observable responses can be distinguished: (a) those responses which take the form of overt changes in behavior and (b) those responses which take the form of less readily observable physiological changes. Such objective evidence, though it undoubtedly avoids the difficulties of the verbalization n of subjective feelings and emotions, presents other difficulties n) less perplexing.

In the first place, emotional responses need not result in overt, observable behavior. As Henry Aiken points out,[7] one of the special characteristics of our responses to aesthetic objects is the very fact that, due to our beliefs as to the nature of aesthetic experience, we tend to suppress overt behavior. Furthermore, as an important adjunct to this point it should be noted that emotion-felt or affect is most intense precisely in those cases where feeling does not result in or take the form of overt behavior or mental fantasy. This is clear as soon as one considers the tendency of human beings to "work off" or relieve emotional tension in physical effort and bodily behavior. In short, the absence of overt emotional behavior, particularly in response to aesthetic stimuli, is no indication as to either the presence or force of emotional responses.

However, even where overt behavior is present, its interpretation is difficult and problematical. When, on the one hand, overt behavior is the product of particularly powerful emotional tensions, it tends to be diffuse, generalized, or chaotic. Extreme conflict, for example, may result in either motionless rigidity or frenzied activity; weeping may be the product of either profound grief or extreme joy. Unless we have accurate knowledge of the stimulus situation before-hand, such behavior can tell us little or nothing as to the significance of the response or of its relation to the stimulus.

On the other hand, when emotional behavior does become differentiated it tends to be standardized—to become part of more general patterns of social behavior. Thus although the philosophical aspect of the stimulus situation, the fact that an aesthetic object is being considered, tends toward the suppression of overt behavior, the social aspect of the stimulus situation permits and at times indeed encourages certain standardized types of emotional behavior. This is apparent in the conduct of performers and audiences alike. The jazz performer and his audience, for example, have one mode of socially sanctioned emotional behavior; the concert performer and his audience have another. The difference between the two is more a matter of conventionally determined behavior patterns than it is a matter of musical differences.

Such behavior must be regarded at least in part as a means of communication rather than as a set of natural, reflex reactions. It indicates and designates not only appropriate mental sets but also the proper (i.e., socially acceptable) modes of response. Once this sort of behavior becomes habitual, and it does so very early in life, then it may be activated by the social aspects of the stimulus situation alone, without regard for the stimulus itself. In short, given no theory as to the relation of musical stimuli to affective responses, observed behavior can provide little information as to either the nature of the stimulus, the significance of the response, or the relation between them. For conduct which might to an observer appear to indicate the presence of an emotional response might in point of fact be the result of the subject's day dreams, his observation and imitation of the behavior of others, or his beliefs as to the kind of behavior appropriate and expected in the given social situation.

Objective Evidence: Physiological Responses

On the physiological level music evokes definite and impressive responses. It "has a marked effect on pulse, respiration and external blood pressure. . . . [It] delays the onset of muscular fatigue . . . [and] has a marked effect upon the psychogalvanic reflex. . . ."[8] In spite of the fact that these changes are the very ones which normally accompany emotional experience, the significance of these data is not completely clear. Two principal difficulties are involved.

To begin with, no relation can be found between the character or pattern of the musical selection evoking the response and the particular physiological changes which take place. These changes appear to be completely independent of any particular style, form, medium, or general character. The same responses will take place whether the music is fast or slow, exciting or soothing, instrumental or vocal, classical or jazz.

Because tonal stimulation is a constant factor of all musical stimuli, Mursell is led to conclude that the power of "tone as such" must be the cause of the physiological changes observed.[9]

There is, however, another constant involved in the perception of music; namely, the mental attitude of the audience. The listener brings to the act of perception definite beliefs in the affective power of music. Even before the first sound is heard, these beliefs activate dispositions to respond in an emotional way, bringing expectant ideomotor sets into play. And it seems more reasonable to suppose that the physiological changes observed are a response to the listener's mental set rather than to assume that tone as such can, in some mysterious and unexplained way, bring these changes about directly. For while the relationship between mental sets and physiological changes has been demonstrated beyond doubt, the effect of "tone as such" has not.

This does not imply that the presence of a physiological environment, which is a necessary condition for the arousal of emotion, is not a significant fact. The existence of this necessary condition increases the likelihood that emotional responses do take place—a fact which some critics have sought to deny. What this analysis indicates is that not only are these physiological adjustments pre-emotional, as Mursell would admit, but they are also premusical.

Furthermore, even the conclusions just reached about the significance of the physiological data are probably an exaggeration, if not from a psychological point of view, at least, from a logical one. For such adjustments not only accompany affective responses, but they are also concomitants of clearly nonemotional responses.

In the light of present knowledge it seems clear that though physiological adjustments are probably necessary adjuncts of affective responses they cannot be shown to be sufficient causes for such responses and have, in fact, been able to throw very little light upon the relationship between affective responses and the stimuli which produce them. The situation is concisely summarized by Rapaport:

> (a) On the basis of the material surveyed nothing can be definitely stated as to the relation to "emotion felt" of physiological processes concomitant with emotions. Proof has not been offered to show that the usually described physiological processes are *always* present when emotion is felt. (b) Nothing is known about the physiological processes *underlying* emotional experience. However, sufficient proof has been adduced that neither the James-Lange theory nor the hypothalamic theory explains the origin of "emotion felt." (c) The investigations into the physiology and the neural correlates of emotional expression are of importance; their relation to the psychic process designated as "emotion felt" is the crucial point of every theory of emotions. However, the knowledge concerning this relation is so scant that investigations into the influence of emotions on other physiological processes will have to be based rather on what is known about the psychology of emotions. [10]

There is one basic problem with all the objective data discussed: namely, that even when affective experiences result in objective adjustments, whether behavioral or physiological, what can be observed is not the emotion-felt, the affect, but only its adjuncts and concomitants, which in the case of behavior tend to become standardized and in the case of physiological changes are not specific to emotion. What we wish to consider, however, is that which is most vital and essential in emotional experience: the feeling-tone accompanying emotional experience, that is, the affect.

Here we face a dilemma. On the one hand, the response with which we are concerned is profoundly and permanently subjective and hence of necessity concealed from the scrutiny of even the most scrupulous observers; and, on the other hand, we have found that the subjective data available, taken by themselves, provide no definite and unequivocal information about the musical stimulus, the affective response, or the relation between them. This difficulty can be resolved only if the subjective data available, including the responses of the readers and the author of this study, can be examined, sifted, and studied in the light of a general hypothesis as to the nature of affective experience and the processes by which musical stimuli might arouse such experience.

Such a hypothesis is provided by the psychological theory of emotions. For although much work undoubtedly remains to be done in the field of emotional theory, there appears to be general agreement among psychologists and psychiatrists at least as to the conditions under which emotional responses arise and as to the relationship between the affective stimulus and the affective response.

The Psychological Theory of Emotions

Since the physiological changes which accompany emotional experience, whatever their importance, do not provide a basis for differentiating affective from nonaffective states, the differentia must be sought in the realm of mental activity.

However, not all mental responses are affective. We speak of dispassionate observation, calm deliberation, and cool calculation. These are nonemotional states of mind.

If we then ask what distinguishes nonemotional states from emotional ones, it is clear that the difference does not lie in the stimulus alone. The same stimulus may excite emotion in one person but not in another. Nor does the difference lie in the responding individual. The same individual may respond emotionally to a given stimulus in one situation but not in another. The difference lies in the relationship between the stimulus and the responding individual.

This relationship must first of all be such that the stimulus produces a tendency in the organism to think or act in a particular way. An object or situation which evokes no tendency, to which the organism is indifferent, can only result in a nonemotional state of mind.

But even when a tendency is aroused, emotion may not result. If, for example, a habitual smoker wants a cigarette and, reaching into his pocket, finds one, there will be no affective response. If the tendency is satisfied without delay, no emotional response will take place. If, however, the man finds no cigarette in his pocket, discovers that there are none in the house, and then remembers that the stores are closed and he cannot purchase any, he will very likely begin to respond in an emotional way. He will feel restless, excited, then irritated, and finally angry.

This brings us to the central thesis of the psychological theory of emotions. Namely: Emotion or affect is aroused when a tendency to respond is arrested or inhibited.

Supporting Theories

In 1894 John Dewey set forth what has since become known as the conflict theory of emotions.[11]

In an article entitled "The Conflict Theory of Emotions,"[12] Angier shows that this general position has been adopted, in more or less modified form, by many psychologists of widely different viewpoints. For instance, the behaviorists, who emphasize the excitement and confusion which disrupt behavior as important characteristics of emotional conduct, would seem to be describing objectively what others view as the result of inner conflict. But the difficulty with examining emotions from the point of view of behaviorism is that, as we have seen, emotion may be felt without becoming manifest as overt behavior.

MacCurdy, whose own attitude is psychoanalytical, points out that it is precisely "when instinctive reactions are stimulated that do not gain expression either in conduct, emotional expression, or fantasy, that affect is most intense. It is the prevention of the expression of instinct either in behavior or conscious thought that leads to intense affect. In other words the energy of the organism, activating an instinct process, must be blocked by repression before poignant feeling is excited."[13] MacCurdy's analysis involves three separate phases: (a) the arousal of nervous energy in connection with the instinct or tendency;[14] (b) the propensity for this energy to become manifest as behavior or conscious thought once the tendency is blocked; and (c) the manifestation of the energy as emotion-felt or affect if behavior and conscious thought are also inhibited. Of course, if the stimulation is so powerful that the total energy cannot be absorbed by either behavior or affect alone, both will result.[15]

It is obvious that a shift of emphasis has taken place in the statement of the theory of emotions. Dewey and his followers tended to stress the conflict or opposition of tendencies as being the cause of emotional response. MacCurdy and most of the more recent workers in the field believe that it is the blocking or inhibiting of a tendency which arouses affect. Actually the concept of conflict through the opposition of simultaneously aroused conflicting tendencies may be regarded as a special and more complicated case of the arrest of tendency.

This point was made in Paulhan's brilliant work, which in 1887, almost 10 years before Dewey's formulation, set forth a highly sophisticated theory of emotions. "If we ascend in the hierarchy of human needs and deal with desires of a higher order, we still find that they only give rise to affective phenomena when the tendency awakened undergoes inhibition."[16]

However, more complex phenomena are possible as the result of "the simultaneous or almost simultaneous coming into play of systems which tend toward opposite or different actions and which cannot both culminate in action at the same time; always provided that the psychical systems brought into play do not differ too widely in intensity. . . ."[17] Such a situation results, according to Paulhan, in an emotion or affect characterized by confusion and lack of clarity.

In other words, in one case a tendency is inhibited not by another opposed tendency but simply by the fact that for some reason, whether physical or mental, it cannot reach completion. This is the situation of the inveterate smoker in the example given earlier. In the other case two tendencies which cannot both reach fruition at the same time are brought into play almost simultaneously. If they are about equal in strength, each tendency will block the completion of the other. The result is not only affect, as a product of inhibition, but doubt, confusion, and uncertainty as well.

These latter concomitants of conflict are of importance because they may themselves become the basis for further tendencies. For to the human mind such states of doubt and confusion are abhorrent; and, when confronted with them, the mind attempts to resolve them into clarity and certainty, even if this means abandoning all other previously activated tendencies.

Thus confusion and lack of clarity, growing out of conflicting tendencies, may themselves become stimuli producing further tendencies—tendencies toward clarification—which may become independent of the originally conflicting tendencies. Such tendencies need not be definite in the sense that the ultimate resolution of the doubt and confusion is specified. Some resolution of the confusion may be more important than this or that particular solution, assuming that the final result is not in conflict with other aspects of the stimulus situation or other mental sets.

Furthermore, it should be noted that uncertainty and lack of clarity may be products not only of conflicting tendencies but also of a situation which itself is structurally confused and ambiguous. This is of capital importance because it indicates that a situation which is structurally weak and doubtful in organization may directly create tendencies toward clarification. Delay in such a generalized tendency toward clarification may also give rise to affect.

Although the main tenets of the psychological theory of emotions have been widely accepted, there have, needless to say, been criticisms of the theory. In the main these have come from those who have sought, as yet without success, to account for, describe, and distinguish emotions in purely physiological terms. The theory of emotions, it is objected, does not tell us what an emotion is; it does not tell us precisely what takes place in the body to make us feel.

This objection, though valid, is irrelevant for our purposes. For just as the physicist long defined magnetism in terms of the laws of its operation and was able to deal with the phenomena without knowing the nature of the magnetic states so, too, the psychologist can define emotion in terms of the laws governing its operation, without stipulating precisely what, in physiological terms, constitutes feeling—what makes affect felt.

The Differentiation of Affect

Thus far we have considered emotion as though it were a general, undifferentiated response, a feeling whose character and quality were always more or less the same. While there is a good deal of evidence for this view, it is nevertheless clear that in common speech and everyday experience we do recognize a variety of emotional states—love, fear, anger, jealousy, and the like.[18] The whole problem of whether undifferentiated feelings, affects per se, exist, of their relation to differentiated emotional experience, and of the basis for such differentiation is of importance in the present study. For while music theorists and aestheticians have found it difficult to explain how music designates particular emotions, they have found it almost impossible to account for the existence of less specific affective experience.

Were the evidence to show that each affect or type of affect had its own peculiar physiological composition, then obviously undifferentiated feeling would be out of the question. However, Woodworth's summary of the work in this field makes it clear that this is not the case.[19]

The evidence in the case of "emotional (affective) behavior" (the term which will henceforth be used to designate the overt and observable aspects of emotional conduct) is more complex. Much emotional behavior, though habitual and hence seemingly automatic and natural, is actually learned. Because this aspect of behavior serves in the main as a means of communication, it will be called "designative (denotative) behavior." To this category belong most of the postural sets, facial expressions, and motor responses accompanying emotional behavior. Though designative behavior is definitely and clearly differentiated, the differentiation is not a necessary one and indicates nothing as to the possible differentiation of the affect itself.

Other aspects of affective behavior, such as skeletal and muscular adjustments, have been said to be automatic, natural concomitants of the affective response. These will be called "emotional reactions." Supposing that such automatic reactions do exist, a fact that has been debated, it has not been definitely shown that they are differentiated as between types of affective experience.

However, even if it were demonstrated that emotional reactions were differentiated, this would not necessarily prove or even indicate that the affects which they accompany are also differentiated. For the reaction is a response made to the total emotion-provoking situation and not necessarily a product of affect itself. In other words, it may well be that such automatic behavior is called forth by the peculiar nature of the objective situation rather than by the operation of the law of affect itself. Were this the case, such a reaction would be independent of affect and might indeed take place, as does designative emotional behavior, in the absence of affect.

The suppositions that behavior reactions are essentially undifferentiated, becoming characteristic only in certain stimulus situations, and that affect itself is basically undifferentiated are given added plausibility when one considers the following:

a. The more intense emotional behavior is, and presumably therefore the more intense the affective stimulation, the less the control exerted by the ego over behavior and the greater the probability that the behavior is automatic and natural.

b. The more intense affective behavior is, the less differentiated such behavior tends to be. In general, the total inhibition of powerful tendencies produces diffuse and characterless activity. For example, extreme conflict may result in either complete immobility or in frenzied activity, while weeping may accompany deepest grief, tremendous joy, or probably any particularly intense emotion.

c. Thus the more automatic affective behavior is, the less differentiated it tends to be.

It seems reasonable then to conclude that automatic reflex reactions not only fail to provide reasons for believing that affect itself is differentiated but the evidence seems to point to just the opposite conclusion.

Finally, our own introspective experience and the reports of the experiences of others testify to the existence of undifferentiated emotions. It is affect as such which Cassirer is discussing when he writes: "Art gives us the motions of the human soul in all their depth and variety. But the form, the measure and rhythm, of these motions is not comparable to any single state of emotion. What we feel in art is not a simple or single emotional quality. It is the dynamic process of life itself."[20]

The conclusion that affect itself is undifferentiated does not mean that affective experience is a kind of disembodied generality. For the affective experience, as distinguished from affect per se, includes an awareness and cognition of a stimulus situation which always involves particular responding individuals and specific stimuli.

Not only do we become aware of and know our own emotions in terms of a particular stimulus situation but we interpret and characterize the behavior of others in these terms. "When an organism is in a situation which results in a disturbed or wrought-up condition, then the situation plus the reaction gives us the name or word which characterizes the whole as a specific emotion. The reaction itself is not sufficient to differentiate the emotion, the character of the situation is involved in this differentiation."[21]

Thus while affects and emotions are in themselves undifferentiated, affective experience is differentiated because it involves awareness and cognition of a stimulus situation which itself is necessarily differentiated. The affective states for which we have names are grouped and named because of similarities of the stimulus situation, not because the affects of different groups are per se different. Love and fear are not different affects, but they are different affective experiences.

Awareness of the nature of the stimulus situation also seems to be the real basis for the distinction which Hebb draws between "pleasant" and "unpleasant" emotions. According to the present analysis, there are no pleasant or unpleasant emotions. There are only pleasant or unpleasant emotional experiences. This is of importance in understanding the distinction made by Hebb.

According to Hebb, the difference between pleasant and unpleasant emotions lies in the fact that pleasant emotions (or, in our terminology, pleasant emotional experiences) are always resolved. They depend "on first arousing apprehension, then dispelling it."[22] But were this actually the case we could only know whether an emotion were pleasant or unpleasant after it was over. Yet, surely, we know more than this while we are experiencing affect. The pleasantness of an emotion seems to lie not so much in the fact of resolution itself as in the belief in resolution—the knowledge, whether true or false, that there will be a resolution. It is not, as Hebb seems to assert when he cites as pleasurable the "mildly frustrating or the mildly fear-provoking,"[23] the control actually exercised over a situation which distinguishes pleasant from unpleasant emotions. It is the control which is believed to exist over the situation.

The sensation of falling through space, unconditioned by any belief or knowledge as to the ultimate outcome, will, for instance, arouse highly unpleasant emotions. Yet a similar fall experienced as a parachute jump in an amusement park may, because of our belief in the presence of control and in the nature of the resolution, prove most pleasurable.

The foregoing analysis is of genuine importance in the present study because it explains and accounts for the existence and nature of the intangible, non-referential affective states experienced in response to music. For insofar as the stimulus situation, the music, is nonreferential (in the sense that it pictures, describes, or symbolizes none of the actions, persons, passions, and concepts ordinarily associated with human experience), there is no reason to expect that our emotional experience of it should be referential. The affective experience made in response to music is specific and differentiated, but it is so in terms of the musical stimulus situation rather than in terms of extramusical stimuli.[24]

In the light of this discussion it is evident that, though it is wrong to assert, as some have done, that emotions exist which are *sui generis* musical or aesthetic, it is possible to contend that there are emotional experiences which are so.[25] By the same token, however, any number of emotional experiences can be grouped together so long as their stimulus situations are in some respects similar. Musical affective experiences, for example, might be differentiated into operatic, orchestral, baroque, and so forth. But the most significant distinction would still lie in the fact that musical stimuli, and hence musical affective experiences, are nonreferential.

Emotional Designation

Although emotional behavior is frequently characterless and diffuse, often it is differentiated and intelligible. Even without knowledge of the stimulus situation, motor behavior, facial expression, tone of voice, and manner of speaking can tell us not only that an individual is responding in an emotional way but also something of the character of his feelings or, more accurately, of the character of his affective experience.

Differentiated behavior, as we have seen, is not an automatic or a necessary concomitant of affect itself or even of affective experience. The more automatic behavior is, the less likely it is to be differentiated. Differentiation involves control, and control implies purpose.

The purpose of emotionally differentiated behavior is communication. The individual responding, having an affective experience or simulating one, seeks to make others aware of his experience through a series of nonverbal behavioral signs. Because the gestures and signs which differentiate such behavior are purposeful, this mode of behavior will be called "emotional designation" or "designative behavior."[26]

Such signs not only act as cues for appropriate behavior in the social situation but are probably, at least in part, aimed at making other individuals respond in an empathetic way. As the saying goes: Misery loves company. And so do other emotional states. Not only do we dislike physical isolation, but we want to share our emotional life with others. And, indeed, such sharing does take place. For an observer, recalling a situation in his own experience similar to the one signified by the behavior of another, may respond to the remembered situation in an affective way. Though designative affective behavior may, through constant use, become habitual and automatic so that it is almost invariably called up as part of the total emotional response, it is not basically a necessary concomitant of the response but one brought into play as a result of a desire to communicate.

Designative behavior is differentiated largely by custom and tradition. It varies from culture to culture and among different groups within a single culture. This does not mean that there are no features of such behavior which are natural and widespread. In all probability there are. However, three points should be kept in mind: (1) There is no real evidence to show that there is only one single natural mode of behavior relevant to a given stimulus situation. When alternative modes of behavior are possible, cultural selection probably determines the composition of any particular pattern of affective designation. (2) Whatever natural tendencies toward a particular pattern of behavior exist may be altered or suppressed by the demands of the larger behavior patterns of the culture. (3) Even where natural behavior is retained in the pattern of emotional behavior, it inevitably becomes codified and standardized for the sake of more efficient communication.

Above all, we understand and make appropriate responses to designative behavior as a total behavior pattern, not just to some features of it, whether natural or otherwise. As a total pattern designative behavior is a cultural phenomenon, not a natural one. It is, in the final analysis, learned.

This is important as it takes most of the sting out of the criticism that music which attempts to designate emotional states depends for its effect upon the learning of conventional signs and symbols. For this fact is not peculiar to music but is characteristic of all emotional designation. If one excludes such designation as a legitimate means of musical communication, one must by the same token exclude it as a means of human communication in general.[27]

The Theory of Emotions Related to Musical Experience

An Assumption

An examination of the psychological theory of emotions was made because the evidence furnished by the introspections of musicians, aestheticians, and listeners and the objective data gathered from the observation of behavior and the study of the physiological responses to musical stimuli did not yield reliable information about the musical stimulus or the affective responses made to it. Implicit in this examination was an assumption which must now be made explicit: Though the stimulus situation may vary indefinitely, the conditions which evoke affect are general and are, therefore, applicable to music. In other words, it was assumed that the law of affect, which states that emotion is evoked when a tendency to respond is inhibited, is a general proposition relevant to human psychology in all realms of experience.

This assumption does not, however, imply or stipulate that musical affective experiences are the same as the affective experiences made in response to other stimulus situations. Musical experience differs from nonmusical or, more specifically, nonaesthetic experience in three important ways.

First, as we have seen, affective experience includes an awareness and knowledge of the stimulus situation. This being so, the affective experience of music will differ from other types of affective experience, particularly insofar as musical stimuli are nonreferential.

Second, in everyday experience the tensions created by the inhibition of tendencies often go unresolved. They are merely dissipated in the press of irrelevant events. In this sense daily experience is meaningless and accidental. In art inhibition of tendency becomes meaningful because the relationship between the tendency and its necessary resolution is made explicit and apparent. Tendencies do not simply cease to exist: they are resolved, they conclude.[28]

Third, in life the factors which keep a tendency from reaching completion may be different in kind from those which activated the tendency in the first place. The stimulus activating a tendency may, for example, be a physical or psychic need of the organism, while the inhibiting factors may simply be a series of external circumstances which keep the organism from satisfying the need. This is the situation in the case of the habitual smoker who can find no cigarette. Or the situation may be reversed; that is, a tendency activated by an external stimulus may be inhibited by the psychic processes of the organism.

Furthermore, in everyday experience the resolutions of the tensions brought into play by inhibition may be irrelevant to the tendencies themselves. Tensions arising from psychic needs may be "worked off" in sheer physical activity which is without meaningful relation to the original stimulus or to the tendency itself.

In music, on the other hand, the same stimulus, the music, activates tendencies, inhibits them, and provides meaningful and relevant resolutions.

Tendency and Expectation in Music

The assumption that the same basic psychological processes underlie all affective responses, whether the stimulus be musical or of some other kind, has been implicit in much musical theory and in the speculations of many aestheticians. But this does not in itself increase our understanding of the nature of musical experience and of the musical processes which form it. It does not explain the nature of the relationships which exist between the stimulus, the listener's perceptions and mental processes, and his responses. To do this it is necessary to demonstrate precisely how musical stimuli do, in fact, arouse and inhibit tendencies and thereby give rise to emotions.

What is meant by a tendency to respond? A "tendency" or, as MacCurdy uses the term, an "instinct" "is a pattern reaction that operates, or tends to operate, when activated, in an automatic way."[29] A pattern reaction consists of a set or series of regularly coincident mental or motor responses which, once brought into play as part of the response to a given stimulus, follow a previously ordered course, unless inhibited or blocked in some way. The order established by a pattern reaction is both temporal and structural; that is, the series involves not only the relation of the parts of the total pattern to each other but also their timing. Thus a series may be disturbed either because the succession of the parts of the pattern is upset or because the timing of the series is upset or both.

The term "tendency," as used in this study, comprises all automatic response patterns, whether natural or learned. Since habit is "a mechanism of action, physiologically ingrained, which operates spontaneously and automatically,"[30] the term "tendency" also "includes habit reactions and, inevitably, acquired concepts and meanings."[31]

The tendency to respond may be either conscious or unconscious. If the pattern reaction runs its normal course to completion, then the whole process may be completely unconscious. Countless reaction patterns, of which the responding individual is unaware, are initiated and completed each hour. The more automatic behavior becomes, the less conscious it is. The tendency to respond becomes conscious where inhibition of some sort is present, when the normal course of the reaction pattern is disturbed or its final completion is inhibited. Such conscious and self-conscious tendencies are often thought of and referred to as "expectations."

In a broader sense all tendencies, even those which never reach the level of consciousness, are expectations. For since a tendency is a kind of chain reaction in which a present stimulus leads through a series of adjustments to a more or less specified consequent, the consequent is always implied in the tendency, once the tendency has been brought into play. Thus while our conscious minds do not actively expect a consequent unless the pattern reaction is disturbed, our habits and tendencies are expectant in the sense that each seeks out or "expects" the consequents relevant and appropriate to itself. Though he may never become aware of his expectations as he reaches in his pocket for a pack of cigarettes, the behavior of the habitual smoker shows that he does expect or, perhaps more accurately, his habits expect for him.

If tendencies are pattern reactions that are expectant in the broad sense, including unconscious as well as conscious anticipations, then it is not difficult to see how music is able to evoke tendencies. For it has been generally acknowledged that music arouses expectations, some conscious and others unconscious, which may or may not be directly and immediately satisfied.

> . . . the pleasure . . . arises from the perception of the artist's play with forms and conventions which are ingrained as *habits* of perception both in the artist and his audience. Without such habits . . . there would be no awareness whatever of the artist's fulfillment of and subtle departures from established forms. . . . But the pleasure which we derive from style is not an intellectual interest in detecting similarities and differences, but an immediate aesthetic delight in perception which results from the arousal and suspension or fulfillment of expectations which are the products of many previous encounters with works of art.[32]

Expectation, Suspense, and the Unexpected

Sometimes a very specific consequent is expected. In Western music of the eighteenth century, for example, we expect a specific chord, namely, the tonic (C major), to follow this sequence of harmonies (see example). Furthermore, the consequent chord is expected to arrive at a particular time, i.e., on the first beat of the next measure.

Of course, the consequent which is actually forthcoming, though it must be possible within the style, need not be the one which was specifically expected. Nor is it necessary that the consequent arrive at the expected time. It may arrive too soon or it may be delayed. But no matter which of these forms the consequent actually takes, the crucial point to be noted is that the ultimate and particular effect of the total pattern is clearly conditioned by the specificity of the original expectation.

At other times, expectation is more general; that is, though our expectations may be definite, in the sense of being marked, they are nonspecific, in that we are not sure precisely how they will be fulfilled. The antecedent stimulus situation may be such that several consequents may be almost equally probable. For instance, after a melodic fragment has been repeated several times, we begin to expect a change and also the completion of the fragment. A change is expected because we believe that the composer is not so illogical as to repeat the figure indefinitely and because we look forward to the completion of the incomplete figure. But precisely what the change will be or how the completion will be accomplished cannot perhaps be anticipated. The introductions to many movements written in the eighteenth or nineteenth centuries create expectation in this way, e.g., the opening measures of Beethoven's Ninth Symphony or the opening measures of the "March to the Gallows" from Berlioz's *Symphonie Fantastique*.

Expectation may also result because the stimulus situation is doubtful or ambiguous. If the musical patterns are less clear than expected, if there is confusion as to the relationship between melody and accompaniment, or if our expectations are continually mistaken or inhibited, then doubt and uncertainty as to the general significance, function, and outcome of the passage will result. As we have already seen, the mind rejects and reacts against such uncomfortable states and, if they are more than momentary, looks forward to and expects a return to the certainty of regularity and clarity. This is particularly striking in the responses made to works of art where, because of a firm belief in the purposefulness and integrity of the artist, we expect that order will in the end triumph, and precision will replace ambiguity.

However, the manner in which clarification and order will be restored may not be predicted or envisaged. Expectation is not specific; the state is one of suspense. In fact, if doubt and uncertainty are strong enough, almost any resolution, within the realm of probability, which returns us to certainty will be acceptable, though no doubt some resolutions will, given the style, seem more natural than others.

The inclusion of suspense arising out of uncertainty may, at first sight, appear to be an extension and amplification of the concept of arrest and inhibition of a tendency. But when the matter is considered more carefully, it will be seen that every inhibition or delay creates uncertainty or suspense, if only briefly, because in the moment of delay we become aware of the possibility of alternative modes of continuation. The difference is one of scale and duration, not of kind. Both arouse uncertainties and anxieties as to coming events.

Suspense is essentially a product of ignorance as to the future course of events. This ignorance may arise either because the present course of events, though in a sense understandable in itself, presents several alternative and equally probable consequents or because the present course of events is itself so unusual and upsetting that, since it cannot be understood, no predictions as to the future can be made.

From the outset ignorance arouses strong mental tendencies toward clarification which are immediately affective. If ignorance persists in spite of all, then the individual is thrown into a state of doubt and uncertainty. He commences to sense his lack of control over the situation, has inability to act on the basis of the knowledge which he supposed that he possessed. In short, he begins to feel apprehensive, even fearful, though there is no object for his fear. Ignorance and its concomitant feelings of impotence breed apprehension and anxiety, even in music. But ignorance also gives rise to more sanguine feelings; for since the outcome cannot be envisaged, it may be pleasant. These feelings are themselves tendencies (the avoidance of painful apprehension and the expectation of a propitious conclusion) which become focused upon an expected resolution of the unpleasant stimulus situation.

The longer doubt and uncertainty persist, the greater the feeling of suspense will tend to be. The stimulus situation creating doubt and uncertainty must, of course, be progressively intensified if suspense is to be maintained or increased. For as we become accustomed to a given stimulus situation, even an unpleasant one, its effectiveness tends to diminish. Moreover, without a change in the stimulus situation in the direction of complication and uncertainty, those vital anticipatory feelings (that a break must come, that doubt and perplexity must give way to knowledge) which make us expect (both apprehensively and hopefully) would be lost.

The greater the buildup of suspense, of tension, the greater the emotional release upon resolution. This observation points up the fact that in aesthetic experience emotional pattern must be considered not only in terms of tension itself but also in terms of the progression from tension to release. And the experience of suspense is aesthetically valueless unless it is followed by a release which is understandable in the given context.

Musical experiences of suspense are very similar to those experienced in real life. Both in life and in music the emotions thus arising have essentially the same stimulus situation: the situation of ignorance, the awareness of the individual's impotence and inability to act where the future course of events is unknown. Because these musical experiences are so very similar to those existing in the drama and in life itself, they are often felt to be particularly powerful and effective.

Musical suspense seems to have direct analogies in experience in general; it makes us feel something of the insignificance and powerlessness of man in the face of the inscrutable workings of destiny. The low, foreboding rumble of distant thunder on an oppressive summer afternoon, its growing intensity as it approaches, the crescendo of the gradually rising wind, the ominous darkening of the sky, all give rise to an emotional experience in which expectation is fraught with powerful uncertainty—the primordial and poignant uncertainty of human existence in the face of the inexorable forces of nature. With mixed feelings of hope and apprehension in the presence of the unknown, we anxiously await the breaking of the storm, the discovery of what unrelenting fate has decreed.

Similarly in music the state of suspense involves an awareness of the powerlessness of man in the face of the unknown.

What is expected in this state of suspense may not be specified, but this does not mean that any consequent is possible. Our expectations are inevitably circumscribed by the possibilities and probabilities of the style of the composition in question. The consequent must, given the circumstances, be possible within what Aiken has called "an ordering system of beliefs and attitudes."[33]

Although the consequent in any musical sequence must, in this sense, be possible, it may nevertheless be unexpected. But the unexpected should not be confused with the surprising. For when expectation is aroused, the unexpected is always considered to be a possibility, and, though it remains the less expected of several alternatives, it is not a complete surprise. Conditions of active expectation (especially general expectation and suspense) are not the most favorable to surprise. For the listener is on guard, anticipating a new and possibly unexpected consequent. Surprise is most intense where no special expectation is active, where, because there has been no inhibition of a tendency, continuity is expected.

As soon as the unexpected, or for that matter the surprising, is experienced, the listener attempts to fit it into the general system of beliefs relevant to the style of the work. This requires a very rapid re-evaluation of either the stimulus situation itself or its cause—the events antecedent to the stimulus. Or it may require a review of the whole system of beliefs that the listener supposed appropriate and relevant to the work. If this mental synthesis does not take place immediately, three things may happen: (1) The mind may suspend judgment, so to speak, trusting that what follows will clarify the meaning of the unexpected consequent. (2) If no clarification takes place, the mind may reject the whole stimulus and irritation will set in.[34] (3) The unexpected consequent may be seen as a purposeful blunder. Whether the listener responds in the first or third manner will depend partly upon the character of the piece, its mood or designative content. The third response might well be made to music whose character was comic or satirical. Beckmesser's music in Wagner's *Die Meistersinger* would probably elicit this type of interpretive understanding.[35] In a piece whose character admitted no such purposeful blunders, the second response would probably be elicited.

Conscious and Unconscious Expectations

In the light of these observations it is clear that an expectation is not a blind, unthinking conditioned reflex. Expectation frequently involves a high order of mental activity. The fulfillment of a habit response, in art as well as in daily life, requires judgment and cognition both of the stimulus itself and of the situation in which it acts. The stimulus as a physical thing becomes a stimulus in the world of behavior only insofar as the mind of the perceiver is able to relate it, on the one hand, to the habit responses which the perceiver has developed and, on the other hand, to the particular stimulus situation. This is clear as soon as one considers that the same physical stimulus may call forth different tendencies in different stylistic contexts or in different situations within one and the same stylistic context. For example, a modal cadential progression will arouse one set of expectations in the musical style of the sixteenth century and quite another in the style of the nineteenth century. Likewise the same musical progression will evoke one set of expectations at the beginning of a piece and another at the end.

Expectation then is a product of the habit responses developed in connection with particular musical styles and of the modes of human perception, cognition, and response—the psychological laws of mental life.[36]

The mental activity involved in the perception of and response to music need not, however, be conscious. ". . . the intellectual satisfaction which the listener derives from continually following and anticipating the composer's intentions— now, to see his expectations fulfilled, and now, to see himself agreeably mistaken . . . this intellectual flux and reflux, this perpetual giving and receiving takes place unconsciously, and with the rapidity of lightning flashes"[37] So long as expectations are satisfied without delay, so long as tendencies are uninhibited, though intelligence is clearly and necessarily involved in the perception and understanding of the stimulus situation, the response will probably remain unconscious.

Mental activity tends to become conscious when reflection and deliberation are involved in the completion of the response pattern, that is, when automatic behavior is disturbed because a tendency has been inhibited. "Impulsion forever boosted on its forward way would run its course thoughtless, and dead to emotion. . . . The only way it can become aware of its nature and its goal is by obstacles surmounted and means employed."[38]

But even when a habit response is inhibited, conscious awareness of the mental activity involved in the perception of and response to the stimulus situation is by no means inevitable. Intellectual experience (the conscious awareness of one's own expectations or, objectively, of the tendencies of the music), as distinguished from intellectual activity, is largely a product of the listener's own attitude toward his responses and hence toward the stimuli and mental activities which bring them into existence. That is to say, some listeners, whether because of training or natural psychological inclination, are disposed to rationalize their responses, to make experience self-conscious; others are not so disposed. If intellectual activity is allowed to remain unconscious, then the mental tensions and the deliberations involved when a tendency is inhibited are experienced as feeling or affect rather than as conscious cognition.

Having shown that music arouses tendencies and thus fulfils the conditions necessary for the arousal of affect and having demonstrated how this is accomplished, we can now state one of the basic hypotheses of this study. Namely: Affect or emotion-felt is aroused when an expectation—a tendency to respond— activated by the musical stimulus situation, is temporarily inhibited or permanently blocked.

As noted earlier, in musical experience the same stimulus, the music, activates tendencies, inhibits them, and provides meaningful and relevant resolutions for them. This is of particular importance from a methodological standpoint. For it means that granted listeners who have developed reaction patterns appropriate to the work in question, the structure of the affective response to a piece of music can be studied by examining the music itself.

Once those sound successions common to a culture, a style, or a particular work have been ascertained, then, if the customary succession is presented and completed without delay, it can be assumed that, since no tendency would have been inhibited, the listener would not respond in an affective way. If, on the other hand, the sound succession fails to follow its customary course, or if it involves obscurity or ambiguity, then it can be assumed that the listener's tendencies would be inhibited or otherwise upset and that the tensions arising in this process would be experienced as affect, provided that they were not rationalized as conscious intellectual experience.

In other words, the customary or expected progression of sounds can be considered as a norm, which from a stylistic point of view it is; and alteration in the expected progression can be considered as a deviation. Hence deviations can be regarded as emotional or affective stimuli.

The importance of this "objective" point of view of musical experience is clear. It means that once the norms of a style have been ascertained, the study and analysis of the affective content of a particular work in that style can be made without continual and explicit reference to the responses of the listener or critic. That is, subjective content can be discussed objectively.[39]

The Meaning of Music

The Problem of Meaning in Music

The meaning of music has of late been the subject of much confused argument and controversy. The controversy has stemmed largely from disagreements as to what music communicates, while the confusion has resulted for the most part from a lack of clarity as to the nature and definition of meaning itself.

The debates as to what music communicates have centered around the question of whether music can designate, depict, or otherwise communicate referential concepts, images, experiences, and emotional states. This is the old argument between the absolutists and the referentialists.

Because it has not appeared problematical to them, the referentialists have not as a rule explicitly considered the problem of musical meaning. Musical meaning according to the referentialists lies in the relationship between a musical symbol or sign and the extramusical thing which it designates.

Since our concern in this study is not primarily with the referential meaning of music, suffice it to say that the disagreement between the referentialists and the absolutists is, as was pointed out at the beginning of this chapter, the result of a tendency toward philosophical monism rather than the result of any logical incompatibility. Both designative and nondesignative meanings arise out of musical experience, just as they do in other types of aesthetic experience.

The absolutists have contended that the meaning of music lies specifically, and some would assert exclusively, in the musical processes themselves. For them musical meaning is nondesignative. But in what sense these processes are meaningful, in what sense a succession or sequence of nonreferential musical stimuli can be said to give rise to meaning, they have been unable to state with either clarity or precision. They have also failed to relate musical meaning to other kinds of meaning—to meaning in general. This failure has led some critics to assert that musical meaning is a thing apart, different in some unexplained way from all other kinds of meaning. This is simply an evasion of the real issue. For it is obvious that if the term "meaning" is to have any signification at all as applied to music, then it must have the same signification as when applied to other kinds of experience.

Without reviewing all the untenable positions to which writers have tenaciously adhered, it seems fair to say that much of the confusion and uncertainty as to the nature of nonreferential musical meaning has resulted from two fallacies. On the one hand, there has been a tendency to locate meaning exclusively in one aspect of the communicative process; on the other hand, there has been a propensity to regard all meanings arising in human communication as designative, as involving symbolism of some sort.

Since these difficulties can be best resolved in the light of a general definition of meaning, let us begin with such a definition: ". . . anything requires meaning if it is connected with, or indicates, or refers to, something beyond itself, so that its full nature points to and is revealed in that connection."[40]

Meaning is thus not a property of things. It cannot be located in the stimulus alone. The same stimulus may have many different meanings. To a geologist a large rock may indicate that at one time a glacier began to recede at a given spot; to a farmer the same rock may point to the necessity of having the field cleared for plowing; and to the sculptor the rock may indicate the possibility of artistic creation. A rock, a word, or motion in and of itself, merely as a stimulus, is meaningless.

Thus it is pointless to ask what the intrinsic meaning of a single tone or a series of tones is. Purely as physical existences they are meaningless. They become meaningful only insofar as they point to, indicate, or imply something beyond themselves.

Nor can meaning be located exclusively in the objects, events, or experiences which the stimulus indicates, refers to, or implies. The meaning of the rock is the product of the relationship between the stimulus and the thing it points to or indicates.

Though the perception of a relationship can only arise as the result of some individual's mental behavior, the relationship itself is not to be located in the mind of the perceiver. The meanings observed are not subjective. Thus the relationships existing between the tones themselves or those existing between the tones and the things they designate or connote, though a product of cultural experience, are real connections existing objectively in culture.[41] They are not arbitrary connections imposed by the capricious mind of the particular listener.

Meaning, then, is not in either the stimulus, or what it points to, or the observer. Rather it arises out of what both Cohen and Mead have called the "triadic" relationship between (1) an object or stimulus; (2) that to which the stimulus points—that which is its consequent; and (3) the conscious observer.

Discussions of the meaning of music have also been muddled by the failure to state explicitly what musical stimuli indicate or point to. A stimulus may indicate events or consequences which are different from itself in kind, as when a word designates or points to an object or action which is not itself a word. Or a stimulus may indicate or imply events or consequences which are of the same kind as the stimulus itself, as when a dim light on the eastern horizon heralds the coming of day. Here both the antecedent stimulus and the consequent event are natural phenomena. The former type of meaning may be called designative, the latter embodied.

Because most of the meanings which arise in human communication are of the designative type, employing linguistic signs or the iconic signs of the plastic arts, numerous critics have failed to realize that this is not necessarily or exclusively the case. This mistake has led even avowed absolutists to allow designation to slip in through the secret door of semantic chicanery.[42]

But even more important than designative meaning is what we have called embodied meaning. From this point of view what a musical stimulus or a series of stimuli indicate and point to are not extramusical concepts and objects but other musical events which are about to happen. That is, one musical event (be it a tone, a phrase, or a whole section) has meaning because it points to and makes us expect another musical event. This is what music means from the viewpoint of the absolutist.

Music and Meaning

Embodied musical meaning is, in short, a product of expectation. If, on the basis of past experience, a present stimulus leads us to expect a more or less definite consequent musical event, then that stimulus has meaning.[43]

From this it follows that a stimulus or gesture which does not point to or arouse expectations of a subsequent musical event or consequent is meaningless. Because expectation is largely a product of stylistic experience, music in a style with which we are totally unfamiliar is meaningless.[44]

However, once the aesthetic attitude has been brought into play, very few gestures actually appear to be meaningless so long as the listener has some experience with the style of the work in question. For so long as a stimulus is possible within any known style, the listener will do his best to relate it to the style, to understand its meaning.

In and of themselves, for example, the opening chords of Beethoven's Third Symphony have no particular musical stylistic tendency. They establish no pattern of motion, arouse no tensions toward a particular fulfillment. Yet as part of the total aesthetic cultural act of attention they are meaningful. For since they are the first chords of a piece, we not only expect more music but our expectations are circumscribed by the limitations of the style which we believe the piece to be in and by the psychological demand for a more palpable pattern.

Thus the phrase "past experience," used in the definition of meaning given above, must be understood in a broad sense. It includes the immediate past of the particular stimulus or gesture, that which has already taken place in this particular work to condition the listener's opinion of the stimulus and hence his expectations as to the impending, consequent event. In the example given above, the past was silence. But this fact of the past is just as potent in conditioning expectation as a whole section of past events.[45] The phrase "past experience" also refers to the more remote, but ever present, past experience of similar musical stimuli and similar musical situations in other works. That is, it refers to those past experiences which constitute our sense and knowledge of style. The phrase also comprehends the dispositions and beliefs which the listener brings to the musical experience as well as the laws of mental behavior which govern his organization of stimuli into patterns and the expectations aroused on the basis of those patterns.

The words "consequent musical event" must be understood to include: (1) those consequents which are envisaged or expected; (2) the events which do, in fact, follow the stimulus, whether they were the ones envisaged or not; and (3) the more distant ramifications or events which, because the total series of gestures is presumed to be causally connected, are considered as being the later consequences of the stimulus in question. Seen in this light, the meaning of the stimulus is not confined to or limited by the initial triadic relationship out of which it arises. As the later stages of the musical process establish new relationships with the stimulus, new meanings arise. These later meanings coexist in memory with the earlier ones and, combining with them, constitute the meaning of the work as a total experience.

In this development three stages of meaning may be distinguished.

"Hypothetical meanings" are those which arise during the act of expectation. Since what is envisaged is a product of the probability relationships which exist as part of style, and since these probability relationships always involve the possibility of alternative consequences, a given stimulus invariably gives rise to several alternative hypothetical meanings. One consequent may, of course, be so much more probable than any other that the listener, though aware of the possibility of less likely consequences, is really set and ready only for the most probable. In such a case hypothetical meaning is without ambiguity. In other cases several consequents may be almost equally probable, and, since the listener is in doubt as to which alternative will actually materialize, meaning is ambiguous, though not necessarily less forceful and marked.[46]

Though the consequent which is actually forthcoming must be possible within the style, it may or may not be one of those which was most probable. Or it may arrive only after a delay or a deceptive diversion through alternative consequences. But whether our expectations are confirmed or not, a new stage of meaning is reached when the consequent becomes actualized as a concrete musical event.

"Evident meanings" are those which are attributed to the antecedent gesture when the consequent becomes a physicopsychic fact and when the relationship between the antecedent and consequent is perceived. Since the consequent of a stimulus itself becomes a stimulus with consequents, evident meaning also includes the later stages of musical development which are presumed to be the products of a chain of causality. Thus in the following sequence, where a stimulus (S) leads to a consequent (C), which is also a stimulus that indicates and is actualized in further consequences,

$$S_1 \ldots \ldots C_1 S_2 \ldots \ldots C_1 S_3 \ldots \ldots \text{etc.}$$

evident meaning arises not only out of the relationship between S_1 and C_1 but also out of the relationships between S_1 and all subsequent consequences, insofar as these are considered to issue from S_1. It is also important to realize that the motion S_1 . . . . . . C_1 may itself become a gesture that gives rise to envisaged and actual consequents and hence becomes a term or gesture on another level of triadic relationships. In other words, both evident and hypothetical meanings come into being and exist on several architectonic levels.

Evident meaning is colored and conditioned by hypothetical meaning. For the actual relationship between the gesture and its consequent is always considered in the light of the expected relationship. In a sense the listener even revises his opinion of the hypothetical meaning when the stimulus does not move to the expected consequent.

"Determinate meanings" are those meanings which arise out of the relationships existing between hypothetical meaning, evident meaning, and the later stages of the musical development. In other words, determinate meaning arises only after the experience of the work is timeless in memory, only when all the meanings which the stimulus has had in the particular experience are realized and their relationships to one another comprehended as fully as possible.

The Objectification of Meaning

A distinction must be drawn between the understanding of musical meaning which involves the awareness of the tendencies, resistances, tensions, and fulfilments embodied in a work and the self-conscious objectification of that meaning in the mind of the individual listener. The former may be said to involve a meaningful experience, the latter involves knowing what that meaning is, considering it as an objective thing in consciousness.

The operation of intelligence in listening to music need never become self-conscious. We are continually behaving in an intelligent way, comprehending meanings and acting upon our perceptions, cognitions, and evaluations without ever making the meanings themselves the objects of our scrutiny—without ever becoming self-conscious about what experience means. What Bertrand Russell says about understanding language also applies to the understanding of music: "Understanding language is . . . like understanding cricket: it is a matter of habits acquired in oneself and rightly presumed in others."[47]

Meanings become objectified only under conditions of self-consciousness and when reflection takes place. "One attains self-consciousness only as he takes, or finds himself stimulated to take, the attitude of the other."[48] Though training may make for a generally self-conscious attitude, one is stimulated to take the attitude of the other when the normal habits of response are disturbed in some way; when one is driven to ask one's self: What does this mean, what is the intention of this passage? Reflection is likewise brought into play where some tendency is delayed, some pattern of habitual behavior disturbed. So long as behavior is automatic and habitual there is no urge for it to become self-conscious, though it may become so. If meaning is to become objectified at all, it will as a rule become so when difficulties are encountered that make normal, automatic behavior impossible. In other words, given a mind disposed toward objectification, meaning will become the focus of attention, an object of conscious consideration, when a tendency or habit reaction is delayed or inhibited.

Meaning and Affect

It thus appears that the same processes which were said to give rise to affect are now said to give rise to the objectification of embodied meaning.

But this is a dilemma only so long as the traditional dichotomy between reason and emotion and the parent polarity between mind and body are adopted. Once it is recognized that affective experience is just as dependent upon intelligent cognition as conscious intellection, that both involve perception, taking account of, envisaging, and so forth, then thinking and feeling need not be viewed as polar opposites but as different manifestations of a single psychological process.

There is no diametric opposition, no inseparable gulf, between the affective and the intellectual responses made to music. Though they are psychologically differentiated as responses, both depend upon the same perceptive processes, the same stylistic habits, the same modes of mental organization; and the same musical processes give rise to and shape both types of experience. Seen in this light, the formalist's conception of musical experience and the expressionist's conception of it appear as complementary rather than contradictory positions. They are considering not different processes but different ways of experiencing the same process.

Whether a piece of music gives rise to affective experience or to intellectual experience depends upon the disposition and training of the listener. To some minds the disembodied feeling of affective experience is uncanny and unpleasant and a process of rationalization is undertaken in which the musical processes are objectified as conscious meaning. Belief also probably plays an important role in determining the character of the response. Those who have been taught to believe that musical experience is primarily emotional and who are therefore disposed to respond affectively will probably do so. Those listeners who have learned to understand music in technical terms will tend to make musical processes an object of conscious consideration. This probably accounts for the fact that most trained critics and aestheticians favor the formalist position. Thus while the trained musician consciously waits for the expected resolution of a dominant seventh chord the untrained, but practiced, listener feels the delay as affect.

Music and Communication

Meanings and affects may, however, arise without communication taking place. Individual A observes another individual B wink and interprets the wink as a friendly gesture. It has meaning for A who observes it. But if the wink was not intentional—if, for instance, B simply has a nervous tic—then no communication has taken place, for to B the act had no meaning. Communication, as Mead has pointed out, takes place only where the gesture made has the same meaning for the individual who makes it that it has for the individual who responds to it.[49]

It is this internalization of gestures, what Mead calls "taking the attitude of the other"[50] (the audience), which enables the creative artist, the composer, to communicate with listeners. It is because the composer is also a listener that he is able to control his inspiration with reference to the listener.[51] For instance, the composer knows how the listener will respond to a deceptive cadence and controls the later stages of the composition with reference to that supposed response. The performer too is continually "taking the attitude of the other"—of the listener. As Leopold Mozart puts it, the performer "must play everything in such a way that he will himself be moved by it."[52]

It is precisely because he is continually taking the attitude of the listener that the composer becomes aware and conscious of his own self, his ego, in the process of creation. In this process of differentiation between himself as composer and himself as audience, the composer becomes self-conscious and objective.[53]

But though the listener participates in the musical process, assuming the role which the composer envisaged for him, and though he must, in some sense, create his own experience, yet he need not take the attitude of the composer in order to do so. He need not ask: How will someone else respond to this stimulus? Nor is he obliged to objectify his own responses, to ask, How am I responding? Unlike the composer, the listener may and frequently does "lose himself in the music"; and, in following and responding to the sound gestures made by the composer, the listener may become oblivious of his own ego, which has literally become one with that of the music.

We must, then, be wary of easy and high-sounding statements to the effect that "we cannot understand a work of art without, to a certain degree, repeating and reconstructing the creative process by which it has come into being."[54] Certainly the listener must respond to the work of art as the artist intended, and the listener's experience of the work must be similar to that which the composer envisaged for him. But this is a different thing from experiencing the "creative process which brought it into being."

However, the listener may take the attitude of the composer. He may be self-conscious in the act of listening. Those trained in music, and perhaps those trained in the other arts as well, tend, because of the critical attitudes which they have developed in connection with their own artistic efforts, to become self-conscious and objective in all their aesthetic experiences. And it is no doubt partly for this reason that, as noted above, trained musicians tend to objectify meaning, to consider it as an object of conscious cognition.

Finally, and perhaps most important of all, this analysis of communication emphasizes the absolute necessity of a common universe of discourse in art. For without a set of gestures common to the social group, and without common habit responses to those gestures, no communication whatsoever would be possible. Communication depends upon, presupposes, and arises out of the universe of discourse which in the aesthetics of music is called style.

NOTES

1. Norman Cazden, "Musical Consonance and Dissonance: A Cultural Criterion," *Journal of Aesthetics*, IV (1945), 3–11.

2. Paul R. Farnsworth, "Sacred Cows in the Psychology of Music," *Journal of Aesthetics*, VII (1948), 48–51.

3. Susanne K. Langer, *Philosophy in a New Key* (New York: Mentor Book Co., 1951).

4. *Ibid.*, p. 171.

5. H. P. Weld, "An Experimental Study in Musical Enjoyment," *American Journal of Psychology*, XXIII (1912), 283.

6. C. S. Myers, "Individual Differences in Listening to Music," in *The Effects of Music*, ed. Max Schoen (New York: Harcourt, Brace & Co., 1927), p. 14.

7. See H. D. Aiken, "The Aesthetic Relevance of Belief," *Journal of Aesthetics*, IX (1950), 301–15.

8. James L. Mursell, *The Psychology of Music* (New York: W. W. Norton & Co., Inc., 1937), pp. 27–28.

9. *Ibid.*, p. 37.

10. David Rapaport, *Emotions and Memory* (New York: International Universities Press Inc., 1950), p. 21.

11. John Dewey, "The Theory of Emotion," *Psychological Review*, I (1894), 553–69; II (1895), 13–32.

12. R. P. Angier, "The Conflict Theory of Emotions," *American Journal of Psychology*, XXXIX (1927), 390–401.

13. J. T. MacCurdy, *The Psychology of Emotion* (New York: Harcourt, Brace & Co., 1925), p. 475.

14. For MacCurdy the term "instinct" includes learned habit responses.

15. Notice that this analysis makes apparent the great significance of Aiken's contention that our beliefs as to the nature of aesthetic experience lead to the suppression of overt responses; for such inhibiting of overt behavior tends to intensify the affective response.

16. F. Paulhan, *The Laws of Feeling*, trans. C. K. Ogden (New York: Harcourt, Brace & Co., 1930), p. 19.

17. *Ibid.*, p. 123.

18. The term affective or emotional "state" will henceforth be used to designate those aspects of emotional experience which have been given names and which are in one way or another fairly standardized in a broad sense.

19. See Robert S. Woodworth, "How Emotions Are Identified and Classified," in *Feelings and Emotions: The Wittenberg Symposium*, ed. M. L. Reymert (Worcester, Mass.: Clark University Press, 1928), p. 224.

20. Ernst Cassirer, *An Essay on Man: An Introduction to a Philosophy of Human Culture* (New York: Doubleday & Co., 1953), p. 190. This admirable statement like so many of its kind suffers at the end from an irritating vagueness in which an intangible "the

dynamic process of life itself" is substituted for a definite account of how and why the emotions of art are not comparable to any single state of emotion. It is for a solution to this problem that we are searching in the present discussion of emotional differentiation.

21. C. Landis, "Studies in Emotional Reactions: II, General Behavior and Facial Expression," *Journal of Comparative Psychology*, IV (1924), 496.

22. Donald O. Hebb, *The Organization of Behavior* (New York: John Wiley & Sons, 1952), p. 258.

23. *Ibid.*, p. 232.

24. This statement must be qualified by the reservation that insofar as it can designate or represent extramusical stimuli, music can be said to evoke such affective states as are normally connected with the situations represented.

25. It is also clear that since the world of emotions is not composed of a series of separate compartments, a given listener may feel that a purely musical emotion is comparable or analogous to affects experienced in real life.

26. The term "emotional expression" is misleading in that it implies that such behavior is the direct, necessary expression of affect.

27. Though not within the province of this study, it can, I believe, be shown that similar aspects of experience are involved in musical and other designation. Both, for example, utilize the generality of motion (fast or slow, continuous or interrupted, smooth or disjunct, intense or weak) in such designation. And musical designation, though probably in some respects natural, is, like designative behavior, in the last analysis a product of culture and learning rather than a product of nature.

28. See John Dewey, *Art as Experience* (New York: Minton, Balch & Co., 1934), pp. 35, 56.

29. MacCurdy, *op. cit.*, p. 556.

30. John Dewey, *Intelligence in the Modern World*, ed. J. Ratner ("Modern Library" [New York: Random House, 1939]), p. 733.

31. MacCurdy, *op. cit.*, p. 556.

32. Aiken, *op. cit.*, p. 313; also see Arthur D. Bissell, *The Role of Expectation in Music* (New Haven: Yale University Press, 1921), p. vii; and Hugo Riemann, *Catechism of Musical Aesthetics*, trans. H. Bewerung (London: Augener & Co., n.d.), p. 29.

33. Aiken, *op. cit.*, p. 305.

34. If this takes place, the listener may shift his attention to another aspect of the musical materials, or he may simply abandon the attempt to make sense of the music altogether.

35. Thus the designation of mood and character, whether accomplished in purely musical terms or with the aid of a program or text, is important not only for its own sake, as a source of enjoyment, but also because, as part of the stimulus situation, it is necessary for the proper understanding of the musical processes in progress.

36. Both these aspects of the process of expectation are discussed in later chapters of *Emotion and Meaning in Music*, where much of the preceding discussion is treated in more detail.

37. Eduard Hanslick, *The Beautiful in Music*, trans. E. Cohen (London: Novello, Ewer & Co., 1901), p. 135. The difficulty with this statement is that Hanslick confuses intellectual satisfaction with intellectual activity. For although intellectual activity, in the sense of mental awareness and cognition, may, as we shall see, be unconscious, intellectual satisfaction implies a self-conscious awareness of the activity taking place.

38. Dewey, *Art as Experience*, p. 59; also see *Intelligence in the Modern World*, pp. 755 ff. Robert Penn Warren writes to much the same effect: ". . . a poem, to be good, must earn itself. It is a motion toward a point of rest, but if it is not a resisted motion, it is a motion of no consequence" ("Pure and Impure Poetry," *Kenyon Review*, V [1943], 251).

39. It is clear that the terms "norm" and "deviation" are being used in a very broad and general sense. Deviation includes all delays and inhibitions which give rise to expectation within the context of the particular style in question.

40. Morris R. Cohen, *A Preface to Logic* (New York: Henry Holt & Co., 1944), p. 47.

41. See George H. Mead, *Mind, Self, and Society* (Chicago: University of Chicago Press, 1934), p. 76.

42. Thus Pratt, while maintaining that the ideas aroused in association with music "have little to do with the intrinsic nature of musical sound" (C. C. Pratt, "Music and Meaning," *Proceedings of the Music Teacher's National Association*, Series XXXVII [1942], p. 113), does contend that "music *sounds* the way emotions *feel*" (*Ibid.*, p. 117), a statement which seems to be a disguised form of referentialism.

Incidentally though Pratt's first statement is undoubtedly true, its implications are not. For while our associations may have nothing to do with the intrinsic nature of sound, whatever that may be, they do have something to do with our experience of sound.

43. The term "stimulus" as used here includes any tone or combination of tones which are marked off as a unitary event which is related to other musical events. It is, to use Mead's terminology, "a musical gesture." Or it is a "sound term." In this sense, a single tone, a phrase, or a whole composition may be considered to be a gesture, a stimulus, or a sound term. In other words, meaning must be considered as being architectonic as well as consecutive.

44. Of course, it may have designative meaning. The more difficult it is to grasp the embodied meaning of a work, the greater the tendency to search for designative meanings.

45. Notice, too, that the final tones of a piece, conditioned by all that has gone before, lead us to expect silence and that it is this expectation which makes them meaningful.

46. Note that hypothetical meanings as well as the other kinds of meaning are architectonic. If we are set to listen to a Haydn rondo, then the idea we have of Haydn rondos is, in a sense, the hypothetical meaning of that particular rondo; it is what we envisage and what points to the impinging stimulus.

47. Bertrand Russell, *Selected Papers* ("Modern Library," [New York: Random House, n.d.]), p. 358.

48. Mead, *op. cit.*, p. 194.

49. Mead, *op. cit.*, p. 42–75.

50. *Ibid.*, p. 47.

51. Of course, if the composer is developing a relatively new style, as many contemporary composers have tried to do, the imagined listener may correspond to no listener who actually exists. He is rather one whom the composer hopes to create as his style becomes part of the general style, part of the listening public's stock of habit responses.

52. Leopold Mozart, *Versuch einer gründlichen Violinschule*, quoted in *Source Readings in Music History*, ed. Oliver Strunk (New York: W. W. Norton & Co., Inc., 1950), p. 602.

53. Generally speaking this study is not concerned with the creative act but rather

with the experience which the art work brings into being. This aspect of the composer's creative life is discussed because it clearly concerns the problem of aesthetic experience. Obviously many other mental processes and attitudes which have not been touched upon are involved in the act of composition.

54. Cassirer, *op. cit.*, p. 191.

2

Music and Language: Parallels and Contrasts

RITA AIELLO

Introduction

The relationship between music and language has been addressed by musicians, philosophers, and scholars (Bernstein, 1976; Langer, 1956; see Winn, 1981, for a rich historical account on this topic). The musicologist Curt Sachs (1943) proposed that "music began with singing." Comparisons between music and language are prompted by the strong similarities between the two. Both have an inherent structure and evolve over a temporal continuum, both have a meaning for the listener, and are innate expressions of human capacities. In music and in language there is a phonetic, a syntactic, and a semantic level.

The research in psycholinguistics has influenced the research in the perception of music (Clarke, 1989; Lerdahl & Jackendoff, 1983; Sloboda, 1985). Psychologists have applied some of the experimental designs used to investigate the perception of language to research the perception of music (De Witt & Samuel, 1990; Locke & Kellar, 1973; Tan, Aiello, & Bever, 1985). Drawing on the psychological literature, this chapter discusses phonetic, syntactic, and semantic comparisons between language and music and urges that there be a greater emphasis on research in the emotional meaning of music.

REFERENCES

Bernstein, L. (1976). *The unanswered question: Six talks at Harvard*. Cambridge, MA: Harvard University Press.
Clarke, E. F. (1989). Issues in language and music. *Contemporary Music Review, 4,* 9–22.

De Witt, L., & Samuel, A. (1990). The role of knowledge-based expectations in music perception: Evidence from musical restoration. *Journal of Experimental Psychology: General, 119*(2), 123–44.

Langer, S. (1956). *Philosophy in a new key* (3rd ed.). Cambridge, MA: Harvard University Press.

Lerdahl, F., & Jackendoff, R. (1983). *A generative theory of tonal music.* Cambridge, MA: MIT Press.

Locke, S., & Kellar, L. (1973). Categorical perception in a non-linguistic mode. *Cortex, 9,* 355–69.

Sachs, C. (1943). *The rise of music in the ancient world.* New York: Norton.

Sloboda, J. A. (1985). *The musical mind.* Oxford: Oxford University Press.

Tan, N., Aiello, R., & Bever, T. G. (1985). Harmonic structure as a determinant of melodic organization. *Memory and Cognition, 9,* 533–39.

Winn, J. A. (1981). *Unsuspected eloquence: A history of the relation between poetry and music.* New Haven, CT: Yale University Press.

Music begins where words end. Johann Wolfgang von Goethe (attr.)

Similarities Between Music and Language

Music and language are universal, innate expressions of human cognition and communication (Clarke, 1989b; McAdams, 1987; Sloboda, 1985). Their universality is evident in the fact that all cultures express themselves verbally and musically. Both are innate abilities that develop through personal interaction, as can be observed in the spontaneity with which children learn to act and interact musically and verbally from a very young age. But, specifically, how does the child acquire a language? In his book *Reflections on Language*, Noam Chomsky (1975) writes:

> [The child] quite effortlessly makes use of an intricate structure of specific rules and guiding principles to convey his thoughts and feelings to others, arousing in them novel ideas and subtle perception and judgments. . . . [I]t remains a distant goal to reconstruct and comprehend what the child has done intuitively and with minimal effort. Thus language is a mirror of the mind in a deep and significant sense. It is a product of human intelligence, created anew in each individual by operations that lie far beyond the reach of will or consciousness. (p. 4)

To learn a language, then, the child subconsciously abstracts the rules of the language structure and utilizes them to create his or her own novel sentences.

Children do not just repeat the sentences they hear, but create new sentences by applying the rules they have abstracted from their language. A similar proposal can be made for the way in which children learn and create music. Along these lines, music, too, can be viewed as "a mirror of the mind in a deep and significant sense." In order to learn and to create music, children abstract some of the rules of their musical culture and use them creatively. Just as they learn spontaneously the rules that allow them to originate an unlimited number of sentences, so they seem to learn the musical rules that allow them to create novel sequences in music. The musical growth of children occurs in stages that have been compared to stages of their cognitive and symbolic development (Gardner, 1973; Hargreaves, 1986; Serafine, 1980; see also Chapters 4 and 5 in this volume).

Although music and language vary across cultures, they share several significant cognitive characteristics (Clarke, 1989b; McAdams, 1987; Sloboda, 1985). Both evolve over time and involve a meaningful use of sound patterns. Throughout the world people use sound patterns to create words, motives, scales, ragas, and drones. The psychologist George Miller (1956) brilliantly showed that our capacity for segmenting and remembering verbal units is approximately seven items: "The magical number seven, plus or minus two;" as he called it. And to a great extent this limit also exists in music if we consider that the pentatonic scale (five pitches) and the diatonic scale (seven pitches) serve as the bases for most of the world's music. The finite length of words, of musical motives, and of verbal and musical phrases reflects our need to segment along the temporal continuum so that we may process most effectively the sounds we hear and create.

Music and language are both modes of communication, yet they have different goals. Generally speaking, while the primary aim of language is to communicate thought, one of the main goals of music is to heighten emotions and express them aesthetically. Music is born out of the need to express ourselves and to communicate aesthetically through the abstractness and the characteristics of sound:

Meter and rhythm are at the heart of music and poetry. Indeed, accents and stresses are the means used to define linguistic and musical patterns. In processing language and music as sensory data, we make use of many of the characteristics of sound—pitch, tone, and dynamics. Some Oriental languages offer striking evidence of the importance that pitch and tone can have, and we find that syllables may be pronounced with different pitch contours. For example, in the Peking dialect of the Chinese language, there are four tones: flat, rising, falling-rising, and falling. The same syllable has different meaning depending on the tone with which it is pronounced: mā (pronounced at the level tone) can mean "mother", má (rising tone) can mean "hemp", mǎ (falling-rising tone) can mean "horse," and mà (falling tone) can mean "scold" (Miller, 1981: 59). The dynamic level with which one speaks may be particularly revealing of one's emotions, and in some Western languages (e.g., Italian) the intonation alone of a sentence, not its grammatical structure, conveys whether it is a declarative sentence or a question.

The music of several African cultures shows a close bond between the pitches played by some instruments and the language itself. In west and central Africa, talking drums are used both as musical instruments and as speech surrogates. These instruments reproduce the intonation of words and the rhythms of spoken texts (Nketia, 1974). In the African languages of Kele and Mbane, each syllable possesses a fixed tone, which is high or low. The talking drum sends messages imitating the patterns of high and low that occur in the words (Carrington, 1969: 18). And the *masengo* and *endingidi* fiddles of Ethiopia and Uganda appear even to imitate vocal timbre (Wachsmann & Cooke, 1980).

Words and music are close neighbors physiologically and perceptually (Burrows, 1990). The link is so ingrained that some theories of the origin of music propose that music is a form of heightened speech (Bernstein, 1976; Revesz, 1953; Stacey, 1989). In 1974, Leonard Bernstein devoted the Norton lectures which he delivered at Harvard University to a comparison of the origins of music and language and to an exploration of the similarities in the ways in which we create and process them. These thought-provoking lectures have been recorded in the book *The Unanswered Question* (Bernstein, 1976), which borrows its title from a composition by Charles Ives. Seeking to answer the question "Whither music?" these lectures have influenced research on the similarities of music and language by both musicians and psychologists (Clarke, 1989b; Lerdahl & Jackendoff, 1983; Sloboda, 1985).

Bernstein proposed that, since sound is based on the harmonic series, it functions as a universal for all types of music. He compared the harmonic series to the monogenesis of language: just as languages can be traced to a common origin, so tones can be traced to the harmonic series. Moreover, Bernstein emphasized that the order in which the partials occur in the harmonic series is responsible for the fact that certain intervals, such of the octave, the fifth, and the minor third, are so prevalent the world over, and he compared this recurrence with that of certain syllables (e.g., *ma*) in many of the world's languages.

Many musicologists have mused over the origins of music. Curt Sachs proposed that music sprang from singing (1943: 21). Indeed, the presence and importance of singing in most of the world's cultures attest to the universal binding of music and speech. The word *melody* derives from the musical intonation of a cadenced phrase. As Stravinsky noted, "*melodia* in Greek, is the intonation of *melos*, which signifies a fragment, a part of a phrase" (1947: 42). The singing styles of *recitativo* and *sprechstimme*, for example, are particularly vivid examples of how speech and Western music can be fused.

Classical Greece gave special attention to the union of music and language. The Greeks used singing and instrumental accompaniments to heighten the significance of poetry and drama, a tradition that is at the core of opera. Not until the late Middle Ages did music emerge as an autonomous art form transcending the scope of language. In the splendid book *Unsuspected Eloquence: A History of the Relations Between Poetry and Music*, James Anderson Winn (1981) describes the birth of medieval polyphony:

The fact that music could achieve actual simultaneity, that it could have vertical as well as horizontal events, was a revolutionary discovery. . . . In literature, one could claim that a line of poetry had four layers of meaning, but in music one could actually write four simultaneous parts . . . . Until this point in history, both the recitation of a poem and the singing or playing of a piece of music had reached the ear as a single series of sounds in time; now music had a new kind of interest, the accidental or contrived vertical combination of two or more pitches. (p. 89)

Until the late sixteenth century, a major role of instrumental accompaniments was to enhance the poignancy of the sung word and of dance. Given today's vast repertoire of instrumental music, it may be easy to forget when instrumental music began to acquire its own independence from the vocal line and to develop into an autonomous art form. Before then, instruments mostly accompanied or imitated dance and song. Igor Stravinsky (1947) in *Poetics of Music in the Form of Six Lessons* remarked: "Music of the kind that has meaning for us today is the youngest of all the arts, although its origin may be as old as man's" (p. 28).

Musical Phonology: Some Comparisons with Language Phonology

The linguist seeks to describe the structure of language just as the music theorist seeks to describe the structure of music. The psycholinguist and the psycho-musicologist investigate in their respective domains the psychological processes by which language and music are created and understood. Psycholinguists study how language is created and processed according to three fundamental components: phonetics (the speech sounds of a language), syntax (the way in which words are put together to form phrases, clauses, or sentences), and semantics (the meanings of words). To understand a language, the listener must sufficiently process all three components of the language. Given the fundamental cognitive characteristics shared by music and language, a number of researchers investigating the perception of music have utilized some of the techniques that were developed to study the perception of language. In this section I will discuss two perceptual phenomena that occur in the perception of language and music at the phonetic level: categorical perception and phonemic restoration.

The phonetics of a language are the sound units that constitute the language itself. A phoneme is the smallest phonetic unit. It distinguishes one utterance from another and is roughly the same as a written letter of the alphabet (e.g., b, c, f). The words *bat* and *cat* and *fat* begin with three different phonemes, *b*, *c*, and *f*, but share others. The analysis of speech sounds into phonemes, as well as the division of phonemes into distinctive features, is critical for any analysis of speech perception.

How do we perceive a language at the phonetic level? Partly by categorizing the sounds that we hear. Categorical perception is the way in which we categor-ize what we hear. Jusczyk (1986) explains: "Generally speaking, categorical per-ception is said to occur when the ability to discriminate among members of the same category is very poor, whereas the ability to discriminate among members of different categories is very good. As applied to speech sounds, categorical perception implies that discrimination of sounds from two different categories such as /b/ and /p/ should be relatively easy, but that the discrimination of two different tokens of /p/ from the same speaker should be almost nonexistent" (27-11).

This ability to categorize is strikingly similar to a musical phenomenon. Musicians categorize musical sounds more accurately than nonmusicians just as native speakers categorize speech sounds that are phonemic in their language more accurately than nonspeakers do (for a review of these latter data see Repp, 1984).

A musical note can roughly be compared to a phoneme (Bernstein, 1976; Sloboda, 1985). Locke and Kellar (1973) investigated the categorical perception of musicians and nonmusicians in detecting a difference between an A minor triad and an A major triad. They asked subjects to compare pairs of sine wave triads. The outer notes of the stimuli were always 440 Hz (A) and 659 Hz (E) while the middle note varied by 2, 4, 6, or 8 Hz, ranging from 523 Hz (C) to 554 Hz (C-sharp). It was found that the musicians discriminated better across catego-ry boundaries than the nonmusicians. They were more sensitive to the differ-ences between the chords and were able to discriminate between the triads when the middle pitch varied by 4 Hz. In general, nonmusicians require a greater difference between the triads to perceive a change. The superiority of musicians in categorizing musical sounds has been proven using different types of musical stimuli (Wapnick, Bourassa, & Sampson, 1982; Zatorre & Halpern, 1979).

The perceptual phenomenon of phonemic restoration also occurs in both language and music; it describes the ability of listeners to use their previous knowledge to supply what is missing (Warren, 1970). De Witt and Samuel (1990) explain that if a phoneme occurring within a word is replaced with noise, listeners cannot indicate which phoneme has been distorted because their knowledge of the word supplies the missing information; therefore, they perceive having heard the intact word with nothing missing. Similarly, in the musical case, restoration occurs when listeners believe they have heard an auditory signal intact when in fact noise has replaced some of the notes.

De Witt and Samuel (1990: experiment 1) asked subjects to hear a series of familiar melodies and indicate whether a noise replaced or coincided with a musical pitch. The researchers found that the subjects' specific expectations about a particular musical sequence allowed them to notice disruptions to that sequence. The musical training of the listeners affected their perception of the stimuli as well: overall, musicians showed better discrimination performance than the less trained subjects. What one expects to hear influences the nature of what one hears. As De Witt and Samuel note, "musical restoration is an example of a more general perceptual phenomenon in which prior knowledge and expectations lead to a filling in of a missing information" (p. 142). The perception of music is not simply a passive reception of tones but an active process. The occurrence of categorical perception and of restoration effects in speech and music demonstrates a certain level of commonality of processing across these two domains.

Musical Syntax: Some Comparisons with Language Syntax

Consciously or subconsciously, one listens to music according to some stylistic and perceptual laws. Music is composed and improvised according to a style, and even the musically untutored listeners acquire a musical syntax, a system of rules by which they make sense of music. Despite varying degrees of awareness, listeners understand the syntactic complexity of composition and the arguments of musical form (Spender, 1987: 502).

In music as in language, we are aware of the grammatical features of the stimulus. Experiments show that there are strong similarities in the way in which people perceive structure in music and in language. Deutsch (1981, 1982) asked musically trained subjects to recall sequences of 12 pitches by writing them down in musical notation. She found that the subjects' performance depended on the degree of structure in the stimuli. Sequences that were tonally structured were easier to write down than sequences that were not tonally structured. In addition, the placement of rests within the sequences also had an effect. The subjects' performance decreased when the rests were placed in locations that did not coincide with the tonal structure of the sequences.

A number of experiments have applied techniques that were developed to investigate the syntactical aspects of language perception to study the syntactical aspects of music perception. I will describe three categories of experiments that show that listeners are aware of the grammatical features of the stimuli, and whose results are rather similar in the language and the music domain: reading experiments, phrase boundary experiments, and experiments that consider the location of clicks within sequences.

Reading Experiments

A number of studies (Levin & Kaplan, 1970; Sloboda, 1974, 1977) have investigated the span (i.e., the number of words or notes) that readers take in ahead of time when reading language or sight-reading music. In language reading, experienced readers tend to take in material extending up to a phrase boundary, wait until the complete processing of that phrase, and then rapidly sweep to the next phrase boundary to take in the material of the next phrase. We tend to pause the longest after reading complete major grammatical units (Sloboda, 1985).

FIGURE 2.1. Brahms, Cappriccio, op. 76, no. 2, bars 76–78.

In sight-reading music, experienced readers identify significant structural units and scan them differently, according to whether the music is homophonic or contrapuntal. Experienced sight readers do not read note-by-note but shape the music as they read it by emphasizing patterns, thus creating a meaningful interpretation. They create meaningful patterns by imposing performance markers onto the music they play. Although an experienced language reader reads a text roughly in the same way as an experienced musician sight-reads music, the proficiency of the musician is evident in one additional way: in the skill with which he or she eliminates some material from the score so that the sight-reading will be heard as being both technically proficient and musically coherent. It is very interesting that in sight-reading a score musicians tend to commit "proof-readers'" errors. Pianists fail to notice the errors that may be in a score and subconsciously correct them, possibly on the basis of their tacit knowledge of the stylistic norms of the music (Sloboda, 1985: 75)

In the second measure of Figure 2.1, most pianists will play the G as if it were written G-sharp. The fact that it is actually a G-natural will easily go unnoticed. It is the *inexperienced* pianist who, lacking the musical intuition, will tend to sight-read this passage as it is printed.

Phrase Boundary Experiments

We segment language and music in locations that reflect the grammatical structure of the stimuli. A phrase, whether it occurs in language or in music, is a psychological unit. Experiments indicate that, in both music and language processing, we tend to process more effectively material belonging to one phrase than material that integrates two phrases. Tan, Aiello, and Bever (1985) asked musicians and nonmusicians to listen to single-line melodies that used only equal-duration notes and that formed a two-phrase musical period. Using a psycholinguistic paradigm, the subjects were asked to recognize a two-note probe that either (1) occurred at the end of the first phrase, (2) straddled the phrase boundary, or (3) occurred at the beginning of the second phrase. All subjects, regardless of their musical training, perceived with greater difficulty the two-note probe that straddled the phrase boundary. The familiarity with the harmonic structure influenced the listener's perceptual organization of the melodies in ways analogous to the perceptual organization of clauses or sentences. This result, however, was more accentuated for the musicians.

Click Experiments

Additional evidence of the syntactical similarities between language and music comes from studies that investigate the location of clicks (Fodor & Bever, 1965; Gregory, 1978). These experiments look at the perceived location of clicks and reveal the strategies that subjects use in processing the auditory material. Click experiments have shown that subjects use basically the same strategies in processing verbal and musical sequences because the grammatical structure of the stimuli guides the listeners' perception. In click experiments, a click is presented at one or more strategic locations while the subjects hear some verbal or musical material; the subjects' task is to indicate the syllables or notes that occurred simultaneously with the click (or clicks). Frequently listeners report the location of the clicks inaccurately. They believe they heard them at the end of phrases, regardless of the location where the clicks actually occurred. It is as if the clicks *migrated* toward the direction of the phrase boundary. This result illustrates that phrase boundaries are important in the perception of language and music.

Musical Grammars

The theories of language proposed by the linguist Noam Chomsky (1957) have been utilized by psychologists and musicians in making comparisons between the nature of music and language. Chomsky postulated that every possible sentence consists of two levels: a surface structure and a deep structure. The surface structure is closely related to the string of words that we hear or see, while the deep structure is closely related to the underlying meaning of the string of words. Let us consider an example. Although at the surface the sentences *John is easy to please* and *John is eager to please* differ in only one word, we understand that there is a substantial difference in their meaning. Indeed, they have different underlying deep structures. On the other hand, we understand that "the dog chased the cat" and "the cat was chased by the dog" are related in meaning (that is, have the same underlying deep structure) despite the dissimilarities in their surface structures.

Chomsky proposed that by applying various transformational rules to the deep structure—for example, *John + Love + Mary*—we can derive all the sentences that are related to this deep structure, such as *John loves Mary, John does not love Mary, Does John love Mary?* and so on. As I pointed out at the beginning of this chapter, we do not store the sentences that we would like to say but, rather, the rules that give rise to the sentences. If language were based exclusively on repeating what we heard, we could *only* repeat what we had heard before and say nothing new. Instead, we abstract the grammatical rules from the previously heard sentences and use them to generate new sentences, thus expressing our own novel thoughts. And, in a general sense, the same can be said for music.

Leonard Bernstein (1976) was among the musicians seeking analogies between aspects of Chomskian theories and the structure of music (other interesting proposals have also been made by Lerdahl & Jackendoff, 1983; Sloboda, 1985; and Clarke, 1989b). Bernstein illustrated how a Chomskian transformational grammar could be compared, in some fashion, to the theories of music proposed by Heinrich Schenker (1935/1979). For Bernstein, Schenker's analyses trace what happens in a piece of music to a basic chordal structure, just as Chomskian transformational theories trace what we hear as the surface of language to the deep structure of language. In this vein, the melody (Schenker's *urline*) is equivalent to the surface structure of the language, and the harmonic structure (Schenker's *bassbrechung*) can be compared to the deep language structure.

One must keep in mind that while Schenker's musical analyses are based on long structures of music that can reflect as much as an entire piece (Schenker, 1969), Chomsky's theories of language are based on strings of words that are relatively short. Nevertheless, there is validity in the Chomsky-Schenker comparison because there is a relationship between the melody and the harmony that can be compared to the deep and the surface structure of language. But although this language-music analogy is attractive and stimulating, I believe that it fails to do justice to a major distinctive element between language grammar and music grammar: ambiguity. Ambiguity occurs rather seldom in language because language is based on communication (I will discuss ambiguity again later in this chapter with reference to the meaning of music). On the other hand, ambiguity is a major element of the grammar and aesthetics of music. Chomskian transformational theories of language explain that what is ambiguous in language is the result of two possible, but different, deep structures. For example, the sentence *they are visiting firemen* could be interpreted as *(they) ([are] [visiting firemen])* or *(they) [are visiting] [firemen])*.

In music, however, a specific harmonic progression can give rise to many melodies *and* the same melody can be harmonized by several different harmonies. Figures 2.2 and 2.3 present the Cantabile movement from Beethoven's Quartet, op. 18, no. 5, and two settings of the chorale "O Ewigkeit, du Donnerwort" by J. S. Bach which illustrate this last point.

Moreover, when listening to music there are many possible perceptions. Many elements occur simultaneously, and each musical element may have a specific syntax of its own. When listening to music we are subconsciously aware that there are *many* grammatical possibilities between the parts. The grammar of music allows for complexity and simultaneity. Overall, the syntax of music has much more latitude than that of language. Thus, in comparing the syntaxes of music and of language, we must remember that music is by far more flexible and ambiguous than language, almost regardless of style.

Let us look at an example where the syntactical ambiguity occurs because of

FIGURE 2.2. Beethoven, Andante Cantabile from Quartet, op. 18, no. 5, theme and variation 4.

FIGURE 2.3. J. S. Bach, two settings of the chorale "O Ewigkeit, du Donnerwort."

the tonality of the piece: Chopin's Mazurka, op. 17, no. 4. What key is this mazurka in? We do not know until later in the piece when we finally realize that it is in the key of A minor. Clearly, in this case, it is the harmony that provides the element of ambiguity to the piece[1] (Figure 2.4).

In returning to Bernstein's analogy that the deep structure and the surface structure of language can be compared to the harmonic structure and the melody of music, I would like to propose that the deep structure of language be compared to a musical theme, and that the surface structure be compared to the musical variations that can be made with the theme. In this vein, by applying rhythmic, melodic, and harmonic transformations to the theme (the deep structure) the composer creates musical variations that reflect their original source but that, at the same time, have the freedom and the ambiguity which are characteristic of music.

For the psycholinguist, a grammar is a set of rules capable of generating an aspect of a structure of language. Grammars are collections of strategies for understanding and producing sentences. The developments in the psychology of music have influenced many researchers to write about musical grammars (Baroni, 1983; Roads, 1979). In recent years, grammars have been proposed for generating Swedish nursery songs (Lindblom & Sundberg, 1970), J. S. Bach's chorales (Baroni & Jacoboni, 1978), chord progressions in jazz (Steedman, 1984), and the setting of words to Gregorian chant (Chen, 1983), to mention only a few. And in A Generative Theory of Tonal Music, Lerdahl and Jackendoff (1983) combined principles of Chomskian transformational grammar and Schenkerian theory and proposed a theory of how listeners familiar with the tonal style listen to tonal music. This theory takes into account principles of: (1) grouping, (2) meter, (3) time-span reduction (a system that assigns the relative dominance of each surface event according to a tree structure), and (4) prolongation reduction (a system that describes the patterns of harmonic tension and relaxation). To date, however, only parts of this theory have found experimental support (Bigard, 1990; Deliège, 1987).

Although the proposal of musical grammars has been very instrumental in advancing research in the psychology of music as a whole, a psychology of music must be sensitive to features that are *unique* to music, because the application of psycholinguistic paradigms alone cannot answer the questions that are at the core of music itself (see also Clarke, 1989a, 1989b). A grammar prescribes an order, a set of rules; it does not guarantee an aesthetic reaction, it is not a prescription for it. Productive research in the psychology of music will need to address not only how the mind perceives the sounds, but the aesthetic and emotional meaning that the sounds give rise to.

Musically speaking, the style of a piece reflects its musical grammar. If the grammar of a musical composition is too taxing perceptually, will listeners relate well to the piece? David Smith and Jordan Witt (1989, see also Smith, 1987) tested how listeners react aesthetically to tonal and serial compositions. They asked subjects classified as "nonexperts who enjoyed classical music" to listen to

FIGURE 2.4. Chopin, Mazurka, op. 17, no. 4.

FIGURE 2.4 (continued)

53

brief excerpts from the beginning and the end of tonal and serial works by Schoenberg and Webern and to describe them using a set of 26 adjectives and a rating scale from 1 to 7. Thus, it became possible to draw an aesthetic profile of each musical excerpt. The results showed that listeners find serial music, with its atonality and rather unfamiliar grammar, to be less rich emotionally than tonal pieces written by the same composers. Smith and Witt, therefore, found that if the stylistic constraints of a piece are perceptually too demanding, listeners may not be able to understand the music and thus may not derive as much enjoyment from what they hear.

This is indeed the general reaction that many listeners will have, at least in the beginning. They will tend to perceive that the stylistic complexity of a serial piece is the result only of the composer's intellectualism. When that happens, the music loses its aesthetic and emotional message for many listeners. In this context, I am reminded of the remarks made by the writer Isaac Bashevis Singer on literature: "The very essence of literature is the war between emotion and intellect. When literature becomes too intellectual—when it begins to ignore the passions, the emotions—it becomes sterile, silly, and actually without any substance" (Page, *The New York Times*, July 26, 1991).

Listening to Music: Where Is the Meaning?

What is musical meaning? Specifically, how does the listener derive a meaning from music? Earlier I discussed some comparisons between language and music at the phonetic and the syntactical level. But, semantically, where is the musical meaning to be found? Is the semantic level of music to be found in the emotions that music elicits? To a great extent, *Yes*. But ultimately, *why* do we listen to music? To follow a grammar? To abide by a perceptual theory? Probably not. Most of us listen to music to partake of the emotional and aesthetic experience that music offers.

Unfortunately, there is a wide gap between the progress that has been made in understanding how music is perceived and what it means to listeners. A close link clearly exists between music cognition and the emotions that music elicits, but an evaluation of this link is yet to be researched thoroughly. Meaning, in all its complexity, most likely lies hidden in the emotional content of music, and all of us, consciously or not, perceive it.

Language is based on understanding the interaction of its phonetic, syntactic, and semantic levels. And while music conveys meanings, its semantic level is not as uniformly defined as that of language. Language is the means through which verbal information is shared, and at the level of literature and poetry, it becomes the art form through which we express ourselves verbally. Music is the art form that expresses feelings and meanings through the qualities of sounds and the relationships between sounds. In language, the specificity of the semantic component provides information. Indeed, verbal communication cannot take place if the listener does not understand the semantic meaning. But in music this is not necessarily the case. Although the meaning of music is enhanced by our knowledge of musical styles and practices, musical meaning remains both pluralistic and personal.

To understand a language, the listener combines the sounds into words that have a semantic meaning and places them within an organized structure (i.e., a grammar). To understand music we combine sounds into motives, melodies, and phrases and listen with various degrees of awareness to many musical elements occurring simultaneously: rhythm, tonality, dynamics, interpretation, all within an overall structure that reflects stylistic influences. There is not one single, uniform meaning that can be attached to a musical composition by all listeners at all times with the same certainty as there is a semantic meaning in a language composition. Broadly speaking, the lack of a specific semantic component leaves the listeners quite free to select from the meanings created by the combinations of the musical elements, and to attach their own meanings to the musical composition as a whole. Because of the lack of a uniformly defined semantic meaning and the multiplicity of elements occurring in a musical piece, music has a plasticity and a richness that language does not.

Music contains a simultaneity of meanings and a plurality of meanings. The simultaneity of meanings exists because each musical element has its own line, its own importance, yet all contribute to an overall form and significance. In music many musical elements occur, simultaneously creating musical shapes and giving rise to musical meanings. The combination of the musical elements and the effect of the performer's interpretation create an exceptionally rich and complex stimulus.

Although our tone of voice and the dynamics of our speech influence very much the nuances of meaning that we wish to convey, communication through language is possible because of the specificity of the semantic level. For example, pronounce "good morning" placing a different emphasis each time on one of the two words. Now pronounce it using a variety of speech dynamics from a bitter, sarcastic comment to an affectionate greeting. Because music is not based on a unified semantic level, we become particularly sensitive to the specific combinations of the musical elements, the nuances, and the dynamics of each performance. Lewers (1980) writes: "If inflection and nuance *enhance* the effect of spoken language, in music they *create* the meaning of the notes. Unlike words, notes and rests do not point to ideas beyond themselves; their meaning lies precisely in the quality of the sounds and silences, so that the exact rendering of the notes, the nuances, the inflection, the intensity and energy with which notes are performed *become* their musical meaning" (p. 67). Indeed, a composition may take a particular meaning just because of the interpretation of a performer.

How many musical elements contribute to create a single measure of music? One of the principal reasons we can keep listening over and over again to a brief piece of music is because of the multiplicity of patterns that potentially we can attend to, and because of the potentially great number of meanings that listening to music can offer us. The art of listening is the art of discovery, and it motivates us to listen again. Consciously or subconsciously, listeners realize that they could discover different degrees of saliency for specific elements in the music with every hearing. The simultaneity with which lines and elements occur in music is different from that of language; this influences the way in which we listen to music perceptually and influences the way in which we retrieve a meaning from music emotionally. When several people speak different words at the same time, they produce cacophony. But when they sing different words at the same time, it may result in immense beauty if the individual parts are coordinated harmonically, melodically, and rhythmically.

The knowledge of a musical style or tradition can be of great importance in relating the intent of the music. In listening to music, the meaning can be derived from (1) the intellectual appreciation of the musical elements, (2) the emotional, aesthetic reaction that results in the appreciation of the stylistic characteristics of the music (Meyer, 1956, see also Chapter 1 in this volume), and (3) the association of a piece with a specific event or place (what John Booth Davis called the "*Darling, they are playing our tune*" theory, 1978: 69). In the book *The Open Work*, Umberto Eco (1989) writes: "the form of the work of art gains its aesthetic validity precisely in proportion to the number of different perspectives from which it can be viewed and understood. These give it a wealth of different resonances and echoes without impairing its original essence" (p. 3).

In some way, then, listening to music is like looking into a prism: to appreciate its light, we view it from different angles since we may only observe the prism's light one way at a time. This does not deprive the prism of its multiplicity of splendors, but attests to our limitation in being able to focus on one side at a time. In this sense, we are always "correct" when we listen to music because there is no exclusive meaning that can be attributed to a piece. How many elements could we potentially focus on, and how many meanings could a musical composition potentially have?

Researchers have probed extensively into the relationship between music and semiotics, the philosophical theory that deals with the interpretation of signs and symbols. A number of writers have proposed that music, too, may be interpreted semiotically (Clarke, 1989b; Eco, 1979, 1989; Nattiez, 1990; Stefani, 1974). From this perspective, musical excerpts or entire musical compositions may be interpreted by listeners as signs having an explicit meaning because of their structure or their historical association. Umberto Eco (1979) explains:

> [M]usic presents, on the one hand, the problem of a semiotic system without a semantic level . . . on the other hand, however, there are musical signs . . . with an explicit denotative value (trumpet signals in the army) and there are . . . entire "texts" possessing pre-culturalized connotative value ("pastoral" or "thrilling music," etc.). In some historical eras music was conceived as conveying precise emotional and conceptual meanings, established by codes, or at least, "repertoires." (p. 11)

Information Theory

One reason people listen to music is that the listening confirms one's expectations. From this perspective, the listeners' awareness of the patterns of musical tensions and resolutions is what gives music its significance. The listeners' knowledge of the musical style allows them to partake of the tensions and resolutions of the music. As Meyer (1956, see also Chapter 1 in this volume) has proposed: "in music . . . the same stimulus, the music, activates tendencies, inhibits them and provides meaningful and relevant resolutions" (p. 23). In an insightful commentary on the first movement of Beethoven's Fifth Symphony, titled "Music, Mind and Meaning," Marvin Minsky (1981) asks: "Why do we like music? . . . everyone knows how it touches our emotions, but few think of how music touches other kinds of thoughts" (p. 28). He goes on to describe how listening to music engages the previously acquired personal knowledge of the listener. Specifically, Minsky asks: "Why do we like certain tunes? Because they have certain structural features. Because they resemble other tunes we like" (p. 34).

The views of Meyer and Minsky (see also Moles, 1968; Pinkerton, 1956; Youngblood, 1958) are rooted in information theory, the theory based on the mathematical probabilities of what will occur next in a chain of events. In brief, research in the applications of information theory to music examines the probabilities that a musical message will be understood by the listener considering the arousal, the satisfaction, and the frustration of the expectations of the listener. In music there are units (i.e., chords, isolated notes, etc.) that represent meaningful events. How can the listener predict what will happen in hearing the chain of musical events? And which specific predictions can the listener make? Events in music form patterns, and these occur especially at meaningful moments in the unfolding of the music (Coons & Kraehenbuehl, 1985; Kraehenbuehl & Coons, 1959; for a summary on information theory and music, see Bent, 1987). The listener, then, searches for a musical meaning by constantly interpreting what is occurring in the music. This view is consistent with research in the psychology of emotions as proposed by Mandler (1984).

In listening to music, the listener seeks an equilibrium: there must be a proportion of novelty within a background of predictability. So the meaning of music is based on the enigma: on the tension of hearing simultaneously the old and the new, in rejoicing in what we recognize, yet in being fascinated and intrigued by the new possibilities that the composer presents us. The theme from "Frère Jacques," as it appears in the beginning of the third movement of Mahler's First Symphony, is an example of how a familiar melody may present us with a completely different meaning because of the context in which it is heard, and because of the way in which the composer has altered it. Here the French children's song is in a minor key, at a slower tempo than the usual one, and accompanied by the poignant ostinato of the timpani. Our emotions in recognizing the "Frere Jacques" theme are likely to reflect our ambiguity—on the one hand, recalling the way we heard it before and, on the other, wanting to embrace the way Mahler presents it now (Figure 2.5).

III

FIGURE 2.5. Mahler, Symphony No. 1, beginning of the third movement.

Experimental Research in the Meaning of Music

The scarcity of research in musical meaning must be attributed in part to the difficulties of the methods that would be needed to investigate this topic, the major one being caused by the fact that there is no uniform meaning in music for all listeners at all times, and that the meaning that the listeners derive from a piece of music may change over time. But, overall, when subjects are asked to assign a title or a descriptive adjective to musical excerpts, their responses do fall within broad clusters of agreement (Hevner, 1936; Wedin, 1972).

In the book *The Language of Music*, Deryck Cooke (1959) proposed that the intervals of the diatonic scale suggest different emotional qualities and described how some basic melodic tonal combinations give rise to specific emotions. Cooke based his theory on the music of the classic and romantic periods, focusing only on the tonal structure of recurring, brief, melodic motives, without taking into account the importance of their orchestration, tempo, rhythm, dynamics, and the broader musical context in which these motivic fragments occurred.

Recently, Sloboda (1991a, 1991b) has begun to investigate whether emotional reaction may be related to specific musical events. He asked listeners to fill out a questionnaire naming the particular pieces of music to which they could recall having experienced physical manifestations commonly associated with emotions. Sloboda found that there was much agreement in the subjects' responses, and that their emotional reactions could be linked to particular structural features of the musical score. Listeners attributed feelings associated with tears to passages containing appoggiaturas and melodic or harmonic sequences (such as the opening of Albinoni's Adagio for Strings), and they associated shivers with musical passages containing new or unprepared harmonies, or sudden shifts in tonality.

Many listeners emphasized how music promoted an intensification or a release of their existing emotions (Sloboda, 1991a). The comments of these listeners link pertinently with the words of the philosopher Susanne Langer. For Langer, musical structure logically resembles the dynamic pattern of human experience. In her book *Philosophy in a New Key* (1956), she writes: "Music is not the cause or the cure of feelings, but their logical expression. It is not usually derived from affects nor intended for them; but . . . it is about them" (p. 218). Thus Langer finds that music "is not self-expression. It is the expression of feelings" (p. 221).

Summary

Some analogies can be drawn between music and language, and a number of experiments have shown similarities between the perception of music and language at the phonetic and syntactic levels. Unlike language, which is attached to semantic structure, music can truly be seen as a universal language in the sense that music has meaning for everyone who listens to it. This meaning is not static, but can change for each person with each listening as our focus shifts from melody to harmony to rhythm to form to the subtleties of the performer's interpretation.

NOTE

1. Bernstein (1976) also used this Chopin mazurka as an example of ambiguity, although his discussion had a different emphasis.

REFERENCES

Baroni, M. (1983). The concept of musical grammar. *Music Analysis*, 2(2), 175–207.

Baroni, M., & Jacoboni, C. (1978). *Proposal for a grammar of melody: The Bach chorales.* Montreal: University of Montreal Press.

Bent, I. (1987). *Analysis.* New York: Norton.

Bernstein, L. (1976). *The unanswered question: Six talks at Harvard.* Cambridge, MA: Harvard University Press.

Bigard, E. (1990). Abstraction of two forms of underlying structure in a tonal melody. *Psychology of Music*, 18(1), 45–59.

Burrows, D. (1990). *Sound, speech and music.* Amherst, MA: University of Massachusetts Press.

Carrington, J. (1969). *Talking drums of Africa.* New York: Negro University Press.

Chen, M. (1983). Toward a grammar of singing: The tune text association in Gregorian chant. *Music Perception*, 1, 84–122.

Chomsky, N. (1957). *Syntactic structures.* The Hague: Mouton.

Chomsky, N. (1975). *Reflections on language.* New York: Pantheon Books.

Clarke, E. F. (1989a). Mind the gap: Formal structures and psychological processes in music. *Contemporary Music Review*, 3, 1–13.

Clarke, E. F. (1989b). Issues in language and music. *Contemporary Music Review*, 4, 9–22.

Cooke, D. (1959). *The language of music.* Oxford: Oxford University Press.

Coons, E., & Kraehenbuehl, D. (1958). Information as a measure of structure in music. *Journal of Music Theory*, 2, 127–61.

Davis, J. B. (1978). *The psychology of music.* Stanford, CA: University of Stanford Press.

Deliège, I. (1987). Grouping conditions in listening to music: An approach to Lerdahl and Jackendoff's grouping preference rules. *Music Perception*, 4, 325–60.

Deutsch, D. (1981). The processing of structured and unstructured tonal sequences. *Perception and Psychophysics*, 28, 381–89.

Deutsch, D. (1982). The processing of pitch combinations. In D. Deutsch (Ed.), *The psychology of music.* New York: Academic Press.

De Witt, L., & Samuel, A. (1990). The role of knowledge-based expectations in music perception: Evidence from musical restoration. *Journal of Experimental Psychology: General*, 119(2), 123–44.

Eco, U. (1979). *A theory of semiotics* (1st Midland Book Ed.). Bloomington: Indiana University Press.

Eco, U. (1989). *The open work* (A. Cancogni, Trans.). Cambridge, MA: Harvard University Press.

Fodor, J. A., & Bever, T. G. (1965). The psychological reality of linguistic segments. *Journal of Verbal Learning and Verbal Behavior, 4,* 414–21.

Gardner, H. (1973). *The arts and human development.* New York: Wiley.

Gregory, A. H. (1978). Perception of clicks in music. *Perception and Psychophysics, 24,* 171–74.

Hargreaves, D. (1986). *The developmental psychology of music.* Cambridge: Cambridge University Press.

Hevner, K. (1936). Experimental studies in the elements of expression in music. *American Journal of Psychology, 48,* 246–68.

Jusczyk, P. (1986). Speech perception. In K. R. Boff, L. Kaufman, & J. P. Thomas (Eds.), *Handbook of perception and human performance: Vol. 2. Cognitive processes and performance.* New York: Wiley.

Kraehenbuehl, D., & Coons, E. (1959). Information as a measure of experience in music. *Journal of Aesthetics and Art Criticism, 17,* 510–22.

Langer, S. (1956). *Philosophy in a new key* (3rd ed.). Cambridge, MA: Harvard University Press.

Lerdahl, F., & Jackendoff, R. (1983). *A generative theory of tonal music.* Cambridge, MA: MIT Press.

Levin, H., & Kaplan, E. (1970). Grammatical structure and reading. In H. Levin and J. Williams (Eds.), *Basic studies in reading.* New York: Basic Books.

Lewers, J. M. (1980). *Rehearsal as the search for expressiveness: Implications for music reading in the high school mixed chorus.* Unpublished doctoral dissertation, Teachers College, Columbia University, New York.

Lindblom, B., & Sundberg, J. (1970). Towards a generative theory of melody. *Swedish Journal of Music, 52,* 71–88.

Locke, S., & Kellar, L. (1973). Categorical perception in a non-linguistic mode. *Cortex, 9,* 355–69.

Mandler, G. (1984). *Mind and body: Psychology of emotion and stress.* New York: Norton.

McAdams, S. (1987). Music: A science of the mind? *Contemporary Music Review, 2,* 1–61.

Meyer, L. B. (1956). *Emotion and meaning in music.* Chicago: University of Chicago Press.

Miller, G. (1956). The magical number seven plus or minus two: Some limits on our capacity for processing information. *Psychological Review, 63,* 81–97.

Miller, G. (1981). *Language and speech.* San Francisco: W. H. Freeman.

Minsky, M. (1981). Music, mind and meaning. *Computer Music Journal, 5*(3), 28–44.

Moles, A. (1968). *Information theory and esthetic perception* (J. E. Cohen, Trans.). Urbana: University of Illinois Press.

Nattiez, J. J. (1990). *Music and discourse: Toward a semiology of music* (C. Abbate, Trans.). Princeton, NJ: Princeton University Press.

Nketia, K. (1974). *The music of Africa.* New York: Norton.

Page, E. (1991, July 26). Isaac Bashevis Singer, Nobel Laureate for his Yiddish stories, is dead at 87. *The New York Times,* p. B 5.

Pinkerton, R. (1956). Information theory and melody. *Scientific American, 194*(2), 77–86.

Repp, B. (1984). Categorical perception: Issues, methods, findings. In N. J. Lass (Ed.), *Speech and language: Advances in basic research and practice* (Vol. 10). New York: Academic Press.

Revesz, G. (1953). *Introduction to the psychology of music* (G. I. C. De Courcy, Trans.). London: Longmans, Green.

Roads, C. (1979). Grammars as representations for music. *Computer Music Journal, 3*(1), 48–56.

Sachs, C. (1943). *The rise of music in the ancient world.* New York: Norton.

Schenker, H. (1979). *Free composition* (E. Oster, Trans.). New York: Longman. (Original work published 1935)

Schenker, H. (1969). *Five graphic music analyses.* New York: Dover Publications.

Serafine, M. L. (1980). *Music as cognition.* New York: Columbia University Press.

Sloboda, J. (1974). The eye-hand span: An approach to the study of sight-reading. *Psychology of Music, 2,* 4–10.

Sloboda, J. (1977). Phrase units as determinants of visual processing in music reading. *British Journal of Psychology, 68,* 117–24.

Sloboda, J. (1985). *The musical mind: The cognitive psychology of music.* Oxford: Oxford University Press.

Sloboda, J. (1991a). Empirical studies of emotional responses to music. In M. R. Jones and S. Halloran (Eds.), *Cognitive bases of musical communication.* Washington, DC: American Psychological Association.

Sloboda, J. (1991b). Music structure and emotional response: Some empirical findings. *Psychology of Music, 19,* 110–20.

Smith, D. (1987). Conflicting aesthetic ideals in a musical culture. *Music Perception, 4*(4), 373–92.

Smith, D., & Witt, J. (1989). Spun steel and stardust: The rejection of contemporary compositions. *Music Perception, 7*(2), 169–86.

Spender, N. (1987). Psychology of music. In R. L. Gregory (Ed.), *Oxford companion to the mind.* Oxford: Oxford University Press.

Stacey, P. (1989). Towards the analysis of the relationship of music and text in contemporary compositions. *Contemporary Music Review, 5,* 9–27.

Steedman, M. (1984). A generative grammar for jazz chord sequences. *Music Perception, 2,* 52–77.

Stefani, G. (1974). Progetto semiotico di una musicologia sistematica. *International Review of the Aesthetics and Sociology of Music, 5,* 277–89.

Stravinsky, I. (1947). *Poetics of music in the form of six lessons.* New York: Vintage Books.

Tan, N., Aiello, R., & Bever, T. G. (1985). Harmonic structure as a determinant of melodic organization. *Memory and Cognition, 9,* 533–39.

Wachsmann, K., & Cooke, P. (1980). Africa. In S. Sadie (Ed.), *The new Grove dictionary of music and musicians* (pp. 144–53). London: Macmillan.

Wapnick, J., Bourassa, G., & Sampson, J. (1982). The perception of tonal intervals in isolation and in melodic context. *Psychomusicology, 2*(1), 21–36.

Warren, R. (1970). Perceptual restoration of missing speech sounds. *Science, 167,* 392–93.

Wedin, L. (1972). A multidimensional study of perceptual-emotional qualities of music. *Scandinavian Journal of Psychology, 13,* 1–17.

Winn, J. A. (1981). *Unsuspected eloquence: A history of the relations between poetry and music.* New Haven, CT: Yale University Press.

Youngblood, J. (1958). Style as information. *Journal of Music Theory, 2,* 24–35.

Zatorre, R., & Halpern, A. (1979). Identification, discrimination and selective adaptation of simultaneous musical intervals. *Perception and Psychophysics, 26,* 384–95.

3

Perception: A Perspective from Music Theory

NICHOLAS COOK

Introduction

The study of the relationship between music theory and psychology can be traced to the work of Leonard Meyer (1956, see also Chapter 1 in this volume) and Christopher Longuet-Higgins (1976, 1978). It can also be traced to Marvin Minsky, a leading exponent of artificial intelligence, who in 1981 asked: "What might we discover if we were to study musical thinking? Have we the tools for such work?" And then went on to recommend that "music theory is not only about music, but about how people process it. To understand any art, we must look below its surface into the psychological details of its creation and absorption" (pp. 28–29).

The last decade has seen a blossoming of the research in the cognitive psychology of music (see Deutsch, 1982; Dowling & Harwood, 1986; Howell, Cross, & West, 1985; Jones & Holleran, 1992; Longuet-Higgins & Lisle, 1989; McAdams, 1987; Sloboda, 1985). Indeed, psychologists have become interested in music because the perception and cognition of music reflect mental structures. Their work has yielded models to test music theory empirically, and at the same time, some music theorists have placed musical analysis within a wide spectrum of knowledge that draws from linguistics and information theory (see Bent, 1987; and Lerdahl & Jackendoff, 1983).

Broadly speaking, musicians and music psychologists have a similar goal: to know how music is perceived and understood. The interest of music theorists and musicians is in understanding better the musical structure and musical interpretation of actual compositions; cognitive psychologists, on the other hand, have been more interested in researching mental theories of how specific musical events may be perceived. Their emphasis has been primarily to investigate the perception of separate musical parameters rather than the musical experience.

In this chapter, Nicholas Cook acknowledges the growing interest in the psychology of music, but argues that cognitive psychology and music theory are two disciplines with essentially different and mutually incompatible aims. Cook challenges the notion that music theory ought to be considered a branch of psychology. He bases his position on the fact that psychological research has placed too much emphasis on the psychoacoustical parameters of music and has not addressed questions intrinsic to the meaning and the cultural value of music. Throughout this chapter, Cook points out that there are potential pitfalls in applying general psychological theories to music without taking into account what listeners actually hear, and why.

As an example of this research, Cook refers to *A Generative Theory of Tonal Music* by Lerdahl and Jackendoff (1983), which proposes that tonal music is based on a grammar. They suggest that in order to understand tonal music the listener needs to know its grammar. Since their book provides a model of the knowledge necessary to listen to tonal music, it is a contribution to both music theory and psychology. For Lerdahl and Jackendoff, the same grammatical principles of tonal music apply whether one listens to individual musical phrases or to entire tonal compositions.

Cook here argues with several aspects of Lerdahl and Jackendoff's theory and quotes experimental evidence demonstrating that people do not listen to music according to large-scale structures. In addition, Cook points out that studies on the recognition of intervals, chord progressions, and key centers are merely tests of ear training. They do not consider the significance of music. He laments: "[P]erceptual psychologists assume that music is made out of notes." Cook concludes by proposing that there be a more careful translation of the concepts from one discipline to the other.

REFERENCES

Bent, I. (1987). *Analysis.* New York: Norton.

Deutsch, D. (Ed.). (1982). *The psychology of music.* Orlando, FL: Academic Press.

Dowling, W. J., & Harwood, D. (1986). *Music cognition.* Orlando, FL: Academic Press.

Howell, O., Cross, I., & West, R. (Eds.). (1985). *Musical structure and cognition.* London: Academic Press.

Jones, M. R., & Holleran, S. (Eds.). (1992). *Cognitive bases of musical communication.* Washington, DC: American Psychological Association.

Lerdahl, F., & Jackendoff, R. (1983). *A generative theory of tonal music.* Cambridge, MA: MIT Press.

Longuet-Higgins, C. (1976). Perception of melodies. *Nature, 263,* 646–53.

Longuet-Higgins, C. (1978). Perception of music. *Interdisciplinary Science Review, 3,* 148–56.

Longuet-Higgins, C., & Lisle, E. R. (1989). Modeling musical cognition. *Contemporary Music Review, 3*, 15–27.

McAdams, S. (1987). Music: A science of the mind? *Contemporary Music Review, 2*, 1–61.

Meyer, L. B. (1956). *Emotion and meaning in music.* Chicago: University of Chicago Press.

Minsky, M. (1981). Music, mind, and meaning. *Computer Music Journal, 5*(3), 28–44.

Sloboda, J. A. (1985). *The music mind: A cognitive psychology of music.* Oxford: Clarendon Press.

Music and Psychology: A Mutual Regard?

There is no doubt that music theorists and perceptual psychologists have become better acquainted with one another's work in recent years. Journals have been set up, such as *Music Perception*, which welcome contributions from either camp. There have been conferences with titles such as "Music and Cognition" which are equally cross-disciplinary in thrust. And, as one might expect, there have been friendly and cooperative programs for cross-disciplinary research. David Clarke, a music theorist, recommends Schenkerian analysis to psychologists as a source of formal theories that may be transformed into empirically testable hypotheses (1989: 130). Carol Krumhansl, a psychologist, recommends empirical data to music theorists as an aid to framing theory in more psychologically relevant terms (1990a: 287). And Jay Dowling puts this picture of mutual cooperation into a nutshell: "Experiments provide tests of theories, and theories show experiments how to define phenomena" (1989: 249).

Of course, the relationship between music psychology and theory is not always so harmonious. One problem has been when musicians draw on perceptual data to justify their theoretical edifices. A classic example of this is the composer and theorist Milton Babbitt, who justified his theory of combinatorial serialism by saying that the system is built out of interval classes, and therefore anyone who can identify pitch classes can hear combinatorial structure (1962: 120). Another is the composer Karlheinz Stockhausen (1959), who justified his use of logarithmic relationships of duration on the grounds that logarithmic relationships are found in the perception of pitch, and that pitch is simply duration transferred to a higher level;[1] therefore, Stockhausen concluded, logarithmic duration structures are perceptually privileged. In each case, the argument—Eric Clarke (1989a: 11) calls it "sleight of hand"—works the same way. A perceptual principle that applies to one set of circumstances (identifying an interval in an ear-training class in Babbitt's case, the logarithmic nature of pitch perception in Stockhausen's) is generalized to a quite different situation, without any consideration as to whether the generalization in fact has any perceptual validity. These are merely extreme and notorious examples of a quite general music-theoretical ploy, the purpose of which is essentially rhetorical: make an initial bow in the direction of the psychology of perception and then carry on with your theorizing regardless, but claiming the enduring benediction of psychology.

Psychologists of music have on occasion lost patience with theorists' cavalier attitudes toward perception. Vladimir Konečni and Heidi Gotlieb (hereafter referred to jointly as Konečni) carried out a number of tests in which well-known works from the classical canon—Bach's *Goldberg* Variations, Beethoven's sonatas—were played with their movements in the wrong order. College-level listeners showed no preference for the original ordering of the movements over the modified one (Konečni, 1984; Gotlieb & Konečni, 1985). Konečni then quoted a number of assertions by theorists to the effect that the movements *had* to be in the order the composer put them in because of considerations of higher unity. (It is worth pointing out that, as is often the case in psychological writings on music, the theoretical sources cited are not held in high regard by contemporary practitioners; genuine theories of intermovemental ordering, as opposed to the kind of old-fashioned pontificating Konečni cited, are in fact quite rare.) And from the contrast between what the theorists said and what the experiments showed, Konečni concluded sourly that "[a] greater degree of caution, moderation, and humility in the music critics' and theorists' often sweeping claims— mere speculations really—would be a welcome consequence of the type of research in the psychology of music that this article advocates" (Gotlieb & Konečni 1985: 98). Or to put it another way: let theorists submit their findings to the psychological tribunal.

Musicians have generally been less vocal in their complaints about music psychologists; they are inclined to mutter that psychologists do not understand music (or, as Eugene Narmour [1989: 97] puts it, "most music psychologists are not sufficiently well-trained to understand how hierarchical patterning emerges in music"), and leave it at that. One symptom of this is the tendency for psychologists to use test materials which are so musically impoverished that they do not really provide a context for *musical* perception at all. This has been widely criticized, and I am not going to repeat the arguments here.[2] There are other respects, too, in which psychological work can strike musicians as being unrealistic. And here a specific example may help.

The basic message of Rita Wolpert's article "Recognition of Melody, Harmonic Accompaniment, and Instrumentation: Musicians vs. Nonmusicians" (1990) is similar to Konečni's: untrained listeners do not listen to music in the same way that musicians do, and what matters to them is not the same as what matters to music theorists. Wolpert's starting point is that theorists view melody, harmony, and rhythm as the essential constituents of music, with instrumentation having a secondary function. (This is as much as to say that "Twinkle, Twinkle, Little Star" is "Twinkle, Twinkle, Little Star" regardless of whether it's played on a soprano saxophone, a sitar, or a sine wave generator.) The aim of Wolpert's research was to find out whether this corresponds to the perceptions of untrained listeners. She carried out a series of experiments, in the first of which trained and untrained subjects heard (1) a tune played on a given instrument (for instance, "Twinkle, Twinkle, Little Star" played on a celesta), then (2) the same tune played on another instrument ("Twinkle, Twinkle, Little Star" played on an oboe), and finally (3) a different tune played on the first instrument ("Hot Cross Buns" played on a celesta).[3] The subjects had to say whether (2) or (3) was "most like" (1). Whereas all the musicians chose (2)—that is, they chose the same tune on a different instrument—nearly half the nonmusicians chose (3)—that is, they chose the same instrument playing a different tune.

Wolpert then conducted two further experiments. In one of them, the same tunes were played as before, but this time they were played with simple harmonic accompaniments; the results were much the same as in the case of the melodies alone. In the other, listeners heard (1) a tune on a given instrument, (2) the same tune on a different instrument, and (3) the same tune on the original instrument, but now with the accompaniment transposed down a fifth, so that it was in a different key from the tune. This time 40 of the 42 nonmusicians chose (3); for them, the identity of the instrument outweighed any changes they noticed in the accompaniment. The musicians, on the other hand, continued to choose (2); for them, playing the accompaniment in the wrong key made a bigger difference than playing the music on a different instrument.

What does all this mean? According to Wolpert (pp. 103–4), it shows that

> Musicians and nonmusicians do not . . . listen by the same rules. Musicians consistently chose melody and correct harmonic accompaniment over instrumentation when matching an excerpt to a model, but nonmusicians did not do so. . . . This choice of instrumentation over correct harmonic accompaniment . . . has important ramifications. It suggests a profound overestimation of what it is that most listeners hear. . . . The implications of these findings are sobering. . . . Music educators may need to teach a new awareness of harmonic accompaniment and key relationships in a more systematic way than they are doing at present. Further, this research may lend empirical verification to what music therapists have long known: instrumentation is attended to and found of interest. . . . The need for empirical verification of what it is that untrained listeners actually attend to can and should inform music professionals.

But a musician might be inclined to retort that it shows nothing of the sort. What it shows is how different listeners respond to questions as to whether one musical extract is more or less like another. Wolpert anticipates objections regarding what she asked the subjects to do: "It was necessary to make the instructions vague, because it was important that the instructions not direct the subject's attention to any one aspect of the music, nor in any way make clear the musical assumptions of the culture" (p. 102). But the result is that the two groups of listeners in Wolpert's tests may well have been engaged in different tasks.

To be a musician trained in the Western tradition means to operate within a language game organized around the concept of "things to play," with a "thing to play" being defined primarily in notational terms (that is, in terms of pitch and duration). You play "the same piece" in one key or another, in one style or another, on one instrument or another—and often to very different effect. When Western musicians, then, are asked whether "Twinkle, Twinkle, Little Star" played on a celesta is most like "Twinkle, Twinkle, Little Star" played on an oboe or "Hot Cross Buns" played on a celesta, they will generally choose "Twinkle, Twinkle, Little Star" played on an oboe because, for them, it is the same piece. This does not mean that they do not care whether the tune is played on a celesta or an oboe. It does not mean that they think other listeners do not care whether the tune is played on a celesta or an oboe. It does *not* mean that they are unaware that "instrumentation is attended to and found of interest." It just means that, when they reply to questions about what they have heard, they do so in terms of the language game of Western musicianship.[4]

But there is no corresponding language game to govern the responses of untrained listeners; that is part of what it means to say that they are untrained. Asking such listeners whether extract (1) is most like extract (2) or extract (3) is rather like asking them whether a melon is most like a banana or a football. It is a bit like both, only in different ways. In culinary and botanical terms, melons are much more like bananas than footballs. On the other hand, imagine an Englishman trying to order fruit in a Tunisian restaurant: "No, no, *not* a banana, what I want is like a *football!*" It is the situation that gives content to the comparison; posed in the abstract, the question whether a melon is more like a banana or a football is pretty meaningless and can be answered equally well either way. The same applies to Wolpert's tunes. Of the untrained listeners in the first two experiments, roughly half said that one excerpt was like another because it had the same tune, and roughly half said it was like another because it was played on the same instrument. In the third experiment, the untrained listeners may or may not have noticed that something had gone wrong with the accompaniment, but most of them said that one excerpt was like another when it had the same tune and was played on the same instrument. This all seems quite straightforward, and it is not an adequate basis for Wolpert's conclusion that "musicians and nonmusicians do not . . . listen by the same rules." In fact, it is not really an adequate basis for saying anything about how people listen to music.

What we have here, as often in psychological writings about music, is an attempt to give a purely psychological explanation for what are in part social phenomena. As I have tried to show, how people respond to psychologists' questions about music is largely a matter of language games, which are essentially social; how they listen to music (for instance, when there are no psychologists about) is quite a different matter. It is because Wolpert does not distinguish between these two things that she arrives at an astonishing conclusion: "There is an immense gulf between the creative intent of the composer or improviser and the perception of the audience. Harmonic practice in classical music, as well as popular, rock, country, jazz, and middle of the road music, shares a similar traditional relationship between melody and harmonic accompaniment of which these listeners are unaware" (p. 104). According to Wolpert, then, even easy-listening music passes over the heads of its listeners; music educators please take note!

In saying this, Wolpert introduces an additional idea, again one that is frequently referred to in the music-psychological literature: the idea of the com-poser's intent being realized in perception. And this raises the question of how far music succeeds in communicating something from composer to listener.

Do People Hear Tonal Structure?

A good way to approach this question is by focusing on cases in which there is an apparent failure of communication between composer and listener. In his article "Cognitive Constraints on Compositional Systems" (1988a), Fred Lerdahl cites Pierre Boulez's *Le Marteau sans Maître* as an example of such a failure. As he says, *Le Marteau*, which was completed in 1954, was widely hailed as a master-piece of postwar serialism, yet for years nobody could figure out just how the serial structure worked. Only recently has the code been cracked. But nobody hears the music differently because of this; the serial structure of *Le Marteau* is so complex and abstract that you cannot hear it, even if you make a special effort to. Here, then, we have a mismatch between the structure the composer puts into the piece and the mental representation of it that the listener forms; Boulez wrote a serial composition, but all that listeners hear is more or less pretty sounds. Lerdahl refers to this as a disjunction between "compositional grammar" and "listening grammar."

As Lerdahl's terminology makes clear, the idea that music involves the en-coding and decoding of some kind of message—something that passes from the composer's brain to the listener's—is based on an analogy with language, and this analogy is central to the interaction between music theory and psychology with which this chapter is concerned. Lerdahl is the co-author, with Ray Jacken-doff, of A *Generative Theory of Tonal Music*,[5] which might be described (not quite accurately) as a reformulation of established theoretical thinking on pitch and rhythm within the general framework of transformational grammar. This means that they are presenting insights drawn from Schenkerian analysis, Coo-per and Meyer's rhythmic theory, and other sources as contributions toward "an explicit formal musical grammar that models the listener's connection between the presented musical surface of a piece and the structure he attributes to the piece" (1983: 3). In other words, Lerdahl and Jackendoff are saying that music theory is really a branch of psychology: "A piece of music is a mentally constructed entity, of which scores and performances are partial representations by which the piece is transmitted. . . . The central task of music theory should be to explicate this mentally produced organization" (p. 2).

Lerdahl and Jackendoff offer their theory to psychologists as a source of predictions regarding the perception of music (1984: 230)—predictions that can be subjected to empirical investigation, along the cooperative lines that I mentioned at the beginning of the chapter. Psychologists have responded to the challenge, and indeed a cursory survey of current writing in music psychology might suggest that *GTTM* is the dominant model in tonal music theory, almost to the exclusion of any other. (The picture is rather different in the music-theoretical literature, where Lerdahl and Jackendoff's work is widely admired, but people tend to stick to the established analytical methodologies or invent their own.) The first major experiment testing Lerdahl and Jackendoff's predictions was carried out by Irène Deliège (1987), who played both musicians and nonmusicians a series of short musical extracts ranging from Bach to Stravinsky. The listeners were supplied with simplified scores of the music, in which each melody note was represented by a dot; they had to draw vertical lines on these scores to show how the music fell into separate phrases or other segments. The subjects' responses were then compared with the segmentation predicted by *GTTM*. On the whole, there was a reasonable correspondence between the two; the theory worked better with musicians than nonmusicians, but Deliège comments that "musical training does not appear to induce the emergence of a grouping behavior radically different from the one used by the naïve listener" (1987: 344).

Now it is almost always possible to raise objections to psychological tests of musical listening, for the simple reason that listeners do not generally listen to music under test conditions, and there is therefore a problem as to how far the results of tests can be generalized to normal listening. (In this case, the question would be to what extent information about how people divide up dots on paper tells us about how people listen to music in the ordinary way.) If, however, we accept Deliège's conclusions—and they seem plausible enough—then how much of *GTTM* have we validated? The answer is: the initial segmentation of the musical surface, but not the larger hierarchical structure that Lerdahl and Jackendoff derive from the initial segmentation. From the standpoint of the music theorist, it is this hierarchical structure that lies at the heart of *GTTM*, because it shows how compositions can be coherent in a specifically *tonal* manner. We can clarify this by referring to the way in which Lerdahl has extended the original *GTTM* to cover atonal music. The essential part of his argument runs as follows (1989: 73–74):

> Given that two events connect, the more *stable* is the one that is more consonant or spatially closer to the (local) tonic; the more *salient* is the one that is in a strong metrical position, at a registral extreme, or more significant motivically. If one event turns out to be more stable and more salient, it unambiguously dominates the other. But if one event is more stable and the other is more salient, there is a

> conflict in the rules. In tonal music stability almost always overrides salience. One might say that the grammatical force of tonal pitch structures can be gauged by their ability to override surface salience. Atonal music may not have stability conditions, but it does project the relative salience of events. The absence of stability conditions makes salience cognitively all the more important. I argue that listeners organize atonal surfaces by means of it. As a result, atonal music collapses the distinction between salience and structural importance.

And a few pages later Lerdahl remarks that this "amounts to an acknowledgement that atonal music is not very grammatical" (p. 94).

Several psychologists have carried out tests showing how this kind of salience influences segmentation. Deliège's (1987) experiments, mentioned above, document the role of such attributes as timbre, register, and dynamics on segmentation. Again, in an experiment where listeners were asked to match musical excerpts with middle-ground reductions, Serafine, Glassman, and Overbeeke found that "metric accent is a major determiner of the structural importance given to tones" (1989: 405). And in tests where musically trained listeners had to rate the strength of boundaries between segments in Mozart's Fantasie in C minor (K. 475), Eric Clarke and Carol Krumhansl found that segmentation was based on such salience-related criteria as change of texture, change of dynamics, and change of register; moreover, they found that these same criteria operated on different levels of structure, from the musical surface to higher-level grouping involving durations of 30–50 seconds (1990: 248–9).

But there is a problem. All these tests were based on tonal music—music, that is, in which criteria based on salience should (according to Lerdahl's theory) have been overridden by criteria based on stability. This emerges with particular clarity from Clarke and Krumhansl's experiments, which compared responses to the Mozart Fantasie with responses to a highly atonal piece: Stockhausen's *Klavierstück IX*. Listeners (and remember these were musically trained listeners) used very much the same criteria in segmenting the Stockhausen piece as the Mozart; in fact, the tables in which Clarke and Krumhansl summarize these criteria for the two pieces are strikingly similar (pp. 227, 243). As the authors comment, there are only two differences between them: "the greater emphasis on pauses and silences as grouping factors in the *Klavierstück* than in the Fantasie, which is a direct result of the more continuous nature of the music in the Mozart, and the greater importance of repetition as a boundary indicator in the Stockhausen" (p. 249). What is strikingly absent from the criteria adopted in the Mozart is any sign of specifically *tonal* features, such as modulations, cadence points, or tonal closure (the return of a tonal excursion to the chord or key with which it began). The conclusion seems inescapable: if people (musically trained people) listen to tonal and atonal music in much the same way, and if atonal music is not very grammatical, then tonal music cannot be very grammatical either.

A few years ago, I carried out a series of tests designed to address the perception of tonal closure in a more direct manner. The significance of tonal closure is that it represents the basic principle of virtually all theories of tonal music—not just Lerdahl and Jackendoff's, but Meyer's, Schenker's, and Schoenberg's. (It is a much more important principle for music theorists than the issue of intermovemental ordering that Gotlieb and Konečni were dealing with.) Put rather too simply, the theory works like this. Tonal compositions begin and end in the same key; that is, a sonata or a symphony is in G major or F-sharp minor, even though it may well contain movements in other keys. Similarly, an individual movement will be in a given key, even though it will probably contain passages in other keys. The idea is that the "home" key, or tonic, represents a point of stability; excursions to other keys represent an increase of tension, which is resolved by the return to the tonic. So the typical sonata movement, which begins on the tonic, moves to the dominant and passes through a series of other keys before returning to the tonic, represents an archlike increase and decrease of tension. The theory, then, purports to explain the practice of tonal composers in terms of the psychological effects that their music has on listeners.

As an illustration of this, consider the third of Liszt's *Fünf kleine Klavierstücke* (Figure 3.1).[6] Bars 1–16 are in F-sharp major, with no more than slight inflections toward the dominant (bars 6–7) and subdominant (bar 11); at the beginning of bar 16 there is a cadence on a diminished seventh, which can be understood as standing for V_7 of F-sharp. Liszt could easily have continued in F-sharp major, for instance by repeating the opening. But he does not do this. Instead, the music shifts unexpectedly into A major. (The voice-leading in the bass—the D of bar 16 falling to C-sharp—means that, although the A major is unexpected, it is not incoherent.) However, the sense of an F-sharp major tonic does not entirely disappear during the A major episode; the B major chord over a C-sharp bass at bar 22, which functions as a modified V_7 of F-sharp and leads to the final tonic, creates a sense of homecoming. The return to F-sharp resolves the tension created by the move to A, and the piece concludes with a satisfying finality. That, at any rate, is the received theoretical wisdom regarding this kind of tonal structure, and similar patterns are found—and explained along the same lines—in much more extended pieces than this *Kleines Klavierstück*.

The question is: do listeners actually respond to this large-scale tonal closure? A simple way to answer this is to play listeners two versions of the piece: the original, as shown in Figure 3.1, and a recomposed version in which the music does not end in the same key as it began in. Figure 3.2 shows such a recomposed version, following on from bar 14 of Figure 3.1; here the music continues, perfectly logically, in F-sharp major. This means that it ends in a rather hard-to-decipher D-sharp major. There is no tonal closure. Tonal theory, then, predicts that the recomposed version of the music will end inconclusively, without creating the satisfying sense of completion engendered by Liszt's version. It might, in fact, lead one to expect a less rich aesthetic experience. My tests, in which the subjects were music students, did not confirm these theoretical predictions.[7] In the case of this particular piece, there was a slight, and not statistically significant, preference for the original version over the recomposed one. In the case of other test pieces there were slight, and not statistically significant, preferences for

FIGURE 3.1. Liszt, *Kleines Klavierstück* no. 3.

the recomposed version over the original one. Only in the case of the two shortest pieces was there a significant correlation of tonal closure and listener preference, and even here preferences were partly the result of ordering effects (listeners tended to prefer whichever version they heard second over the one they heard first). To eliminate the effects of ordering, I carried out further tests. The listeners were divided into groups, each of which heard the two shortest pieces, but with the original and recomposed versions in a different order. This time only the very shortest piece yielded a significant correlation between tonal closure and listener response.

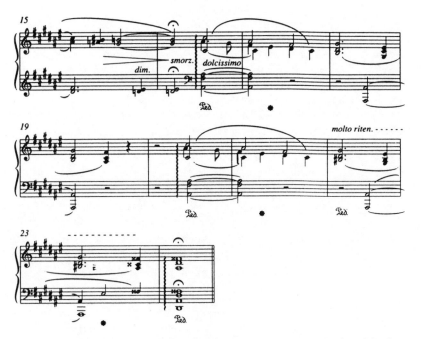

FIGURE 3.2. Liszt, *Kleines Klavierstück* no. 3, bars 15–24 (modified).

The shortest piece of music in these tests was about 30 seconds long,[8] while the next shortest was about 55 seconds. So the tests indicate that tonal closure only has a direct effect on listeners (even musically trained listeners) when the time scale involved is well under a minute. This means that, in perceptual terms, an extended composition cannot have the tonal unity that a single phrase has. Such a conclusion must be disturbing to anybody who expects tonal theory to be psychologically valid, in the sense of correctly predicting the effect of music on listeners. After all, the basic explanatory thrust of theories such as Schenker's or Lerdahl and Jackendoff's is that large-scale musical structures are to be explained along the same lines as small-scale structures. That is what it means to have a hierarchical theory of music; that is what it means to explain music by analogy with the hierarchical structures of transformational grammar.

Burton Rosner and Leonard Meyer have criticized the analogy between musical and linguistic hierarchies from just this point of view; their analysis is so penetrating that it is worth quoting in full (1986: 37).

> Analysts such as Schenker . . . and Lerdahl and Jackendoff . . . may well produce hierarchical diagrams of quite long musical passages. But if "higher" events exert increasingly tenuous perceptual influences, the psychological force of the outputs from such analytical machinery will dwindle quickly, whatever may be their value for the theory of music. In this regard, we must point out a fundamental difference between the tree structures used in linguistics and those presented by music theorists like Lerdahl and Jackendoff. The top node of a grammatical tree is an immediately observed datum: a sentence or an utterance. It represents

some incident, occurring over time, which can be entered completely and rapidly into memory. The associated tree decomposes that uppermost node into parts at several lower levels of a strict hierarchy. The lowest nodes in music-theoretic tree structures, however, represent a datum: an actual stretch of music. Quite often, only fragments of it are held faithfully in memory. The lower nodes in the tree are not decompositions of higher ones. Instead, higher nodes are *selections* from among lower ones. We therefore cannot believe that the increasingly higher nodes, which represent ever more rarified selections, form the core of music perception.

Rosner and Meyer are saying that while the top node of a grammatical tree corresponds to something that is actually said or heard, the musical equivalent has a purely theoretical existence. A related observation—or maybe it is just another way of saying the same thing—is that, whereas the analysis of language converges on semantic content (Chomsky's "deep structure"), the analysis of music does not converge on anything; the "deepest" level of Schenkerian structure, the *Ursatz*, is simply an abstraction. It means nothing at all.

Psychology of Music or Psychology of Ear Training?

One of the major problems in applying models drawn from linguistics to music theory, then, has to do with the significance to be attached to different levels of structure. Another set of problems can be focused around a further concept borrowed from the study of language: pragmatics. Now pragmatics comes in two flavors. What we could call the "mild" flavor means "studying the use of a language as distinct from, but complementary to, the language itself seen as a formal system" (Leech, 1983: x). Or to put it another way, pragmatics deals with what grammar leaves out; to say this is to define pragmatics in terms of grammar. We can focus what is at issue here around Chomsky's well-known distinction between "competence" and "performance." By "competence," Chomsky means the grammatical knowledge that a competent language user has internalized; as the use of the word "internalize" shows, this is considered to be a mental construct. "Performance," on the other hand, refers to the way in which this knowledge is used in actual situations. If theories of competence deal exclusively with perfect, well-formed sentences, theories of performance deal also with interruptions, syntactic breakdowns, failures of comprehension, and the goals that people have in using language in specific contexts (the last of these being the subject matter of pragmatics more narrowly defined). And it is an axiom of formal linguistics that issues of performance cannot be properly understood except on the basis of a theory of competence: as Eytan Agmon puts it, using a different terminology, "one cannot answer the question 'how' before having answered the question 'what'" (1990: 298).

This principle has been transferred intact into linguistically orientated music theory. Lerdahl and Jackendoff state it thus: "In our view it would be fruitless to theorize about mental processing before understanding the organization to which the processing leads" (1983: 4). But there are distinct problems in applying the idea of competence to music. The classic definition of a grammar is a finite set of rules that will generate all, and only, well-formed sentences in a given language; as I said, competence means having internalized such a grammar. Now it is not at all obvious how a clear distinction is to be drawn between musical structures that are well formed and those that are not. To be sure, there are some styles so constrained that one can always say with assurance that this note is right whereas that note is wrong: species counterpoint is one. But then species counterpoint is a pedagogical construct, a demonstration of rules; Palestrina notoriously did things that counterpoint textbooks don't allow. Again, imagine misprints in a Schubert song: some would be obviously wrong (that *can't* be an F-sharp!), but others would be merely questionable (Schumann might write that F-sharp, but surely not Schubert?). To cope with the last case we would need to hypothesize a grammar for Schubert that is different from a grammar for Schumann. And obviously, the process could continue until we had different grammars for early Schubert and late Schubert, for songs and symphonies, for heroic songs and sentimental ones, and so on.

As Eric Clarke (1989b) has said, there are many factors that militate against the usefulness of explaining music in terms of strict grammars: the ways in which composers consciously mix musical styles, the coexistence of different musical styles within a single cultural community, the rate at which style change occurs in music. He explains these things in terms of the different functions served by language and music (p. 19):

> Natural language is essential to the cohesion and survival of human social organization, and hence must make use of structural constraints (grammar) which, by remaining relatively unchanging, ensure successful communication. By contrast, music in European art culture, although serving as an important cultural indicator, does not bear the same functional responsibility, and thus has less need for long-lasting structural constraints. Each piece can make use of a substantial number of principles that are specific only to that work, and which are consequently inexplicable (or at best explicable only at a very general level) in terms of a broad and general structural theory.

Music, in other words, is much more fluid than language. Before you start a conversation, you know what the grammar is going to be; in music, you can never be sure of the grammar until you have heard the piece.

Alan Marsden (1989) has outlined a model of musical listening based on the idea of discovery learning. This model suggests that, as somebody listens to music, certain parsing rules (the kind of rules that *GTTM* is based on) are dynamically strengthened or weakened, according to how well they fit the music. Moreover, the model allows for new rules to be derived. What Marsden is suggesting, then, is that listening to music involves creating a grammar to fit the piece being heard. But to say this is, in effect, to abandon the idea of grammar

altogether, at least as it is understood in formal linguistics. For it means that a
musical grammar is essentially a collection of strategies for understanding music.[9] In other words, it means that the distinction between competence and
performance cannot be sustained as applied to music. So it comes as no surprise
that Lerdahl and Jackendoff fail to sustain it in their own work. As Uwe Seifert
has pointed out (1991), *GTTM* is not really a theory of competence at all. It is a
model of the way in which a structural description may be derived from a
musical surface. It is an input-output mechanism. That is, it is a theory of
performance, though an incomplete one.

   We started with what I called the "mild" flavor of pragmatics. But by now we
have advanced to the "strong" flavor, which maintains that the whole idea of a
formal grammar (and therefore the distinction between performance and competence) is a theoretical artifact, an illegitimate abstraction from the real-world
phenomenon of language. Roy Harris (1980, 1981) is a leading proponent of this
position, and he argues that formal linguistics is a pseudoscience that has come
into being by adopting the principles of traditional grammar (which mainly
means Latin grammar), and then claiming what traditional grammarians never
claimed, that these principles have some kind of psychological validity. In other
words, pedagogical principles (for traditional grammar was a system of teaching)
have been reinterpreted as psychological ones. Harris sees the competence/
performance distinction as playing a crucial role in this transition, because it
means that while grammatical rules are asserted to be "in the brain," it is
impossible to prove or disprove their existence; it is only the *use* of these rules,
that is to say performance, that can be subjected to psychological investigation. If
experiments cast doubt on any given model of language, that need not affect the
issue of competence; it can always be said that, by its nature, performance is
determined by all sorts of factors, and the model under investigation has failed to
make proper allowance for these (1981: 109). In this way the linguist's claim to
be talking about psychological realities is secured against all possible counterevi-
dence from psychologists.

   I am going to argue that there has been a corresponding, if less thoroughgo-
ing, transformation of music theory (which again is in essence a system of
teaching) into a theory of perception. Perhaps the best way to approach this is to
look at a key issue in Harris's account of the transformation of traditional grammar into formal linguistics and see how it applies to music. This is the issue of
scriptism.

   Harris defines scriptism (a word of his own coinage) as "the assumption that
writing is a more ideal form of linguistic representation than speech" (1980: 6).
Modern linguists vociferously disassociate themselves from any such idea, insist-
ing that speech is primary and that the written word is not to be understood as
anything other than a representation of the spoken word. But Harris argues
persuasively that, in reality, linguists analyze speech on the model of writing.
They regard *Mary had a little lamb* as a linguistic unit that can be articulated in
two different ways (depending on whether it is a reply to *What did Mary have?* or

Who had a little lamb?), rather than as two basic linguistic units that happen to be written the same. They regard words as basic linguistic units, and as late as the 1950s were defining them by reference to "potential pauses" in speech—clearly on the model of the space on either side of the written word. They regard phonemes as linguistic units that happen to correspond rather closely to letters, and as late as the 1970s were trying to analyze speech into fixed sound units corresponding to phonemes (1981: 57). Linguistics, as Harris puts it, is cryptoscriptist.

What about music theory? Again, we have the vociferous insistence that the proper object of study is the sound of music, not the written score. Except in a few special instances (say a study of music preserved in an imperfectly understood notation), no music theorist would care—or dare—to say that she was interested in the score as anything other than a representation of the sound, the listener's experience of the sound, or both. In other words, music theorists *use* scores, but they do not *study* scores—they study the music. Or at least that is the claim. But, in fact, it is obvious that the claim is not always true. Consider a set-theoretical analysis of a piece of atonal piano music, say Schoenberg's *Sechs Kleine Klavierstücke*, op. 19, no. 3. Set theory[10] deals with the relationships between the individual notes you can see in the score. Of course, you hear the notes when you listen to the music. Or do you? Well, you hear a succession of composite sounds which, if you have a good musical training, you may be able to distinguish into their component pitches. But then again, you may not; there is no law saying that, in order to do an analysis of atonal piano music, you have to be able to "hear out" each note of the music. Of course, you might hear each note in the sense that if a wrong note was played, or if a note was left out or added, you would recognize that something was wrong. But then again, you might not; in practice it would probably depend on what the note in question was. In other words, there is, to put it mildly, a nonlinear relationship between the notes in the score and what people hear when they listen to a performance of it. Set theory takes no account of this.

At least, in the case of atonal piano pieces, the note is actually there, in the sense that either the pianist plays it or he doesn't. But there is a lot of music in which even this is doubtful proposition. An opera singer sings a rapid scale: does she actually sing every note? Is there a clear transition between each note and the next, or does one slide into the other? If so, how do you tell where one note stops and the next one starts? Or is there just a rather uneven glissando? Is the only way of answering these questions to record the sound and slow it down or print out a time/frequency graph of it? But if you have to do this to decide what notes are there, can you really say they are there in a *musical* sense? Problems of this sort become particularly pressing in the case of the florid singing characteristic of many Asian cultures. Robert Gjerdingen (1988) recently published a computer analysis of extracts, a few seconds long, from recordings made by the South Indian singer Gayathri Kassebaum. As he explains, Kassebaum's voice is constantly in motion; traditional melograms (the ethnomusicologist's word for combined time/frequency and time/intensity graphs) reveal a bewildering multi-plicity of events. Yet comparison between Kassebaum's different recordings of this passage, and between Kassebaum's recordings and students' imitations of her singing, reveals a much smaller number of events that remain invariant between the different performances. It is presumably these that are the notes—that is, if there *are* notes in Kassebaum's singing.

Gjerdingen offers a transcription of the passage into Western notation based, not on traditional melograms, but on graphs of the combined rates of change in frequency and intensity; these graphs throw the invariant events into relief. But he observes that such graphs can provide no more than a "good foundation" for transcription, because any musical notation involves cultural values (pp. 59–60):

> When we move from the analysis of curves, functions, and rates of change to a discussion of notes or particular rhythms, we are moving towards the consideration of cultural units of meaning, not simply pitches and intensities. Sensitivity is required when different cultures have differing ideas about the nature of such units.

Another way to put this is that the notes are not "in" the recording of Kassebaum's singing. Rather, they are constructed *out* of it through appropriate (or inappropriate) interpretation. And this is also true of Western music. There are no notes "in" the opera singer's rapid scale; if we interpret what we hear as a scale, a series of notes, and not as a rather uneven glissando, that is because in most operatic styles we expect scales rather than glissandos. (If she were singing music by Ligeti, we might hear the glissando.) Again, music students often have difficulty when they are asked to write down the inner lines of four-part chorale settings, which is part of the traditional music curriculum. It's not that they hear the lines but can't write them down; it's that they can't hear them. Later, when they have learned more harmony, they find that they can hear the inner lines quite easily. This is because they now know how to "compose" possible inner lines, so to speak, and compare these with what they hear. In other words, they have learned how to *create* notes and lines in what was previously a composite, undifferentiated mass of sound. Untrained listeners, of course, cannot do this. For them, there are no notes in the inner lines. Or rather, there are no inner lines—just, at most, inner parts.

If music theorists really wanted to analyze how music sounds, and only how it sounds, they would put away their scores and forget all about notes. Some phenomenologically minded theorists have tried to do just this. The trouble is that they almost invariably end up creating scores of their own. The only difference is that their scores tend to be relatively impoverished representations of the music, so the analytical results are generally unsatisfying from a musical point of view. This is not really surprising. In the first place, music theorists can no more forget about notes than linguists can forget about letters; they are part of our mental equipment. In the second place, any music theorist who achieves the impossible and forgets about notes "risks being left with a shapeless mass which he does not know what to make of" (Harris, 1980: 17). Harris is talking about language, but what he says applies with no less force to music. For all music has its source in mental representations based either on notation or on kinesthetic imagery derived from singing or playing musical instruments; to compose is to manipulate images (Cook, 1990: Chapters 2, 4). It stands to reason, then, that the kind of full and satisfying comprehension of music at which the theorist aims is unlikely to be attained, except on the basis of a representation as richly determinate as that in terms of which the music was conceived. For this reason, there is nothing wrong in principle with the theorist who carries out a set-theoretical analysis of notes that he could not pick out from the musical sound. And in any case, he may well end up hearing them. It is often claimed that one of the benefits of music theory is that it enables people to hear music better. In fact, you might say that the main point of analyzing music is to enable us to respond to the excess of music over sound. I shall come back to this later.

This kind of defense against charges of scriptism is not available to psychologists, whose studies of musical perception are meant to be descriptive rather than prescriptive (that is, we expect them to tell us how people hear music, not how they might best hear it). And even a cursory examination of the music-psychological literature will show that such charges are warranted. The general picture that emerges is that, as Eric Clarke puts it, listeners "accumulate and integrate individual notes of a performance . . . into successively more abstract and global representations" (1989a: 4); we have studies of how listeners distinguish the voices of polyphonic music, discriminate intervals, follow chord progressions, and judge key centers. Now people can do all these things, at least within certain constraints. They are trained to do these things if they become music students. (They have to be trained, because otherwise they can't do them.) Such training—called ear training, aural training, or aural analysis—creates the interface between musical sound and the theoretical knowledge in terms of which musicians create, notate, and reproduce music. So we have a lot of psychological studies of ear training. The trouble is that they are not called studies of ear training. They are called studies of musical listening. And as such they are thoroughly unsatisfactory, because they begin with the premise that people hear music in terms of music-theoretical categories. They assume what music theory assumes; that music is made out of notes. This is scriptism with a vengeance. I am tempted to improve on Harris's coinage and call it *theorism*.

Theory of Music or Theory of Mind?

Perhaps the most revealing example of theorism is tonal hierarchy theory. This theory, most conspicuously represented by the work of Carol Krumhansl, can be traced to two sources: one theoretical, and the other psychological. The theoretical source is a tradition of representing key relationships in topological terms that originated in eighteenth-century Germany, the best-known example being

the "chart of the regions" in Schoenberg's *Structural Functions of Harmony*
(Figure 3.3). Schoenberg's chart shows a two-dimensional space with minor
thirds on one axis and perfect fifths on the other, and its purpose is to indicate
how closely different tonal regions are related to one another. For instance, the
chart shows the distance from C major to F-sharp major as being much greater
than the distance from C major to G major. What this means is that, in writing
music in the tonal style, it is not easy to make the relationship between C major
and F-sharp major sound coherent; modulating from C to F-sharp major requires a lot more care, if it is to be done convincingly, than modulating from C
to G major. The purpose of the chart, then, is pedagogical. *Structural Functions
of Harmony* is a textbook.

The psychological source of tonal hierarchy theory is a methodological one:
the probe tone technique, introduced by Krumhansl and Roger Shepard in
1979. The purpose of this technique is to find out how the perception of individual pitches is affected by the context in which they are situated. Usually the
contexts provided in experiments of this sort are very simple: subjects may hear a
rising major scale, or 16 notes selected more or less at random from a given
diatonic set. (Some recent work has involved more extensive contexts.) After
listeners have heard these materials, they are played a final note—this is the
probe tone—and asked how well this final note follows from the others "in a
musical sense" (Krumhansl, 1983: 35). Such tests are carried out using a range of
probe tones (usually all the notes of the chromatic set). The results are analyzed
statistically, and this yields a profile showing how well each of the different probe
tones has been judged to fit in that particular context; this is what Krumhansl
calls a tonal hierarchy. For instance, you find that the tonic and fifth are judged
to fit better than other notes in a diatonic major context. Moreover, you can
compare the profiles of different diatonic sets; it turns out that, as you might
expect, C major and G major are much more similar than C and F-sharp major.
Krumhansl and her co-workers take this to be a measure of the distance between
different keys, and if you express the results of such comparisons topologically,
you end up with a chart that is essentially identical to Schoenberg's "chart of the
regions."[11] So these experiments may be said to demonstrate the psychological
reality of Schoenberg's topological representation of key relationships.

Krumhansl's work has come in for a good deal of criticism, some of it

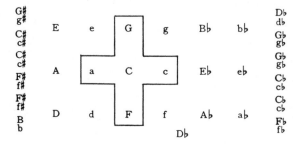

FIGURE 3.3. "Chart of the regions" from Schoenberg, 1969.

acrimonious. One of the main complaints is the one I leveled at Wolpert's experiments: the task required of the subjects is too vague. Just what does it mean to ask how well the probe tone fits "in a musical sense"? In *what* musical sense? One of Krumhansl's experiments highlights the complexities of the response situation: in probe tone tests based on serial contexts, listeners inexperienced in serial music produced profiles similar to those found in tonal music, whereas experienced listeners produced exactly the opposite profiles. Krumhansl and her associates suggest that this was because the experienced listeners adopted "a strategy, whether conscious or not, of relating the serial contexts to tonal hier-archies of major and minor keys, and simply reversing the ordering of the ratings" (Krumhansl, Sandell, & Sergeant, 1987: 73–74). In this case, since the responses were fairly consistent within each group of subjects, it can't have been too hard to see that they were adopting different strategies. In other cases, however, the divergences between response strategies might be much harder to spot. David Butler, who has been foremost among Krumhansl's critics, writes of a particular experiment that "the rating of any probe tone following the contex-tual series of chords might have signaled one listener's judgment of melodic continuation at the same time that it recorded another listener's judgment that the probe tone represented a well- or ill-fitting extrapolation of the roots of the chords in the contextual pattern" (1990: 329). Adding such divergent ratings together would make little sense, because the listeners are not engaged in the same task. Each is judging how well the probe tone fits, but in a *different* musical sense. [12]

Krumhansl responds to such objections by pointing out that there is consider-able consistency in the results obtained by means of the probe tone technique; "Different listeners exhibit similar patterns of responses, and the same individual tends to produce the same or nearly the same response on different occasions when the identical musical stimulus is presented" (1990a: 11). Butler, however, has another explanation for this consistency: the test materials in these experi-ments have been consistently weighted toward the tones that end up with the highest ratings in the profiles. In other words, listeners have generally said that the tonic and the fifth fit best in a major-scale context because there have generally been more tonics and fifths in the test materials than other scale degrees; the resulting profile is "a stimulus artifact . . . rather than a reflection of mental representations of pitch relations" (1989: 230). Now this is at first sight a very damaging claim. Krumhansl, however, agrees that her tests do indeed show that "humans . . . are highly sensitive to information about frequency of occur-rence" (1990b: 315). And she refers to comparative tests of Western and Indian listeners who heard materials taken from North Indian ragas. Although the Western listeners had no experience of Indian music, they produced profiles very similar to those of the Indian listeners, all of whom were trained in Indian music. Krumhansl's (1990a: 262–63) explanation of this result is that the West-ern listeners must have registered the relative salience or emphasis given the various tones in the musical contexts. In this case, this strategy produced style-appropriate tonal hierarchies. Thus, it could be used to achieve a sense of tonal organization that, when refined and solidified through experience, would serve as the basis for appreciating and remembering more complex and subtle structural features. For the Indian listeners, the high correlations between the probe tone ratings and the tone durations reflect the convergence between the surface emphasis given the various tones and the underlying tonal organization of the rāgs.

And in her response to Butler, she cites some statistical measures of the relative frequency of occurrence of different scale degrees in different works by composers like Mozart, Schubert, and Schumann, showing how these note frequencies correspond closely to the profiles for major and minor keys yielded by probe tone studies (1990b: 316, also in 1990a: 68).

By this stage in the argument it is becoming less and less clear what the probe tone studies are actually telling us. How can the same results for Western and Indian listeners in Krumhansl's experiment tell us different things in each case— that Western listeners are responding to surface features, while Indian listeners are responding to the convergence between surface features and underlying tonal organization? If perceived tonal hierarchies are a function of the frequency of occurrence of different notes, chords, or keys, then won't any probe tone experiment yield profiles that simply reflect the test materials and so cannot be generalized to any other musical context? But it isn't this simple; sometimes the attributes of the test materials and the results of probe tone experiments don't go hand in hand. For instance, tests using Balinese materials yielded different results for Western and Balinese listeners (Krumhansl, 1990a: 266–68). Krumhansl explains this in terms of the different knowledge of musical style with which the two groups of listeners approached the task. Her basic assumption is that probe tone tests reveal stable, long-term knowledge that listeners use in processing musical sounds. In an overview of her work written in 1983, she described it as "an initial attempt to understand the kinds of internal representations and processes involved in listening to tonal music. The results provide a quantitative, structural description of the kinds of knowledge listeners have about fundamental aspects of tonal organization" (1983: 59). And she referred to the tonal hierarchy as "the fundamental underlying feature of tonal music, one that is generative of interkey relations" (p. 56). The word "generative" says it all; tonal hierarchy theory was to provide something like a competence theory for tonal music. Krumhansl began her 1983 overview with a reference to Chomsky.

Since then, however, it has become increasingly evident that the static nature of tonal hierarchy theory drastically limits its explanatory scope. In Butler's words, "it is necessarily based on a rigid, time-independent conception of musical consonance in which the tonic is always considered most consonant and most stable, the dominant is next-most consonant and next-most stable, and so on" (1989: 223). But key identification, to take one of the things Krumhansl has tried

to explain in terms of tonal hierarchies, is clearly time-dependent. Whether a given passage projects a specific tonic, say C, does not simply depend on the notes in the passage: it depends on their ordering (which is to say, on their harmonic implications, contour, and so forth). A recent experimental study of key identification grew out of "a class in the psychology of music in which the . . . author had programmed a computer to sound out the notes of a diatonic scale in random succession and, after a minute or so of this continuous stream of notes, asked the class of musically highly educated listeners to hum what they thought was the major-mode tonic. To his (and the class's) surprise, the result was a cacophony" (West and Fryer, 1990: 254). The ensuing experiment, based on a version of the probe tone method in which subjects were asked "to judge the suitability of the probe tone *as a tonic*" (p. 255, my italics), confirmed the impression: responses depend on the order in which the notes are presented. This means that tonal hierarchy theory can capture, at best, only part of the phenomenon of key identification.

In her 1990 response to Butler (who for years has been arguing that key identification is time-dependent), Krumhansl takes an accommodating line over the question of key identification, suggesting that tonal hierarchies constitute just one of several relevant factors (1990b: 317). And her characterization of the general scope of tonal hierarchy theory is also more modest than it was in 1983: "tonal contexts (even simple, schematic ones) evoke listeners' knowledge about how musical entities, such as tones, chords, and keys, are generally used in the style. These abstract pitch relations provide a background that facilitates understanding the organization of a particular piece" (pp. 313–14). As a matter of fact, Lerdahl has recently incorporated tonal hierarchy theory within *GTTM* in a way that is very much in line with this. In the original version of *GTTM*, there were informally stated "stability conditions" favoring certain structural interpretations over others. (The basic idea was that connections are more likely between elements that are tonally close to one another.) In his article "Tonal Pitch Space" (1988b), however, Lerdahl presents a more formal model of these stability conditions; this is, in essence, an amplified and generalized version of Schoenberg's "chart of the regions."[13] And he invokes Krumhansl's experiments as showing the psychological reality of the model. He doesn't express a view as to exactly what the model represents; as a theorist (rather than a psychologist) he doesn't need to. He is using tonal hierarchy theory as a rule of thumb, and you can do this without knowing whether it reflects listeners' long-term knowledge of a given style, or their responses to note distributions in a given passage, or, for that matter, some other factor such as tonal consonance.

Roy Harris says of the transformation of traditional grammar into modern linguistics that "[t]he situation in which an established descriptive format devised for one particular purpose is taken over and adapted to serve some new and quite different purpose is a situation fraught with potential errors and inconsistencies of all kinds" (1981: 54). That a similar situation obtains in the study of music is clear from statements like "the existing body of music theory is essentially a non-formalised cognitive theory" (Marsden and Pople, 1989: 30), or "Rameau's *basse fondamentale* or Schenker's *Ursatz*, and more generally, 'music analysis' of almost any familiar kind, may be convincingly construed as attempted descriptions of underlying mental realities" (Agmon, 1990: 285). The attempt to transform music theory into a theory of mind accounts for some of the most basic characteristics of current music psychology: not just the emphasis on notational categories that I mentioned earlier, but the whole guiding principle that there are specialized psychological mechanisms which process different parameters of the music more or less independently of one another. As Eric Clarke notes (1989a: 4), this approach is derived from music theory; psychologists have taken theoretical constructs and attempted to give them a psychological interpretation. Tonal hierarchy theory is an example of just this process, and the acrimonious debate over it exemplifies the difficulties of which Harris speaks.

Nothing in the practice of Western tonal music suggests that unordered collections of notes, like the C major diatonic set, function in their own right as significant musical structures. It is *ordered* structures that are significant: harmonic progressions, melodic patterns. The diatonic set is simply a theoretical abstraction, a generalization from specific harmonic and melodic contexts. It is a pedagogical construct, like Schoenberg's chart of the regions. Tonal hierarchy theory, then, does not arise from the observable phenomena of music. It arises from the attempt to give a psychological interpretation to concepts drawn from music theory. In this sense, it is theory-driven rather than data-driven. Now in saying this I am going against Krumhansl's own claims regarding her topological representations of tonal structure: they are not theoretical models, she tells David Butler in reply to his criticisms, they are simply descriptions of data. Indeed, she appears to question whether there is such a thing as tonal hierarchy "theory" at all (1990b: 309–10). But there is something disingenuous about this argument. In the first place, what Krumhansl presents as (say) a major-key profile is an extrapolation from test materials in which certain notes of the C major scale appeared in a certain order; the extrapolation is made on the assumption that unordered pitch sets constitute meaningful contexts. This is a theoretical assumption. In the second place, as Eric Clarke says, "there is a strong sense in much of this work that these descriptions or formalisms are regarded as being very close to truly mental structures—not least because they are presented as contributions to the cognitive psychology of music" (1989a: 6). The title of Krumhansl's recent book-length exposition of her work is *Cognitive Foundations of Musical Pitch*.

Why did the debate between Krumhansl and her critics become so acrimonious? The basic reason seems to be that the protagonists could not agree what they were talking about. They could not agree what tonal hierarchy theory was a theory of. They could not agree whether it was a theory at all. The story of tonal hierarchy theory is the story of a description in search of a meaning.

Should Theory Reflect or Challenge
Musical Perceptions?

Jay Dowling writes that "psychologists like myself often assume that cognitive processing (whether consciously explicit or not) proceeds in an analytic mode—that like Schumann's 'ideal listener' the brain reconstructs the score as it goes along" (1989: 250). And he adds: "This assumption feeds a theoretic position built on the experimental analysis of the brain's feature analysis." When he says "theoretic," Dowling is referring to psychological theory. But the same assumption feeds—and is fed by—music theory, which has always had a basically scriptist orientation. The result of the psychologization of music theory (I am tempted to write, the music theorization of psychology) is that it has come to seem natural for both theorists and psychologists to explain music in terms of formal principles or rules—if not actually the rules offered by current music theory, then future rules, better rules, that will be shown to be psychologically valid. Lerdahl and Jackendoff's work obviously represents a giant step in this direction and holds out the promise of a single theory that will be at the same time musical and psychological. What I want to suggest in this final section is that such total convergence between music theory and psychology may not be desirable, or even feasible, because the two disciplines have essentially different and mutually incompatible aims.

Lerdahl and Jackendoff's theory of music is both music theory and psychology because it assumes, not just that there are rules governing both composing and listening to music, but that they are essentially the same rules. Or rather, it assumes that they *ought* to be essentially the same rules, and that to the extent that they are not, there is a failure in the communicative process. Earlier I mentioned how, in his "Cognitive Constraints on Compositional Systems," Lerdahl attacks *Le Marteau sans Maître* on the grounds that there was a mismatch between its "compositional grammar" and its "listening grammar." He goes on to prescribe a number of conditions that must be fulfilled if this kind of mismatch is to be avoided. And he puts forward two general aesthetic laws: "The best music arises from an alliance of a compositional grammar with the listening grammar," and "[t]he best music utilizes the full potential of our cognitive resources" (1988a: 255–56). If the first of these laws excludes *Le Marteau* and serial music in general, the second has still more drastic effects: Ligeti's *Atmosphères* drops out because it blurs distinction between events (p. 239), Balinese gamelan music "falls short with respect to its primitive pitch space" (p. 256), and "[r]ock music fails on grounds of insufficient complexity." (Rock music attracts massive audiences, plays a major role in the personal and social development of young people, and makes fortunes, but it fails all the same.) Such conclusions will strike many people as astonishing; however, this doesn't invalidate Lerdahl's starting point, which is that a composer can't just stuff structure into a piece of music and expect listeners to be able to reconstruct it simply because it is there. There are constraints on the kind of structures that listeners can reconstruct.

But this brings us back to the question that Dowling raised: how far *are* people engaged in reconstructing structure when they listen to music? Dowling continues, "We should not forget that the brain and mind is not always so precise and analytic, and that cognitive processing can operate effectively on a more global level." In other words: even if it is possible for people to listen analytically, they may choose to listen holistically instead. There is plenty of evidence that they do just this. If Lerdahl's account of listening grammar is correct, then the subjects in Clarke and Krumhansl's experiments could have listened to the Mozart Fantasie grammatically—that is, could have reconstructed the structure—in a manner impossible in the case of *Klavierstück IX*; but they apparently listened to both pieces in much the same way. (Similar, though less formal, experiments of my own produced comparable results.)[14] Again, Alan Smith played incomplete movements from Haydn symphonies to a group of music students, and asked them to say at what point in the form the music had stopped; in the first test "[t]he results were not better than might have been expected had the subjects all guessed. However, during two sequent selections the subjects, who now knew what was expected of them, performed well" (1973: 212–13). In other words, the students could perfectly well have listened grammatically the first time, but they *chose* not to. Introspective and anecdotal evidence suggests that this is how most people listen most of the time.[15]

The idea that music is a process of communication in which listeners decode structures that composers have encoded—the idea we saw at its most basic in Wolpert's article—is, then, based on several disputable assumptions: that people choose to listen grammatically; that there is, or ought to be, an equivalence between compositional and listening grammars; and, most fundamentally, that there is such a thing as musical grammar. It seems to me that a strong argument can be made that, if music is like language at all, then it is most like everything in language *except* grammar. In a book entitled *The Violence of Language*, Jean-Jacques Lecercle writes, "Words speak. They alliterate . . . , they proliferate in the inventories of subjects and passions, . . . they quibble . . . , and of course they endlessly pun. Homophony is the law of the remainder" (1990: 98). By "the remainder," Lecercle means the power of words to create signification of their own, to subvert intended meanings, to do violence to their users. He means the "parts of language that no grammar can ever reach" (p. 18). Lecercle, like Harris, does not believe in formal grammars. In fact, he does not believe in grammars at all. Or rather, he believes that they consist of "largely arbitrary and negative frontiers" (p. 52); he sees them as interventions in the world, historical institutions, part of the politics of language. Now Lecercle's analysis is at least equally applicable to music; what is music but the speaking, alliteration, proliferation, quibbling, and endless punning of sounds? What is its basic law, if not homophony? And it seems clear enough that the rules of music theory serve to codify, legitimize, and institutionalize musical styles. They explain music, to be sure, but not in the sense that formal grammars explain language; more in the sense that books of etiquette explain how to behave in public.

I can clarify this by going back to the issue of tonal closure. As I said, theorists explain forms like sonata in terms of tonal excursions creating and resolving tension. But we have seen that listeners do not, in practice, respond to large-scale tonal structure. The theory of tonal closure, then, fails to predict listener responses. It is bad psychology. But then, it was never meant to be psychology. It was meant to be a way of thinking about large-scale musical structure. For the tonal plan of a sonata movement governs the disposition of themes and textures, the patterning of loud and soft and high and low, the pacing of climax and relaxation—all aspects of music that *do* directly bear on the listener's experience (Rosner & Meyer, 1986). The idea of tonal closure allows us to recapture something of the way in which composers of the eighteenth and nineteenth centuries conceived their music. Schenker's reductive graphs, or Lerdahl and Jackendoff's, show how these composers adopted the same principles in shaping the small-scale and the large-scale structure of their music. They built sections and even entire movements on the model of a single phrase, articulating each through the motion of tonic to dominant and back to tonic. They created a hierarchy of closures ranging from the perceptible to the imperceptible. And because of this, it does not really make sense to look upon hierarchical theories of music as theories of perception. At their higher levels, at least, theories such as Schenker's or Lerdahl and Jackendoff's tell us far more about what composers of tonal music did than about what listeners to their music do.

A psychological theory of music is successful to the extent that it reflects perception. Musical perception is pluralistic and fluid; listeners make use of multiple cognitive frameworks (Marsden & Pople, 1989) and shift their strategies from one moment to the next (Hantz, 1984: 255). A psychological model of perception needs to embody these characteristics. But there is no reason why music theory should be like this. When a theorist analyzes a piece of music, she is taking up an interpretive stance in relation to it. She is following through the implications of a particular way of thinking about it. She is aiming, perhaps, to change the way people experience the music. From this point of view, the psychologist's perceptual model is totally inappropriate because, as David Osmond-Smith puts it, "the resultant theoretical construct will be devoid of critical content: it cannot challenge our pre-formed responses because it sets out to reproduce them" (1989: 92). The aim of music theory, then, is to go beyond perception. In fact, you might put the point polemically and say that, from the music-theoretical point of view, an analysis can have value only to the extent that it *deviates* from perception. As an illustration of this, consider Schenker's analysis of the opening theme from Beethoven's Sonata, op. 90 (Figures 3.4, 3.5) Schenker suppresses the most perceptually salient feature of Beethoven's music—the pause on the dominant and registral displacement at bar 16. He

FIGURE 3.4. Beethoven, Sonata, op. 90, first movement, bars 1–24.

reads a tonic prolongation right across this passage. Critics who accuse Schenker of reducing the classics to abstract formulae could have a field day here! But such accusations are the result of looking *at* the analytical graph, instead of looking *through* it to the music. Schenker's graph expresses a stylistic norm, against which Beethoven's music stands out in all its singularity. It casts an oblique light on the music, thus throwing its characteristic features into relief. The content of the analysis, then, lies in the divergence between the graph and the music listeners hear.[16]

Another illustration of this is Charles Rosen's analysis of Haydn's String Quartet in B minor, op. 33, no. 1. This is focused round the interaction of B minor and D major. The tonal ambiguities of the opening (Figure 3.6), leading to the trenchant A-natural/A-sharp clashes of bars 3–4, create a tension that Rosen sees as generating much of the work's large-scale structure. The rest of the movement resolves the dissonant D major, he says, "first by treating it as the dominant or secondary key . . . , and then by expanding this in the 'development' and resolving everything in a recapitulation which—except for two measures at the opening—insists dramatically on the tonic" (1976: 120). But do listeners hear all this? Well, maybe they *do* after they have read Rosen's analysis, which succeeds wonderfully in sharpening perceptions. (It's an obvious fact,

FIGURE 3.5. Schenker's reduction of Beethoven's Sonata, op. 90, first movement, bars 1–24.

FIGURE 3.6. Haydn, Quartet, op. 33, no. 1, movement 1, bars 1–10.

though not often mentioned in the psychological literature, that people hear music differently after they have studied the score.) And maybe Rosen's analysis recaptures something of the refined sensibility of the aristocratic connoisseurs and dilettanti for whom Haydn wrote his quartets. Or maybe it doesn't; there is no way of knowing for sure. But that does not really matter. If we accept Rosen's analysis, we do not do so because we believe it to be in some absolute sense correct. We do so because we find it persuasive. We do so because it contributes to our experience of the music. The value of the analysis, to repeat what I said earlier, is that it enables us to respond to the excess of music over sound.

Only a few years ago, music theorists with an interest in psychology were inclined to complain that psychologists ought to stop reinventing the wheel and learn some theory.[17] Things have changed; psychologists know a lot of music theory nowadays. The problem, as I have argued, is that they have tended to assimilate theory, treating it as a kind of incompletely formed psychology, rather than seeing it as a related but distinct discipline with its own aims and its own methods. Of course we do not want to go back to the bad old days, when psychologists knew little or nothing about theory and theorists knew little or nothing about psychology. But what Clarke (1989a: 2) calls the "rather unstructured 'leakage' between the disciplines" is potentially damaging to both of them. Music psychology risks losing the ability to pose fundamental questions through too ready an acceptance of music-theoretical concepts and categories; it becomes unduly influenced by music theorists' preoccupation with issues of formal structure. And conversely, music theory risks losing its identity in a welter of incompatible claims regarding both procedures and objectives. What is needed is the careful translation—or maybe it would be more accurate to say the careful *mistranslation*—of concepts from one discipline to the other.

NOTES

1. Clap your hands regularly once a second, record the sound, play it back 440 times faster, and you have the pitch A = 440.

2. See, for example, Sloboda 1985: 151–54.

3. The instruments were, in fact, synthesized.

4. This is rather like the musicians in an experiment conducted by Lucy Pollard-Gott; they judged the similarity of different excerpts from Liszt's B minor Sonata purely in thematic terms, because theme is an essential component in the language game of traditional formal analysis. "One expert commented that after the similarity task was over, he realized that there might have been other criteria for judging similarity such as relative loudness. Yet when he heard the passages, their thematic relations were compelling and seemed to be the only natural basis for comparing them" (1983: 81).

5. Often abbreviated GTTM. The first comprehensive statement of the theory was in the book of that name (1983); subsequent extensions to it have appeared in Lerdahl's articles on timbral hierarchies (1987), tonal pitch space (1988b), and atonal prolongational structure (1989). An outline of GTTM will be found in Chapter 2.

6. Also published, minus one piece, as *Vier kleine Klavierstücke*. Examples 1 and 2 are taken from Cook, 1990, where a more detailed discussion of these issues may be found.

7. The tests are fully reported in Cook, 1987. Subjects evaluated the test pieces along four dimensions: coherence, completion, pleasure, and expressiveness. There was, in general, a high level of redundancy between these measures. Bengt Edlund, of the University of Lund, reports similar results from a series of tests carried out in 1991 (unpublished paper, "Tonics and Returns").

8. This was in fact only a fragment: the theme from Brahms's *Haydn Variations*. All other pieces in the tests were complete movements.

9. This is an adaptation of G. Lakoff and H. Thompson's description of language, cited in Hantz, 1984: 247.

10. Short for pitch class set theory, a music-analytical system first described in Forte, 1973.

11. See Figures 2.8 and 7.4 in Krumhansl, 1990.

12. At least the subjects in Krumhansl's experiments probably knew what they were doing, which seems unlikely to have been the case in a cross-cultural study of tone hierarchies carried out by Kessler, Hansen, and Shepard (1984). In what must rank as one of the most farcical episodes in the history of music psychology, the team from Stanford jumped on their motorbikes and set out to find the remotest village in Bali. Eventually they discovered a village whose inhabitants had never heard the Indonesian national anthem, and who regarded the Americans as "Javanese" on the grounds that they obviously were not from Bali. The probe tone tests presented some difficulties, and the rating scale had to be reduced from 7 to 5 so that the villages could respond by holding up their fingers. When processed back at Stanford, the results indicated that the villagers were equally unfamiliar with the tonal hierarchies of Western and Balinese music. Another interpretation might be that the villagers were completely baffled by the whole undertaking and simply gave the first answers that came into their heads in order not to disappoint their visitors. What Kippen (1987: 175) refers to as the "cultural insensitivity" of the whole episode underscores the difficulty of adapting the procedures of experimental psychology to non-Western or non-Westernized cultures.

13. The chart now appears in yet another form: see Lerdahl's Figure 17.

14. See Cook, 1990: 44–45, 56–58.

15. For a particularly telling introspective account of musical listening, see Osmond-Smith, 1989: 95. An extended treatment of this whole topic may be found in Cook, 1990.

16. A fuller version of this argument may be found in Cook, 1989: 131–34. The graph is taken from Schenker, trans. 1979, Example 109a (1).

17. This is the general tenor of, for instance, Walsh, 1984.

REFERENCES

Agmon, E. (1990). Music theory as cognitive science: Some conceptual and methodological issues. *Music Perception*, 7, 285–308.

Babbitt, M. (1962). Twelve-tone invariants as compositional determinants. In P. H. Lang (Ed.), *Problems of modern music* (pp. 108–21), New York.

Butler, D. (1989). Describing the perception of tonality in music: A critique of the tonal hierarchy theory and a proposal for a theory of intervallic rivalry. *Music Perception*, 6, 219–41.

Butler, D. (1990). Response to Carol Krumhansl. *Music Perception*, 7, 325–38.

Clarke, D. (1989). Structural, cognitive and semiotic aspects of the musical present. *Contemporary Music Review*, 3, 111–31.

Clarke, E. (1989a). Mind the gap: Formal structures and psychological processes in music. *Contemporary Music Review*, 3, 1–13.

Clarke, E. (1989b). Issues in language and music. *Contemporary Music Review*, 4, 9–22.

Clarke, E., & Krumhansl, C. (1990). Perceiving musical time. *Music Perception*, 7, 213–51.

Cook, N. (1987). The perception of large-scale tonal closure. *Music Perception*, 5, 197–205.

Cook, N. (1989). Music theory and "good comparison": A Viennese perspective. *Journal of Music Theory*, 33, 117–41.

Cook, N. (1990). *Music, Imagination, and Culture*. Oxford.

Deliège, I. (1987). Grouping conditions in listening to music: An approach to Lerdahl and Jackendoff's grouping preference rules. *Music Perception*, 4, 325–59.

Dowling, W. J. (1989). Simplicity and complexity in music and cognition. *Contemporary Music Review*, 4, 247–53.

Forte, A. (1973). *The structure of atonal music*. New Haven, CT.

Gjerdingen, R. (1988). Shape and motion in the microstructure of song. *Music Perception*, 6, 35–64.

Gotlieb, H., & Konečni, V. (1985). The effects of instrumentation, playing style and structure in the Goldberg Variations by Johann Sebastian Bach. *Music Perception*, 3, 87–101.

Hantz, E. (1984). Studies in musical cognition: Comments from a music theorist. *Music Perception*, 2, 245–64.

Harris, R. (1980). *The language-makers*. Ithaca, NY.

Harris, R. (1981). *The language myth*. London.

Kessler, E., Hansen, C., & Shepard, R. (1984). Tonal schemata in the perception of music in Bali and the West. *Music Perception*, 2, 131–65.

Kippen, J. (1987). An ethnomusicological approach to the analysis of musical cognition. *Music Perception*, 5, 173–95.

Konečni, V. (1984). Elusive effects of artists' "messages." In W. R. Crozier & A. J. Chapman (Eds.), *Cognitive processes in the perception of art* (pp. 71–93), North-Holland.

Krumhansl, C. (1983). Perceptual structures for tonal music. *Music Perception*, 1, 28–62.

Krumhansl, C. (1990a). *Cognitive foundations of musical pitch*. New York.

Krumhansl, C. (1990b). Tonal hierarchies and rare intervals in music cognition. *Music Perception*, 7, 309–24.

Krumhansl, C., Sandell, G., & Sergeant, D. (1987). The perception of tone hierarchies and mirror forms in twelve-tone serial music. *Music Perception*, 5, 31–77.

Lecercle, J.-J. (1990). *The violence of language*. London.

Leech, G. (1983). *Principles of pragmatics*. London.

Lerdahl, F. (1987). Timbral hierarchies. *Contemporary Music Review*, 2, 135–60.

Lerdahl, F. (1988a). Cognitive constraints on compositional systems. In J. A. Sloboda (Ed.), *Generative processes in music: The psychology of performance, improvisation, and composition* (pp. 231–59), Oxford.

Lerdahl, F. (1988b). Tonal pitch space. *Music Perception, 5,* 315–49.

Lerdahl, F. (1989). Atonal prolongational structure. *Contemporary Music Review, 4,* 65–87.

Lerdahl, F., & Jackendoff, R. (1983). *A generative theory of tonal music.* Cambridge, MA.

Lerdahl, F., & Jackendoff, R. (1984). An overview of hierarchical structure in music. *Music Perception, 1,* 229–52.

Marsden, A. (1989). Listening as discovery learning. *Contemporary Music Review, 4,* 327–40.

Marsden, A., & Pople, A. (1989). Modelling musical cognition as a community of experts. *Contemporary Music Review, 3,* 29–42.

Narmour, E. (1989). The future of theory. *Indiana Theory Review, 10,* 95–97.

Osmond-Smith, D. (1989). Between music and language: A view from the bridge. *Contemporary Music Review, 4,* 89–96.

Pollard-Gott, L. (1983). Emergence of thematic concepts in repeated listening to music. *Cognitive Psychology, 15,* 66–94.

Rosen, C. (1976). *The classical style* (rev. ed.). London.

Rosner, B., & Meyer, L. (1986). The perceptual roles of melodic process, contour, and form. *Music Perception, 4,* 1–39.

Schenker, H. (trans. 1979). *Free composition.* New York.

Schoenberg, A. (1969). *Structural functions of harmony* (2nd ed., rev. by L. Stein). London.

Seifert, U. (1991). Competence and performance in cognitive science: On the relation between music-theoretical research and the modelling of musical cognition. Abstract of paper scheduled for presentation at the Computers in music research conference, Queen's University of Belfast, April 7–10, 1991.

Serafine, M. L., Glassman, N., & Overbeeke, C. (1989). The cognitive reality of hierarchic structure in music. *Music Perception, 6,* 397–430.

Sloboda, J. (1985). *The musical mind: The cognitive psychology of music.* Oxford.

Smith, A. (1973). Feasibility of tracking musical form as a cognitive listening objective. *Journal of Research in Music Education, 21,* 200–13.

Stockhausen, K. (1959). How time passes . . . . *Die Reihe, 3,* 10–41.

Walsh, S. (1984). Musical analysis: Hearing is believing? *Music Perception, 2,* 237–44.

West, R., & Fryer, R. (1990). Ratings of suitability of probe tones as tonics after random orderings of notes of the diatonic scale. *Music Perception, 7,* 253–58.

Wolpert, R. (1990). Recognition of melody, harmonic accompaniment, and instrumentation: Musicians vs. nonmusicians. *Music Perception, 8,* 95–105.

Developmental
Perspectives

4

Songsinging by Young and Old: A Developmental Approach to Music

LYLE DAVIDSON

Introduction

There have been many investigations of the musical development and the musical abilities of children in recent years (see overviews by Hargreaves, 1986a; Shuter-Dyson & Gabriel, 1981). Research ought to benefit educational practice, but there have been difficulties in establishing an effective dialogue between the scientific and educational communities (Hargreaves, 1986b; M.E.N.C., 1981; Sloboda, 1986). In Chapter 4 and 5, Lyle Davidson and Jeanne Bamberger discuss issues related to musical development and education. Both writers stress the importance of integrating experimental results in pedagogical practice.

Scientific research in music development has examined the abilities of children from a very young age. Chang and Trehub (1977) found that five-month-old infants are already sensitive to the sequential structure of a melody. The investigations presented a series of short melodies to the babies and, by monitoring their heart rate, noticed that when a new melody was presented some of the infants showed changes in their heart rate, a reliable indicator of perceived novelty. Studies in the perception of tonality have also investigated the young child's sensitivity to tonality. Zenatti (1969) asked five-, six-, and seven-year-old children to listen to a series of three-note tonal or atonal melodies. Each melody was followed by a repetition in which one of the notes had been altered in pitch. While five-year-olds performed equally poorly on both types of melodies, children six and seven years of age performed better on the tonal melodies than on the atonal ones, thus showing that they had extracted some structural information that helped them in comparing the melodies.

The psychologist Jean Piaget (1960, 1967) believed that to study the intellectual growth of the child we must look at growth over a period of years, and his work has led to a developmental model for researching musical growth longitudinally (Serafine, 1980). The research headed by Howard Gardner at Harvard University's Project Zero, has investigated the musical development of children, providing a naturalistic and detailed record of the development of their song output over several years. Gardner (1973) has proposed that the artistic development of children can be traced to their acquisition of symbols and their sensitivity to artistic styles.

Lyle Davidson, a senior investigator on the Project Zero research team, has extensively researched musical development, focusing on songs (Davidson, 1985; Davidson & Scripp, 1988a, 1988b). In Chapter 4 Davidson discusses the development of tonal knowledge, looking at the preschoolers' earliest songs, the singing of musically untrained adults, and the perceptual changes in tonal relationships that a student undergoes in music school. Davidson notes that we do not have a comprehensive view of the goal of musical development and instruction because we fail to learn from the uncoordinated and loosely connected chunks of knowledge that we have. He encourages educators and professional musicians to consider the psychological nature of musical knowledge. Davidson describes the musical growth of the child by showing how the child's early approximations of a song later acquire a definite melodic shape and a stable contour, and he illustrates this process with drawings of the child's musical notation (see also Chapter 7 by Jay Dowling in this volume, and Dowling, 1984, for additional research on the development of children's songs).

REFERENCES

Chang, H., & Trehub, S. E. (1977). Auditory processing of relational information by young infants. *Journal of Experimental Child Psychology, 24*, 324–31.

Davidson, L. (1985). Tonal structures of children's early songs. *Music Perception, 2*(3), 361–74.

Davidson, L., & Scripp, L. (1988a). Young children's musical representations: Windows on music cognition. In J. Sloboda (Ed.), *Generative processes in music: The psychology of performance, improvisation, and composition.* Oxford: Clarendon Press.

Davidson, L., & Scripp, L. (1988b). A developmental view of sight-singing: The internalization of tonal and temporal space. *Journal of Music Theory Pedagogy, 2*(1), 10–23.

Dowling, W. J. (1984). Development of musical schemata in children's spontaneous singing. In W. R. Crozier & A. J. Chapman (Eds.), *Cognitive processes in the perception of art.* Amsterdam: Elsevier.

Gardner, H. (1973). *The arts and human development.* New York: Wiley.

Hargreaves, D. J. (1986a). *The developmental psychology of music.* Cambridge: Cambridge University Press.

Hargreaves, D. J. (1986b). Developmental psychology and music education. *Psychology of Music, 14,* 83–96.

M.E.N.C. (1981). *Documentary report of the Ann Arbor symposium.* Reston, VA: M.E.N.C.

Piaget, J. (1960). *The psychology of intelligence.* Totowa, NJ: Littlefield, Adams.

Piaget, J. (1967). *The child's conception of space.* New York: Norton.

Serafine, M. L. (1980). Piagetian research in music. *Council for Research in Music Education Bulletin, 62,* 1–21.

Shuter-Dyson, R., & Gabriel, C. (1981). *The psychology of musical ability* (2nd ed.). London: Methuen.

Sloboda, J. A. (1986). Achieving our aims in music education research. *Psychology of Music, 14*(2), 144–45.

Zenatti, A. (1969). *Le développement génétique de la perception musicale.* Monographies Françaises de psychologie No. 17.

In this chapter, I argue that taking a developmental perspective reveals a great deal about the nature of musical ability and the nature of effective music instruction. Based on methods of developmental psychology, the development of tonal knowledge is traced by considering preschoolers' earliest songs, the songsinging of musically untrained adults, and finally, the transformation in a student's grasp of tonal relationships in performance, which result from the intensive training that takes place in music schools. Contour schemes—the organizing mental structures of tonal materials in music typical of young children—continue to function beyond the years of childhood, unless there is considerable broad musical training like that typically found in music schools.

Musical Talent: A Determined Ability or a Propensity for Development?

A deep-seated assumption about the nature of musical ability is the belief that musical ability is largely (if not wholly) innate and fixed. From this point of view (I will call it the "talent model"), development is assumed to occur very nearly all by itself—in the person endowed with talent. Environment, training, education, hard work: these are assumed to play little role in musical ability and knowledge. At least two difficulties follow from this assumption: only the gifted and talented are seen as worth the teacher's investment of time and energy, and the scope of the teacher's and the student's activity is reduced. Let's consider each of these issues in turn.

First, the talent model suggests that fine teachers, good instruments, and time devoted to mastering even elementary musical skills are wasted on those not obviously talented. This line of thinking is reinforced by the assumption that an individual's natural gifts should be allowed to develop freely. Unfortunately, a model of education based on the romantic concept of the flowering of talent ultimately fails to recognize and develop the capacities for musical expression and thought in those students who are not identified as gifted.

Research suggests that *the musically untrained have surprisingly sophisticated abilities*. For example, the average child and adult, although unable to read music notation and without any performance training, can represent the musical dimensions of phrase structure, melodic contour, pitch, and rhythmic elements surprisingly well (Davidson & Scripp, 1988a; Davidson, Scripp, & Welsh, 1988) (Figure 4.1). Furthermore, research suggests that the average adult, although unable to read music notation and without any performance training, can solve musical problems *at least* at the level of undergraduate music students who have years of performance experience in their background (Scripp, Meyaard, & Davidson, 1988). *By investigating the development of musical ability,* it is possible to see degrees of difference and similarity among various groups, children and adults. From this more articulated perspective, it is possible to make better arguments in support of teaching music to the general student, and better strategies for teaching students at all levels of education (Davidson & Scripp, 1988a).

Another difficulty is the assumption that the talented student basically learns by herself. This reduces the scope of the teacher's and the student's interaction. There is little incentive to probe deeply into the nature of musical knowledge and understanding. The narrow version of the talent model assumes that instrumental proficiency alone accounts for careers and alone is powerful enough to override the need for strong interpersonal skills. It reduces the opportunity, as well as the motivation, to consider other aspects of musical life and musical thinking. For the student, *the talent model isolates later development from early experience.* The continuity of growth is cut off. Early forms of musical knowing are ignored in favor of the formal, articulated knowledge of the expert. Talent is necessary but not sufficient.

The oversimplification typical of the talent model greatly misrepresents the reality of the engaging and dynamic exchange in music, just as learning in the classroom misrepresents the knowledge required beyond school (Resnick, 1981).

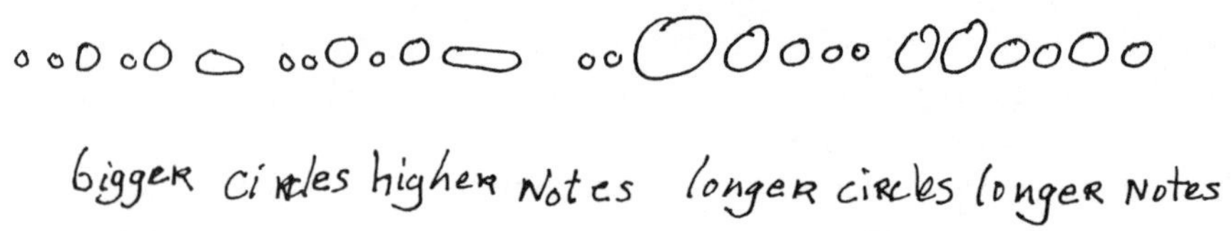

FIGURE 4.1a. Child's invented notation of "Happy Birthday to You."

FIGURE 4.1b. Adult's invented notation of "Happy Birthday to You."

It presents a lean concept of what is involved in the development of a rich form of expression. *It results, in part, because educators and professional musicians do not consider the psychological nature of musical knowledge.*

Development: Knowledge Under Construction

It is axiomatic in developmental psychology that our knowledge changes as it develops and matures (Wohlwill, 1973). As we acquire new degrees of mastery in a skill, our relationship to our former level of skill, knowledge, and understanding changes significantly as well. But, as musicians know if they think about it for a moment, this change is more than a simple addition to an already formed base. Its impact is deeper than adding one more element to what is already known. For example, when I learn second position on the violoncello, I do more than add another finger position to my repertoire of skills. Knowledge of the new position forces me to reinvestigate the notes I mastered in first position. My relationship to the fingerboard changes. My physical connection to the instrument is different. The implications of these changes continue to spiral beyond the moment. The change in my physical position changes my sense of what the issues are when I play a line. My choice of string on which I play a given note now reflects my understanding of the role timbre plays in my interpretation. As my options expand, the choices I make become increasingly significant, their impact increasingly wide ranging.

This dramatically transforms my perspective of the musical experience as well as the nature of performance. For example, as my ability to differentiate among possible physical movements and choices increases, my awareness of the elements of a piece also increases. When second position has become integrated into and extends the knowing represented by first position, I can begin to construct multiple views of a note, a passage, or a section. For instance, I can imagine the note A below middle C on one of two strings, and choose which one to play on the basis of the nature of the passage I am trying to play and on the basis of the musical shape I am trying to project. Finally, in this manner, my ability to consider simultaneously multiple aspects of an event, or concept, reflects considerable transformation in my mental representations of that event or concept. All of this reflects considerable developmental change.

The understanding at various points along the way to mastery is usually not noticed, except when deficient. This is not surprising, because when considering musical knowing, we normally take the most complete knowledge (the expert's) as the point of reference. When we adopt such a perspective from which to develop the musical knowledge of novices, we fail to take into account the knowledge the student brings to the task. The knowledge of an expert is very different from that of the less developed student in at least three ways: the degree of its articulateness, its stability, and the extent of its internalization (Trotter, 1986). Indeed, research shows that, contrary to what we might expect, novices and beginning musicians often confuse distinctions easily made by mature musicians (e.g., pulse and duration, contour and interval) when they make representations of each (Bamberger, 1991; Davidson & Scripp, 1988a).

We have a view of the goal of development and instruction without a corresponding view of the path that leads to the goal, because we fail to learn from the uncoordinated and loosely connected chunks of knowledge. If we don't consider the nature of the diffuse, unstable, and relatively unregulated knowledge of the musically naïve, we have little opportunity for reflecting on the knowing typical of the average nonmusician and the beginning musician as well. The study of development reveals changes in what we know, as well as in how we know it. The process of bridging the gap between the musically sophisticated and the musical novice leads to a transformation of our understanding of issues and origins, and ultimately produces new forms of knowing.

Stages of Musical Development: The Expert's Perspective

> Domains were (previously) broken down into their principles and theories, but not studied in terms of the ways in which individuals move from encounter to engagement, from engagement to mastery of early levels, from apprentice to journeyman, and so on. Feldman, 1980: 168

Musical experts provide the models of pedagogy and set the standards for mastery. Yet unlikely as it may seem, these experts may not be the best sources of information about how knowledge of a domain develops and matures. Developmental psychologist David Feldman argues for a way to bridge the gap that separates the expert and the novice. He makes a strong case for the need to redefine a domain in terms of its psychological reality, not its logical analysis. He advocates looking at how the individual knowledge changes with experience and training, instead of defining what a person needs to know on the basis of expert *a priori* assumptions. Traditionally, developmental psychologists have been concerned with building and refining models of intellectual growth within various domains (Furth, 1969; Fischer, 1980). They seek to describe convincingly, whenever possible, invariant *and* universal stages representing changes in cognitive processes and skills as they develop from novice to expert. Consider children's understanding of how to draw a person.

When children begin to develop a concept of space, what do they use as the reference point around which to organize their picture? Unlike adults, children do not always honor the horizontal baseline as an element in the organization of pictures. Instead, children first work from unit to unit, figure to figure, without an overarching reference system (Piaget & Inhelder, 1967). Thus, they first attend to and create the topological features of a drawing without reference to the whole picture. The integrating structure occurs later. Children work with the contour and more general aspects of depiction in the absence of the physical coordinates that involve the horizontal and vertical relationships which adults and experts assume to form the foundation of spatial perception and formation. So, in children's early drawing of human figures, one sees that the proximities are generally correct: arms and legs are appropriately attached to the body, the eyes are placed on the head, and they may even be placed beside one another. But the overall design is uncoordinated, proportions are unrelated to the subject as they work only from one unit to the next (Goodnow, 1977).

However, as children become able to make reference to multiple dimensions of relationships they can begin to show coordinated and geometrical relations. Thus, only when they are able to consider and honor the relationship of the horizon, the house, the angle of the roof, and the chimney in reference to one another are they able to represent the three-dimensional features necessary to make what would be an acceptable adult-style picture (Piaget & Inhelder, 1967). In music, the ability to relate individual pitches to a highly structured order (the musical scale) and the ability to coordinate the regular pulse and the varied pattern of the rhythmic surface demonstrate levels of integration necessary for an advanced knowledge of music and suggest an advanced stage of musical development which I call operational (Davidson & Scripp, 1989).

Operational Thinking: Performance Accompanied by Awareness and Coordination

> . . . as a result of their internalized and integrated nature, concrete operations are actions accompanied by an awareness on the part of the subject of the techniques and coordinations of his own behavior. Piaget & Inhelder, 1969

Piaget's statement about the quality of actions taken in a context of awareness of techniques and coordination is a useful reference point when considering the further development of musical skills. His concept of operationality is important when considering the evolving mastery of tonal knowledge by children and adults, because it describes what takes place in the training of professional musicians. In Piaget's terms, the difference between the different grasps of tonal relationships involves contrasting aspects of thought: *figurative* and *operational* thinking (Piaget, 1970). The figurative aspect is manifest in the initially passive aspect of knowledge as it relates to perception, imitation, and mental imagery. Mental imagery at this level is internalized imitation. For example, the finger movements that so often accompany the piano student's sightsinging, the arm movements of the trombone player, or the physical feeling of the vocal placement for the singer are examples of representation linked to an auditory image at the figurative level.

Musical training, and not only instrumental training, provides the structure for transforming the more "figurative" thinking represented by contour scheme knowledge and knowledge of tonal relationships as "tunes" into progressively operationalized thinking. This is often achieved by mixing images from different modes of representation. For example, by asking the pianist to "play" the notes while singing them with syllables or note names, the teacher is deliberately combining kinesthetic and symbolic modalities. In solfège classes, the student must initially "call up" and confirm the sounds of notes by naming them while singing melodies. Gradually, more of the sound can be imagined directly from the page, until eventually, the imagined sounds can be transformed mentally with relative ease (without externalized vocal expression). During this process, the student's knowledge of tonal space becomes increasingly articulated and internalized (Davidson & Scripp, 1988c; Scripp & Davidson, 1988; Davidson, Scripp, & Meyaard, 1988).

This provides some indication of the symptoms of what operational thinking in music might sound like. Operational thinking in music is evident in the degree to which one can make transformations and reversals of actions from one state to another (e.g., singing "Happy Birthday" in a major mode and then in a minor mode). Children and adults without musical training cannot do this simple task (except when supported by a great deal of rote imitation) because they lack the stable, yet articulated and internalized, structure on which the transformation is based. Musically untrained adults, who use either contour schemes or their memory of the specific and unique melodic shapes as whole units, can perform their songs in one way, but not both.

Tonal Knowledge: Contour Schemes, Standard Songs, and Scales

The process of making tonal knowledge operational is as long and complex as the developmental profiles of other intelligences (Piaget, 1976). Piaget describes three distinct stages leading to the development of operational and internalized knowledge: sensorimotor, concrete operational, and formal operational (Piaget & Inhelder, 1969). In relation to tonal development, we might think of tonal knowledge as being constructed first through contour schemes, then as phrases of melodies in which the individual relationships of the pitches are not articulated, and finally, as scales which reflect the hierarchical knowledge typical of operational thought.

Examples of the first phase clearly show the process of constructing the schemes or mental tools that precede higher levels of musical knowledge. The sound of the singing is often diffuse and unfocused. Contours of songs are typically reduced. Even if learned correctly, the range of the song usually shrinks with time to match the level of the child's current contour scheme. There is no evidence of key structure.

The second, or concrete operational, phase is different in various ways. The diffuse singing of the beginning years is replaced by discrete pitches. At this level, a singer can usually make transformations on an entire melodic set, but not on elements of the set. For example, a singer may be able to make stylistic shifts, imitate the sound of a specific performer, or sing the entire melody at a different tempo or with a different dynamic. However, other changes will be more difficult, especially changes that affect individual pitches of the melody. Singers during this stage depend on their externalized vocal production to maintain relative intonation of notes of a melody. When they imagine notes without singing them, their tonal reference slips. Their knowledge of music appears to be partitioned as performance, perceptual, or reflective ways of knowing, each one relatively independent and isolated from the other (Davidson & Torff, 1991).

We most often see the final phase of the developmental process (making tonal knowledge operational) in the context of formal music education. In music schools the instrumental lessons are linked to learning and development in several ways: through performing without the aid of one's own instrument (e.g., in the solfège class, the study of a second instrument, or chorus); through specifying one's perception (e.g., when transcribing solos, taking dictation, or making an analysis by ear), and when discussing and critiquing the music and performances of one's peers and mentors. Singers with third-stage operational knowledge do not require explicit vocal monitoring to maintain their tonal orientation or to check their notation when learning by imitation, sightsinging, or taking dictation. They can imagine the notes of a melody, transform or modify them on demand, and sing specific notes with intonation that reflects understanding of the tonal context.

To be useful, a developmental view takes into account the entire range of procedural and discursive knowledge, in a context of productions, perceptions, and reflections. These reflect the intellectual skills necessary for musical expression (Davidson & Scripp, 1992). Mapping how individuals change as they move from the "initial engagement" of their youthful years to the "early mastery" of middle teens, to become mature artists, is the business of developmental psychology. Therefore, we want to place the musical knowledge and skills of children, adolescents, and adults side by side and see what the trajectories of change really are. We ask about the antecedents of adults' musical knowledge by approaching it from a psychological as well as a musical perspective, in the hope that with this experience we will be better able to understand and assess the skill, talent, and artistry that support mature musical expression.

Before we continue, it will be useful to review some of the arguments. First, I will argue that a logical analysis of the elements of music will not reveal the psychological knowledge on which naïve understanding is based. The psychological nature of understanding is not revealed by a logical analysis of features. It can, however, become evident by close comparison of different levels of ability. Second, a psychological analysis of musical development reveals there are plateaus of musical development. Each of the preceding levels prepares the way for the next level, but does not necessarily lead immediately to it.

Showing What We Know:
The "Felt Path" or the Formal System

The pioneering work of Jeanne Bamberger (Bamberger, 1986) provides an indication of the differences between the musically untrained and the musically trained mind. It reveals an unexpected difference between the two groups' use of the tonal reference system. Bamberger reports that untrained children and adults play melodies on Montessori bells by arranging the bells in the order of the notes of the melody as performed (a "felt path" of pitch relationships). For example, the untrained novices require one bell for each of the notes of the melody, *including the repeated tones*. Thus, for them, the first two notes of the opening of "Happy Birthday" require two different bells, one for each note (even though both pitches are the same), and the first phase, therefore, requires six bells. In the novices' understanding of melody, the notes of the tune and the order of the action of bell playing are fused together, making it unthinkable to restrike a bell in order to sound the repetition of a note.

The approach favored by the musically trained is very different. They first construct a scale of eight notes (making a formal system of pitch relationships). They then play the notes of the song, extracting them from an operational scheme of tonality. Only two notes are needed to play the first four notes of "Happy Birthday," and only four bells are required to play the first phrase. The musically sophisticated people begin the task of representing the melody with the bells by constructing an abstract scheme with which they can more efficiently represent all the notes of the melody.

The difference between these two approaches to tonal structure reflects a qualitatively different orientation to musical elements. At one level of development, the functional units of tonal space stand in such fragile relation to one another that issues like key establishment are moot. At the other level of development, the construction of the hierarchical structure of scales makes several issues relevant for consideration: the identity and stability of pitches on the one hand, and the capacity to establish and maintain keys on the other hand.

From this perspective, one index of musical sophistication is the ability to integrate localized pitch knowledge into increasingly less contextualized tonal structures as represented by scales and keys. That is, the untrained subjects can be expected to work only within the context of the sequence of the notes of the tune, whereas the trained subjects can be expected to infer a higher-order structure: a tool with which to integrate the various notes of the tune.

Bamberger's work reveals some of the power that can be attained by comparing the performance of the same task by individuals possessing very different levels of expertise. In the next section, we will consider the songsinging abilities of young children and adults.

Songsinging in Preschoolers:
Constructing a Basic Vocabulary

Let's consider the very beginnings of performance ability, the first songs a child sings. By viewing the prototypes of musical practice as a moment on the path that leads to sophisticated musical thought, it is possible to learn a great deal about music if we watch children's first years of songsinging. Even in the beginning songs, the earliest efforts to participate in musical thinking and practice, musical elements common to all songs emerge. However, during the development of musical knowledge, the significance of various dimensions may change. For example, rhythmic structures appear to be relatively robust at first hearing, especially and when compared with children's grasp of pitch. However, careful analysis of the quality of early rhythmic structures which children use in songs appears to be first closely linked to words (Davidson & Colley, 1987). Later, independence of rhythmic development from words begins to emerge as children become able to hold a note across a beat or pulse (as with a dotted quarter note in common time). Similarly, dimensions that fail to appear early may require considerable support at later stages of development, as in the case of key stability (Davidson & Scripp, 1988c) or music students' knowledge of key use (Davidson & Welsh, 1988).

The following three songs illustrate the kinds of changes that are at issue. Despite their differences, each of these songs is a version of "Twinkle, Twinkle, Little Star," sung by the same child at three different ages (Figure 4.2).

At age three, Jeannie already knows several important things about the way songs combine words and pitches. She knows that in singing, more than in speaking, the voice is consistently modulated in a way that produces a complex contour of ups and downs, and she also knows that the pitches in the melody should be distinct from one another (i.e., not continuous slides). In addition to understanding these general characteristics of music, Jeannie has some more precise knowledge. She duplicates some of the rhythms of the standard version of the song and can divide the song into smaller units or phrases, yet she makes no attempt to measure the interval between the phrases. Where pitch relations are concerned, the contours the child sings do not match the model and her song

FIGURE 4.2(a,b,c).
Jeannie's three versions
of "Twinkle, Twinkle, Little
Star."

lacks the tonal coherence that a stable scale would provide. The song structure is difficult to recognize: Jeannie sings only two of the song's four phrases, and the ends of the phrases are not marked by notes of longer duration.

In the second version of the song, when Jeannie is four, she carries the melodic contour by humming. At the same time, she forms the words with her lips closed, thus sounding all the changing vowel sounds in the text. This suggests that at four, she is still dependent on the text to keep her place in the melody. While the contour of each phrase is closer to the model, some of the notes and intervals remain inaccurate. The way these phrases approximate the model suggests a greater pitch stability. However, the fluctuating intonation and the lack of a note-to-note match across phrases make it difficult to give her credit for having a firm sense of tonality or scale. However, the rhythmic shapes are much sharper in this version. At the end of the phrases, there is a longer note, but the interval of time between phrases is not yet measured by an underlying pulse (i.e., the steady beat of the music).

By six years of age, Jeannie's version of the song matches the model. The contours of the phrases are accurate, and the pitches and intervals suggest regulation by a sense of tonality and scale. She lends a steady pulse to each phrase and this pulse controls the duration of time between the phrases. While the words are in place, the completeness of the music suggests that the text no longer dominates the musical aspects of the performance. It is equally significant that the child now uses the constituent phrases of the song (the first and second phrases) to make a simple three-part form, which can be represented by ABA. The repetition of the melodic material of the A section at the end of the song is exact. Every aspect of the song is related to a structure that governs the whole: a single scale, a regulating pulse and surface pattern, and a specific form that binds the individual phrases into a coherent musical whole.

These three songs provide a sense of the nature of the essential questions in musical development. The streams of pitch and rhythm emerge as primary, for two reasons. First, studying these aspects of musical understanding provides explicit connections between children's songs and those of adult singers. Moreover, as the examples illustrate, each of these, pitch and rhythm, exhibits considerable development in the years between one and six.

With respect to each of these streams, there are critical questions to consider. First, we want to explore how development occurs in pitch: Is it a process of gradual approximation of adult models? Or, do children organize their songs using qualitatively different principles? If the latter is the case, can we describe these principles in terms of rules or stable structures? Is development steady or are there marked shifts in musical abilities?

The three versions of "Twinkle, Twinkle, Little Star" that Jeannie sang suggest that learning to sing songs is a more complex task than it appears at first. Learning to sing songs involves: (1) singing articulate pitches that reflect an underlying scale or tonal structure; (2) performing both surface and underlying rhythmic patterns regulated by a common pulse; (3) mastering the canons of song form that guide standard songs so they can be applied to invented compositions; (4) forming structures that make possible the use of internal reference (repetition, variation, and development).

Development of Pitch Relationships

Three components are basic to the control and understanding of pitch relationships: (1) the capacity to grasp the figurative shape or contour of a phrase; (2) the ability to match individual pitches; and (3) sufficient memory or organizing structure to maintain key stability across the phrases of a song. There has been considerable discussion about the manner in which these various aspects of pitch relations develop. Some earlier research suggests that knowledge of pitch relations may develop through a series of broad levels or phases in which children grasp first the contour, then the specific pitches, then intonation, and finally, key stability. For example, Moorhead and Pond (1941) and Shuter-Dyson (1968) report that contour is perhaps the first aspect of melody to be grasped by the child. Teplov (1966) finds that children sing the contours of the melody first and are only later able to match the specific intervals contained in a model melody. Still other research suggests that tonal knowledge may develop out of the ability to match specific pitches. Specifically, Wing (1963) reports that children's ability to match pitches and intervals precedes their ability to produce the general shape of the melody. However, Sargeant and Roche (1973) report that children's ability to match pitches even declines as their ability to match contours improves.

There is more widespread agreement that the ability to sing in key appears late. Michel (1973) reports that by the end of the preschool years, children are able to perform music in major and minor scales, and even to appreciate harmony. However, this rich description of young children's tonal understanding is questioned by other researchers who report that children even four or five years of age are not able to sing scales at more than chance levels (Bridges, 1965).

Beneath these descriptions lie two difficult, but highly significant, problems in analyzing children's tonal knowledge. First, many analyses have been too narrow in focus insofar as they have examined either the development of interval matching or the growth of the ability to seize the figural shape of a melody. If one studies tonal development by breaking up musical performances into their smallest units or intervals, one loses an important aspect of pitch relationships—the ongoing motion of the melodic impulse. On the other hand, if one focuses only on the motion of unfolding melodies as contours, one misses a close look at the precision, accuracy, and stability of individual intervals.

The second difficulty arises because studies of children's songsinging are often based on an inappropriate unit of analysis (Wertsch, 1985). It is evident that the tonal knowledge of musicians reflects the control of individual contours, pitches, intervals, and keys. However, and this is critically important, these musical organizers are the by-products of considerable and protracted activity constructing pitch relations. Children's early songsinging simply does not depend on linking of fixed pitches or key structures. Because of this, there is little reason to analyze their productions in those terms. Indeed, to analyze the songs of a three-year-old in these terms is akin to applying the rules of point perspective to early drawings or the rules of transformational grammar to one-word utterances. In effect, the key to understanding the development of musical ability lies in discovering a unit which captures the melodic aspect of children's songs but which does not presume that children organize their songs in terms of notes, contours, or keys from the outset. Thus, an early and major focus of our work was to develop a way of describing children's growing understanding of pitches, intervals, and contours which did not assume that the child used fixed pitches, measured intervals in diatonic terms, or organized performances based on knowledge of keys.

So how do children, in fact, learn to control pitches of their songs? Although researchers confirm that musical pitch development follows neither course associated with the adult predictions suggested (Dowling, 1982; Ries, 1982), a systematic and empirical model of pitch development has been offered. Systematic observation of 78 children over a six-year period at Harvard Project Zero suggests that *contour schemes* rather than gradual refinements in the overall contour or interval matching account for the route of emerging tonal knowledge (Davidson, 1985). The term *contour* conveys the importance played by the figurative shape of melody—its contour; while *scheme* conveys the importance of recognizing levels of mental organization. This model, which emerged out of the Project Zero research, suggested five specific levels of pitch development in young children's singing between the ages of one and six years. These levels characterize children's knowledge of tonal relationships as expressed through their performances of songs.

When singing invented and conventional songs, preschool children first use these melodic schemes with a descending direction. Except for the first contour scheme, the phrases children sing are longer than individual notes or intervals, yet, at the same time, smaller than the individual melodic phrases of model songs. With development, the vocabulary of schemes grows from those that span roughly a third to those that span roughly a sixth. It would simplify the story if, as one might assume, development occurred by filling in the initial space with stepwise movement, and then expanding the tonal space by adding more steps. This would be efficient (on the surface of it) and would reflect some models of ear training and sightsinging currently proposed (Adler, 1979). But the path of development is not so neat and tidy. Contour schemes do not develop in ways one might logically predict from interval learning—that is, proceeding from smaller to larger fixed intervals. Although they begin as small, descending motions and expand through a fourth, fifth, and sixth, this simple line of development does not immediately account for the occurrence of stepwise motion within each tonal frame.

Expand the boundaries of the tonal space first, then go back and fill in the gaps in previously acquired schemes with steps—that appears to be the rule. For example, only after developing the next larger contour scheme does the child fill in the gap between the top and bottom of the previous contour scheme with stepwise motion. For example, not until a child has acquired the ability to reliably sing a fourth (as a leap) does she fill in the earlier leap (the third) with stepwise motion. This "backing and filling" process continues until finally the contour scheme of a sixth has been achieved. At this point the accretive process of development stops. Contour schemes do not continue to develop in the same

FIGURE 4.3. Transcription of a typical preschooler's performance of "Row, Row, Row Your Boat" with contour scheme analysis below.

way beyond the span of the sixth. The octave, which emerges only later, appears to arise from fundamentally different processes (perhaps having a great deal to do with memory for register, for example).

Figure 4.3 shows how these schemes function only in very local contexts (i.e., within an individual phrase) when preschool children sing "Row, Row, Row Your Boat." Substantially more developmental change is required to construct a level of tonal stability that can be sustained from phrase to phrase and in a variety of contexts.

The increasing differentiation and stability of pitches are two characteristics of pitch-singing development in the early years. At first, preschool children fail to return to established pitches or reference points in their songs as they generate only the individual contours which form the child's repertory of melodic schemes. As the repertory of contour schemes grows, the number of different reference pitches used when singing a song decreases until there is a relatively stable one-to-one correspondence between the pitches of a model song and the pitches the child sings. However, during the preschool years, the locus of this stability is restricted to pitches within the unit of the phrase. It does not yet extend across all the phrases of songs.

Collecting Songs and Forming a Database

The setting in which musical behavior occurs is very important. Much research is conducted in laboratories in which designated variables can be controlled. However, what is learned from laboratory and clinical settings cannot easily be generalized to everyday experience. By taking a more ecologically sensitive approach to the study of music and how our musical knowledge develops, we can trace the connections between the productions of children, adults, and professional musicians. The songs on which this study is based were collected in the homes as part of a larger study of children's symbolic development. Seeing the children every other week for six years made the researchers "part of the family."

The songs collected during the study include the traditional songs American children learn during the preschool years, as well as some songs that were composed for experimental purposes. In addition, many novel songs were invented by the children under a wide variety of circumstances—sometimes requested as a part of warm-ups to experimental tasks in other domains, sometimes as spontaneous responses to looking at "wordless books." The more than 500 songs that form the corpus were collected under a wide variety of contexts: inventing a song at the request of an observer, singing while playing with the materials of another domain (most often drawing or playing with blocks), singing favorite songs on request, and singing on private occasions when parents thoughtfully made home recordings of their children's performances.

A word about the methods. While the data from this study are rich, the corpus of songs scored includes only those songs which consisted of two or more phrases. The songs were transcribed by experienced musicians and checked by outside experts. Because every attempt was made to reflect the characteristics of the children's performances faithfully, the notations include special symbols. For pitch, in addition to conventional notation, there are symbols for speech, contour, and notes which are half spoken and half sung. The rhythm symbols used reflect free groupings, proportional durations, and more measured and regular rhythmic patterns. Analysis of each song was done from both the notation and a tape of the child's performance.

The transcription and the analysis of the songs were separate processes. Before scoring a song, we determined the number of phrases it contained and, when possible, the tempo at which it was sung. We also classified the song as either invented or standard, and the manner in which it was performed as either spoken, sung with diffuse pitches, or sung with articulated pitches. We then rated each phrase of the song for the way in which the boundaries of the phrases were marked, the type of tonal motion it contained, and finally, the type of song structure that the song exemplified.

What conditions must be present in order to determine that a musical response or behavior is stable? In short, when does a child acquire a behavior as opposed to simply showing an isolated instance of its occurrence? A conservative rule was developed. In order for a musical shape to be counted as a stable part of a child's repertoire of pitch relationships, it had to appear twice in different songs and in different sessions. Separate analysis was carried out on each group, invented and standard songs. This made it possible to distinguish between development within the two different repertoires of songs the children made up and the songs of the culture they were taught. (For more detailed description of the scoring process the reader is referred to Davidson, 1985.)

The following composite picture is based on the findings of a longitudinal study of nine firstborn children who were followed for five years. The first visits—which took place two times each month—were made shortly after the children's first birthdays. The findings of this longitudinal sample were replicated in a cross-sectional study that was made up of 69 children who were grouped by age across the same age range (from a matching socioeconomic class). Among other tasks, the children in the cross-sectional sample were asked to sing their favorite songs and a song was taught to them during three separate visits. These songs were tape-recorded and later scored on the same measures as the songs from the longitudinal study.

Constructing the First Boundaries of Tonal Space

Contour Scheme: The Interval of a Third

There are many ways to tell the story of what is happening in Heather's song, or to put it another way, to determine the units of meaning in this song (Figure 4.4). Here, the danger is that the observer attributes an irrelevant meaning to the child's production. For example, from one perspective, one could argue the child is attempting to use many adult-like goals. One could say that Heather "decided" to invent a new version of the song "A, B, C, D" by beginning on what are "intuitively" more stable notes (the notes of a tonic, G-sharp-E), and closing on less stable notes (notes of its dominant chord, F-sharp-D-sharp). But once stated, this version seems somehow inadequate. For one thing, it at least implies that, since these tonal concepts are already visible in the songs of toddlers, appreciation and understanding of these tonal concepts (tonic and dominant functions) may be genetic givens, independent of culture, and thus musical universals. This story suggests that the child is already considering and using the materials of music in ways which music students find difficult even 17 years later (Davidson & Welsh, 1988). Thus, the unlikeliness of this precocious grasp of the harmonic structure of Western music by any but a very few makes it difficult to argue that the units of meaning for children in their songsinging are derived from the expert's formulations of musical theory and practice.

From another point of view, of the units of meaning a child uses when songsinging can be redirected to address the issue of the musical units of pitch, interval, contour, and phrase. A story based on this perspective might be about how children learn the rudiments of tonal structures by long experience, attempting to match the correct intervals or engaging in "trial and error" approximations of melodic contours, without regard for intervals. In any case, the stability and regularity of contour schemes, revealed by analysis of hundreds of children's songs, argues against such a successive approximation model of learning that controls the tonal materials of music.

The children's songs themselves suggest another possibility for units, the phrases. It is characteristic of young children's songs to *not* reflect a concern for melodic continuity beyond the level of the individual phrase. For example, at

FIGURE 4.4. Heather's "A, B, C, D."

first they do not heed the importance of "reading" or acknowledging the rests and silences between phrases. Instead, they treat the space between phrases as "free" areas which do not need to be measured or regulated, quite unlike adults' performances. Children may develop the ability to control and regulate musical silences most naturally under the focused circumstances of a specific repertoire. The child distinctively segments the musical line into units, taking a breath between the units in order to begin speaking. Thus, phrases are the initial musical units of song.

There is more to say about Heather's version of "A, B, C, D." The reduced range of this song illustrates an important feature of psychological analysis: psychological boundaries in music are different from the physiological boundaries. When children first draw, they work from feature to feature—for example, from head to body to arms, and so on. They work without an overall scheme or design with which to regulate the individual units. They move from one unit to the next and the drawing is the result of a series of localized moves (Goodnow, 1977). When singing, children operate in much the same way. Early songs suggest that children operate on a principle of nearness similar to that found in drawing research: the notes of early songs and melodies are not extremely disjunct, but surprisingly contained within a small register. Regardless of the melodic model, and they appear to be used as repetitive chunks, the notes of individual phrases are relatively close together.

The constrained range children use when singing is not physiological. Children can vocalize across a wide range (Fox, 1990; Jersild & Bienstock, 1931). Yet Heather fails to imitate the melody of the song as she has heard it. This is consistent with the performances of the other children of this study. Unless excited or pushed to do so by an adult, children don't use their full vocal range when singing songs. Instead, they use a psychological unit or scheme as a means of coordinating the tonal aspects of their singing.

There is no evidence of the highly distinctive contour of the song's melodic line. The ascending perfect fifth leap of the first phrase is nowhere to be seen. Typical of children's first songs, the contour of this earliest of melodies is a small descending motion. Greatly reduced in length, in number of words, using a compressed register with a descending contour, Heather's song is representative of the first songs children sing.

There are several more things to notice about Heather's early performance of "A, B, C, D," however. The song is not only reduced in register, it is also severely reduced in length. Only two phrases of the song are sung. The words of the song are very simple, yet only a small portion of them is rendered. Nevertheless, the singer's ability to render the song appears to draw more heavily on the text than on the melody—that is, the song is more fully represented by its text than by its melody. Also typical of the first songs children sing, the text consists of single words. However, the order and sequence of phrases of early songs are not always that of the model. The salience of the text plays an important role in what phrases of the song are going to be produced.

FIGURE 4.5. Heather's "A, B, C, D," showing the construction of contour schemes.

Throughout the development of songsinging there is a consistent pattern in children's grasp of pitch relationships: once a set of boundary pitches has been established and integrated as a stable mental structure, that scheme is used in conjunction with others to reflect more accurately the contour of a given standard song. Contour schemes have several characteristics. First, each contour scheme is identified by a single framing interval: a third, a fourth, a fifth, and a sixth. These "framing intervals" mark the boundaries of the contour of a phrase of song as the child sings it. Thus, the initial contour scheme delineates the interval of a third, and there is a leap between the two notes that form this interval. Later, this leap is filled in, and a more mature form of contour scheme is revealed through stepwise motion. This stepwise motion appears first in the descending form, and with the development and an increasingly operational grasp of the contour scheme, it appears in the ascending form as well. In the initial stages, the pitches of a contour scheme are relatively unstable. Often sounding like a portamento (a special manner of singing with the voice gliding gradually from one tone to the next through all the intermediate pitches; *Harvard Dictionary of Music*), these diffuse pitches become increasingly stable and articulated with development.

Contour schemes appear to represent the tonal structures for the musically untrained child as scales represent the tonal structure of the more musically trained. Children use their repertoire of contour schemes, either singularly or in tandem, to form and control the tonal materials of their songs. Children who are using contour schemes as their mental representation of the pitches of a song will reduce the range of the contour of a song that goes between the range of the most recent contour scheme acquired. In many instances, they will even inappropriately expand the range of a phrase in order to match the size of the framing interval of a new contour scheme under construction. In "A, B, C, D," Heather is using two juxtaposed contour schemes of a third. As Figure 4.5 shows, Heather is using two intervals of a third.

Contour Scheme: The Interval of a Fourth

Kori's version of "Itsy Bitsy Spider" illustrates the contour scheme of a fourth. Throughout the melody the chunks of phrases are bounded by the intervals of a third or fourth. Like "A, B, C, D," the text appears to be driving the content of this song, in that the pitches of the song are not nearly as well represented as the words.

This contour scheme is characterized by a tonal frame of a fourth—that is, the interval of a fourth forms the top and bottom of the unit of measure at this level of development. As with the previous level, the child may imitate larger intervals when they are modeled, but the child will revert to the fourth as the largest stable interval within a phrase when left alone. Leaps larger than the fourth, when they occur in standard songs, are typically compressed to the smaller size (Figure 4.6).

Children appear to construct the contour scheme of a fourth by adding an outside step to the tone of the boundary notes of the already stable contour scheme of a third. The first step of this level is characterized by either descending step-leap, or leap-step, motion, which more or less outlines an interval of a fourth (approximately in perfect or augmented form). As with the contour scheme of a third, this motion still does not reveal an underlying scale structure. The high-low dichotomy functions as it did in the contour scheme of the third, only now expanded to the slightly wider interval. There is still little stability of individual pitches at this stage. During this period of development, the framework of a third and fourth provides the stable structures for songsinging.

The average range of songs sung during this phase of development expands. It includes the notes of an octave, specifically from c′ to c″, or from middle c to c one octave higher. Each song does not use the entire range. Because the contours of standard songs are compressed to fit the framing interval of the contour scheme, however, individual songs can start higher. The contours of the melodies of this level are still sometimes diffuse and unmarked by articulated pitches, and now, both rising and falling contours are sometimes found. However, more of the pitches are clear.

An important milestone of development occurs during this level: individual pitches of songs can now be matched when they are sung in the appropriate range. Even intervals larger than a fourth can be matched if they are sufficiently supported, prompted, or modeled. These larger intervals are not used in songs, however, suggesting that songsinging uses different skills than interval matching; that representations of melody are based on contour scheme rather than intervals. Additional evidence supports this perspective. When the child is learning a

FIGURE 4.6. Kori's "Itsy Bitsy Spider."

new song, or singing a song while performing some other task (such as playing a set of bells, drawing a picture, or moving about the room), the contour scheme currently under development, when it occurs in a song, may itself be replaced by a more stable and smaller scheme—in this case, that of a third.

As noted earlier, the child at this level does not have a reliable way of representing leaps larger than a fourth, so larger leaps in standard songs are compressed. Also typical of this level, there is little evidence of key and pitch stability. Indeed, the tonal structures used at this stage are still extremely local in nature, which means the child does not always match the high or low note within the contour scheme being used.

As with the contour scheme of a third, the second step of this level involves a filling in of the framing interval. This stepwise descending fourth pattern occurs only after the boundary interval of a fourth is stable and after the contour scheme of the fifth is acquired.

Contour Scheme: The Interval of a Fifth

Max's rendition of "Happy Birthday" illustrates the use of the contour scheme of a fifth (Figure 4.7). The range of the first two phrases (d'–a') establishes the framing interval. The notes he uses in the first two phrases (a', g', f-sharp and d') are typical of the first, unfilled form of the contour scheme. They represent the linking of the two forms of the contour scheme of a third (see Figure 4.8).

Like the others, this is another two-step contour scheme—the first unfilled, the second filled. In both, as in the earlier contour schemes, the descending contour initially predominates. Later, the contour can be rendered flexibly (as in Figure 4.7). The shapes that result in this contour scheme are few in number and can be derived from the two previous contour schemes. The framing interval of the fifth coordinates the notes within this register.

When children sing a song using the previous contour schemes, they appear to not return to specific pitches, but only move up or down reflecting the contour of the phrases. Thus, often there are relatively few shared pitches within a song. By contrast, when children use the contour scheme of a fifth to sing a song, they tend to return to specific pitches as they sing the contour of the piece. Thus, now there are more shared pitches across the phrases of the song. This produces songs that begin to sound as though there were a superordinate structure like a scale in place. However, while the effect of this is to create songs that may use as few as five pitches, this should probably not be taken as evidence for a scale or key structure. For one thing, as in the earlier levels, the child may imitate intervals

FIGURE 4.7. Max's "Happy Birthday to You."

FIGURE 4.8. Constructing the contour scheme of a fifth.

larger than those of a fifth when they are modeled, but the fifth is still the largest stable interval. That is, intervals exceeding a fifth are typically compressed to a fifth. Furthermore, although the child may give an appropriate tonic (or ending note) in a completion task (especially if prepared by a stepwise descending motion), as in the last phrase of "Row, Row, Row Your Boat," the use of contour schemes in his invented songs does not show the coordination among pitches or the constraints which go with knowledge represented by scales. The child's use of the contour schemes is the same as in the earlier levels, as a high-low boundary.

When a song contains leaps larger than the interval of a fifth, they are compressed to a fifth. Not only does compression of larger intervals occur, but also smaller intervals are sometimes expanded. In these cases a smaller interval (which we know a child has acquired) may be pulled in the direction of a fifth (or whatever contour scheme is being constructed) and thus distorted in a new way. This illustrates the powerful influence that a mental structure can have on memory, perception, and production.

During this level, the average range of the singing expands very little, up a step from c″ to d″. As in the earlier levels, an individual song probably will not use the entire range. Also during this level, the nature of diffuse singing changes markedly. Diffuse singing does not occur as part of a rising and falling contour, but may sometimes occur as a sliding between two discrete pitches. This may reflect an unstable contour scheme, but the individual pitches are much clearer and more distinct than during the previous contour schemes.

There is another development. The child is now able to differentiate between the starting and ending pitches of phrases by often making the ending pitches lower. There is also evidence that during this level a child begins to use an internal model when singing. The following example shows that the child was able to correct the intervals of the first phrase during the musical repetition in the second phrase.

When learning a new song, the child characteristically reduces the contour of the melody to earlier acquired levels (e.g., contour scheme of a third). Later versions of the song show that the child has replaced those smaller intervals with the appropriate one of a fifth. There are a variety of ways of ordering the internal space of this contour scheme. All of these ways can be related to the previous two levels. For example, one way of constructing this level is to repeat the process of adding on to an already stable contour scheme. This often occurs after the contour scheme of a filled-in third has been acquired. Another way of constructing this contour scheme involves interlocking thirds, which can also be derived from the contour scheme of the third.

As with the contour scheme of a fourth, the second step of this level involves filling in the framing interval. This stepwise descending fifth pattern occurs only after the boundary interval of a fifth is stable. Also, this level occurs relatively late, as anyone who listens carefully to a five-year-old's version of the last phrase of "Row, Row, Row Your Boat" can testify.

Contour Scheme: The Interval of a Sixth

Maja's version of "Jack and Jill" provides a good example of contour schemes at this level (Figure 4.9). She is the only one to acquire the filled-in version of the contour scheme of a sixth. As in the previous levels, the many routes to this contour scheme may be derived from a limited number of strategies, based on previous contour schemes. Phrases of melody that employ a range of tonal frames of more than a fifth, but less than an octave, are characteristic of this level. Some of the ingredients of this level are the result of linking the contour schemes already mastered. Thus, the contents of this contour scheme are less narrowly defined than the earlier ones. Because there is not much evidence of a stable octave, the organization is still based on the local knowledge that contour schemes represent.

The average range of the songs at this level extends a little on both ends, spanning the notes between b and e″. Songs end on pitches that are lower than those on which they begin. As before, individual songs do not use the entire range, but only a portion of the tonal register available. The child sings pitches that are well formed and clear during this level. Diffuse singing is sometimes found around the outer limits of the register, and there may be an occasional sliding between two distinct pitches.

There is a major change in the stability of individual pitches within a phrase and across phrases. At this level, a child can remember a specific pitch and, having left it, can return to it. This makes it possible for the child to sing and resing notes and pitches consistently throughout an entire song. The result is that the songs are much less chromatic than during earlier levels, because the phrases of songs at this level tend to share the same pitches—rather than to use different pitches. Since the child still lacks a scheme for the octave, intervals larger than a sixth are usually reduced to the interval of a sixth. "Somewhere over the Rainbow" shows how this reduction occurs (Figure 4.10).

Another interesting strategy begins to emerge. It shows the role memory can now play in melodic construction. The greater memory capacity that the child now has is used to fix a specific register as a reference point. For example, when

FIGURE 4.9. Maja's "Jack and Jill."

FIGURE 4.10. Jeannie (4:6) "Somewhere Over the Rainbow."

Jeannie now sings "Old MacDonald Had a Farm," she places the melody of the phrase "EIEIO" in a higher register and returns to the same register and same notes whenever the phrase is needed. She does this without regard for the appropriate tonal relationships across phrases. The song appears to exist in two distinct registers, one distinctively low and the other distinctively high. The song is sung maintaining these two registers throughout.

Contour Scheme: The Interval of an Octave

While none of the children sing the interval of an octave before the age of six, there are some single instances that indicate what can be expected. As with earlier levels, the unfilled space appears first. Also, like the earlier levels, this level is constructed by combining earlier contour schemes. The song in Figure 4.11 exemplifies songs that count as instances of this level.

   This song is very different from earlier ones in several ways. First, the only notes present in the song are those of an appropriate scale (i.e., they meet a musician's expectation). For example, Maja's song uses only the notes of the F major scale (or, if you prefer, a pentatonic on F since there is no B-flat in the melody). Second, these songs differ from those of earlier levels in that they tend to begin and end on the tonic of the scale, even though the range is now bound by the vast space of the octave. Another way this level differs from earlier ones is that notes on either side of leaps are discrete—there is rarely any glissandi or diffuse singing. Finally, some completions of target pitch patterns (the child is asked to finish fragments of a descending scale) show that the appropriate tonic can be inferred from the context of a given pattern of notes. It appears that these traits are characteristic of both invented and standard songs.

   This ends the story of how young children construct the tonal space of their songs. It has been argued that children's grasp of tonal relationships undergoes systematic development as they expand their repertory of contour schemes and, correspondingly, as they more often return to individual referent notes of the model song. Additionally, it appears that development does not proceed neatly from steps to leaps, nor does it follow a direct sequence from simple to more complex intervals. Finally, a significant first phase leading to mastery of tonal space appears to be completed by the age of six or seven. What happens next?

FIGURE 4.11. Maja invented song.

Meeting the Culture: Middle Childhood and Beyond

After this phase, development appears to take another direction; knowledge of tonal relationships is linked to the individual's song repertory. In many ways this progression parallels that found in the visual arts, where, after a burst of creative brilliance, young children refocus their drawing efforts toward mastering the somewhat mundane and canonical forms of objects. The resulting flatness of their efforts is dull when compared with their earlier products.

A similar closing down and focusing on cultural forms may also occur in music. Young children, after a long period of eagerly engaging in musical tasks like inventing a song about a rabbit, become shy about singing. Now, after being asked to invent a song, they are likely to respond by throwing back a challenge, "You sing one." One may lament the loss of invention, but there is another interpretation of this phenomenon. This seeming reduction of creativity is perhaps the next important step toward mastery of the materials of the domain. Children have, by now, a rudimentary grasp of the materials of music, pitch, and rhythm. During this new phase, children are becoming aware that there is a cultural bank of standard songs, and they learn that their knowledge of those songs is limited. From this perspective, their response, "You sing one," is social in nature. It reflects a desire to take part in the culture which lies beyond that of their own making. Thus, during the years of middle childhood, the focus of activity shifts away from the materials of music toward practicing the canonic forms, thereby learning the artistic language of culture. There are, doubtless, other interpretations. Yet the parallel in visual arts strongly suggests that in music there may also be something like the "retreat" from free invention into prolonged study of cultural forms.

During the years of early adolescence music becomes extremely important to children. Children now spend an enormous amount of time listening to and learning songs that reflect the repertoire of the culture, usually the favorites of their peer group. During the middle childhood years the focus of musical activity shifts, perhaps beyond the canonical forms of the music of the culture to using music as a means of negotiating and establishing social relationships. What is the effect of so much listening and the singing it generates? Such intensive exposure should have a powerful effect on their understanding of tonal space, but does it? Does this amount of singing result in the construction of a hierarchical tonal structure to be used when performing songs? If contour schemes are characteristic of young children's song performances, at what point in development and under what conditions does a singer's command of tonal space reflect the hierarchical thinking evident in the construction and use of scales?

Song of the Culture: Way Points
to Operational Knowledge

Ongoing work at Project Zero is taking up the issue of the continued development of tonal knowledge into adulthood: How do musically untrained adults use tonal relationships in singing songs? Do adults use scales to integrate pitches when they sing songs, or do they continue to use the looser tonal structure typical of the contour schemes we observed in children (Davidson & Torff, 1991)? Put another way, how do musically untrained adults differ from or resemble the seven- or eight-year-old child's performance of children's songs? Are their performances similar to those of children in spite of years of experience listening to the music of culture?

There are some clues that indicate what we might expect. There is a strong resemblance between the invented notations of seven-year-olds and untrained adults (Davidson, Scripp, & Welsh, 1988), as Bamberger noted in her comparison of musically untrained children and adults (Bamberger, 1986). Surprisingly, there is little difference between the notations made by the two groups, in spite of the fact that adults have had nearly 15 years more experience hearing music than the children.

Turning from children's performance of songs to that of adults, we found that the study of musically untrained adults' songsinging ability has three conditions (Davidson & Torff, 1991). The first one is simple: Sing "Happy Birthday" once, then resing it. Since the second performance might be much better than or different from the first, this controls for the effect of warming up. In the second condition, subjects are asked to sing the song and then listen to a tape of someone else singing the song—this version contains the most frequent errors made by adults. After identifying the location of the errors, they sing the song again. This allows us to look at the relationship of their singing to their perception of errors. The final condition is like the second, except that the tape is of their own singing (not someone else's version). They are asked to reflect on their performance, imagine how the song goes, and compare that with the version they just performed. At the end of the discussion, they are asked to sing the song again.

Although the study is in progress, some of the results already noted have a bearing on the topic of this chapter. In the case of tonal knowledge, it is clear that a significant number of musically untrained adults sing "Happy Birthday" without employing the integrating structure of the scale. As with young children, adults typically compress the range of the third phrase (an octave) and surprisingly end the song in a different key from the opening phrases. These two errors strongly suggest the use of contour schemes, as we saw in our study of children, for these reasons: first, the octave is usually performed as a smaller

FIGURE 4.12. Typical er-
rors in an adult's version of
"Happy Birthday to You."

interval, typically compressed to a fifth or sixth, just as young children do; second, the last phrase is lower than it should be, ending in the register of the starting notes, suggesting that closure depends more on register than on hierarchical tonal relationships (Figure 4.12).

In our ongoing work with adults we are finding that musical performance knowledge is remarkably stable. And there is no significant warm-up effect; repeated singing does not change the quality or accuracy of the first version. Furthermore, even after hearing their flawed version of the song, many subjects report that it represents their "best" version of the song. Others will describe their errors as "not high enough" (for the third phrase) and "got off" (for the ending) and then resing the song without correcting the problems they have clearly identified.

The questions this work raises extend beyond the scope of this chapter, but one question is worth pursuing. What is the nature of the tonal understanding that results from the songsinging of middle childhood?

Musical Study: Continuing the Path of Development

The course of development enters a new phase when music instruction begins around the age of 10 or 11 (for those students who take lessons on an instrument). Contour schemes begin to be integrated into the hierarchical structure provided by the scales of the culture. However, as tonal memory and the use of scalar structures expand, sensitivity to tonal functions increases and the contour schemes are gradually, yet still only somewhat, coordinated with the tonal vocabulary of the culture. Clues about the limitations of this path of development lie in the performance of major scales under a variety of conditions by students entering professional music schools. Their performances suggest they know scales as whole chunks, as melodies. These structures are difficult to pull apart and are unstable if not performed in a manner or speed which allows the student to perform, perceive, or monitor the entire shape as a single unit.

By the time music students enroll in a college-level sightsinging class, they bring with them a vocabulary of contour schemes, a repertoire of standard songs that they share with nonmusicians, the perceptual knowledge of tonal functions, a first-draft knowledge of the scale, and years of instrumental training and exposure to music literature. Given this background, it is odd that when they enter professional schools to begin formal music study, their knowledge of scale systems and tonal melodies is so incomplete and their grasp of tonal structure is so superficial.

Yet this superficial stage of tonal knowledge is easy to demonstrate. Just a few moments with a beginning solfège (sightsinging) class in the United States reveals students' relatively figurative grasp of scales. Although able to sing scales and melodies, many will be unable to easily sing specific notes of a scale on demand, for example, scale degrees four or six. Additionally, if individuals are asked to sing a one-octave span on a neutral syllable starting on scale degree two of a major mode (singing the notes of the C major scale starting on the note D), one of three things happens. Some students will sing the octave but transform the second scale degree into a tonic and sing a major scale. Many more students stop singing when they reach the tonic instead of completing the octave by continuing up one more note. In each case the students often are not aware of what they've done. Still other students use knowledge extrinsic to music—that eight steps make an octave—to determine when to stop. They solve the task by counting up eight notes as they sing.

These responses are evidence that students have not yet learned to partition musical space on demand, nor do they have an articulated and internalized representation of tonal space. They know the scale as a whole performance act, a string of notes linked into specific relationships. Singing the scale as if it were a "melody," they stop where it "feels right," not where they are asked to stop. In other words, they are unable to monitor and control their performance of the scale to show musical understanding of the parts in the context of the whole; merely counting the number of steps is not enough to engage intrinsic musical sensibilities.

Their knowledge of pitches within a scale is initially very much like the nonmusician's grasp of the notes of a song. The nonmusician's understanding of a melody is static, a rote performance without reflection, a recitation without comprehension. The song becomes a sign for music, formulaic and canonical. It is understood as a whole, not as a collection of independent units yoked into special connections. It is as if the smaller units of contour schemes are replaced by the relatively larger, yet completely context dependent, phrases of melodies.

Development and Talent

This chapter looked at the abilities of children and adults to sing tonal songs, but our findings carry implications for the relationship of development to talent. The context for investigation has not been the laboratory, but the natural settings in which nonmusicians first begin songsinging and young musicians first begin training. Given the point of view advanced here, one can begin to appreciate the effect of musical training on the relatively naïve musical knowledge of the novice in unsuspected ways. For one thing, it suggests that, to a remarkable degree, nonmusicians and beginning musicians share the same reference system when they are singing unaccompanied songs. Surprisingly, when deprived of the advantage of their instruments, these young talented musicians look like the nonmusicians. This, in turn, strongly suggests that instrumental training by itself does not guarantee a grasp of musical relationships, and that musical thinking in these cases is constrained to the use of the instrument.

This finding has broad implications for the study of musical talent. A developmental picture of musical knowledge suggests that natural gifts may not develop very far when allowed to grow freely or when students are not encouraged to use their knowledge and skills in ways that promote integration. Instruction focused exclusively on playing an instrument or passing on the masterpiece of the culture fails to carry the mind of the individual far enough beyond the instrument and into musical thought to make integration and operational understanding likely. A far broader program is suggested. A developmental perspective suggests that a range of musical instruments and contexts be explored rather than a restrictive focus of musical study and instruction on an instrument of choice. The differences between younger and more mature musicians suggest that integration does occur, but that it may be dependent on the extent to which knowledge and skills are used in diverse and increasingly complex relationships to one another. Studies designed from this perspective will ensure that young musicians will be able to coordinate their use of musical knowledge and skills across a range of situations.

Finally, for all of us, knowledge of the developmental path that leads to a moving musical performance can help us better understand the remarkableness of the achievement. In addition, it can help us appreciate more fully the meaning and richness of the musical knowledge that supports such a performance.

ACKNOWLEDGMENTS

The basic research in music reported in this chapter has been generously supported by the Spencer Foundation, the Carnegie Corporation, and the Markle Foundation. The applied research is funded by the Rockefeller Foundation.

REFERENCES

Adler, S. (1979). *Sight-singing: Pitch, interval, and rhythm.* New York: Norton.

Bamberger, J. (1986). Cognitive issues in the development of musically gifted children. In R. J. Sternberg, and J. E. Davidson (Eds.), *Conceptions of giftedness.* Cambridge: Cambridge University Press.

Bamberger, J. (1991). *The mind behind the musical ear.* Cambridge: Harvard University Press.

Bridges, V. A. (1965). *An exploratory study of the harmonic discrimination ability of children in kindergarten through grade three in two selected schools.* Unpublished doctoral dissertation, Ohio State University.

Davidson, L. (1985). Tonal structures of children's early songs. *Music Perception, 2*(3), 361–73.

Davidson, L., & Colley, B. (1987). Children's rhythmic development from age 5 to 7: Performance, notation, and reading of rhythmic patterns. In J. C. Peery, I. W. Peery, & T. W. Draper (Eds.), *Music and child development* (pp. 107–36). New York: Springer-Verlag.

Davidson, L., & Scripp, L. (1988a). Young children's musical representations: Windows on music cognition. In J. Sloboda (Ed.), *Generative processes in music* (pp. 195–230). Oxford: Oxford University Press.

Davidson, L., & Scripp, L. (1988b). Sightsinging at New England Conservatory of Music. *Journal of Music Theory Pedagogy, 2*(1), 3–9.

Davidson, L., & Scripp, L. (1988c). A developmental view of sightsinging: The internalization of tonal and temporal space. *Journal of Music Theory Pedagogy, 2*(1), 10–23.

Davidson, L., & Scripp, L. (1989). Education and development in music from a cognitive perspective. In D. J. Hargreaves (Ed.), *Children and arts: The psychology of creative development* (pp. 59–86). Leicester, UK: Open University Press.

Davidson, L., & Scripp, L. (1992). Surveying the coordinates of cognitive skills in music. In R. Colwell (Ed.), *The handbook of music research and learning* (pp. 1293–1328). New York: Macmillan.

Davidson, L., Scripp, L., & Meyaard, J. (1988). Sight-singing ability: A quantitative and a qualitative point of view. *Journal of Music Theory Pedagogy, 2*(1), 51–68.

Davidson, L., Scripp, L., & Welsh, P. (1988). "Happy Birthday": Evidence for conflicts of perceptual knowledge and conceptual understanding. *Journal for Aesthetic Education, 22*(1), 65–74.

Davidson, L., & Torff, B. (1991). *Adult's singing of children's songs.* Unpublished manuscript. Cambridge: Harvard Project Zero.

Davidson, L., & Welsh, P. (1988). From collections to structure: The developmental path of tonal thinking. In J. Sloboda (Ed.), *Generative processes in music* (pp. 260–85). Oxford: Oxford University Press.

Dowling, W. J. (1982). Melodic information processing and its development. In D. Deutsch (Ed.), *The Psychology of Music* (pp. 413–29). New York: Academic Press.

Feldman, D. (1980). *Beyond universals in cognitive development.* Norwood, NJ: Ablex.

Fischer, K. (1980). A theory of cognitive development: The control and construction of hierarchies of skills. *Psychological Review, 87*(6), 477–531.

Fox, D. B. (1990). An analysis of the pitch characteristics of infant vocalizations. *Psychomusicology, 9,* 21–30.

Furth, H. G. (1969). *Piaget and knowledge: Theoretical foundations.* Englewood Cliffs, NJ: Prentice-Hall.

Goodnow, J. (1977). *Children drawing.* Cambridge: Harvard University Press.

Gregg, L. W., & Steinberg, E. R. (1980). *Cognitive processes in writing.* NJ: Lawrence Erlbaum.

Jersild, A. T., & Bienstock, S. F. (1931). The influence of training on the vocal ability of three-year-old children. *Child Development, 2,* 272–91.

Michel, P. (1973). The optimum development of musical abilities in the first years of life. *Psychology of Music, 1,* 1.

Moog, H. (1976). *The musical experience of the pre-school child.* London: Schott.

Moorehead, G. E., & Pond, D. (1941). *Music of young children.* Santa Barbara: Pillsbury Foundation Study.

Piaget, J. (1970). *Genetic epistemology.* New York: Norton.

Piaget, J. (1976). Walking on all fours. In *The Grasp of Consciousness.* Cambridge: Harvard University Press.

Piaget, J., & Inhelder, B. (1967). *The child's conception of space.* New York: Norton.

Piaget, J., & Inhelder, B. (1969). *The psychology of the child.* New York: Norton.

Pond, D., Shelley, S. J., and Wilson, B. D. (1978). The Pillsbury Foundation School Revisited. Paper presented to the 26th Music Educators National Conference, Chicago.

Resnick, L. (1987, December 13–20). Learning in school and out. *Educational Researcher.*

Ries, N. L. L. (1982). *An analysis of the characteristics of infant-child singing expressions.* Unpublished doctoral dissertation, Arizona State University, Tempe.

Sargeant, D. C., & Roche, S. (1973). Perceptual shifts in the auditory information processing of young children. *Psychology of Music, 1.*

Scripp, L., & Davidson, L. (1988). Framing the dimensions of sight-singing: Teaching towards musical development. *Journal of Music Theory Pedagogy,* 2(1), 24–50.

Scripp, L., Meyaard, J., & Davidson, L. (1988). Discerning musical development. *Journal of Aesthetic Education,* 22(1), 75–88.

Shuter-Dyson, R. (1968). *The psychology of musical ability.* London: Methuen.

Teplov, B. M. (1966). *Psychologie des aptitudes musicales.* Paris: Presses Universitaires de France.

Trotter, R. (1986, July). The mystery of mastery. *Psychology Today,* pp. 34–38.

Wertsch, J. V. (1985). *Vygotsky and the social formation of mind.* Cambridge: Harvard University Press.

Wing, H. D. (1963). Is musical aptitude innate? *Psychology of Music, 1,* 1.

Wohlwill, J. F. (1973). *The study of behavioral development.* New York: Academic Press.

Wolf, D., Davidson, L., Davies, M., Walters, J., Hodges, M., & Scripp, L. (1988). Beyond A, B, and C: A broader and deeper view of literacy. In A. D. Pellegrini (Ed.), *Psychological basis for early education* (pp. 123–54). New York: Wiley.

5

Coming to Hear
in a New Way

JEANNE BAMBERGER

Introduction

In the second developmental chapter "Coming to Hear in a New Way," Jeanne Bamberger focuses on the relationship between the description of music and the perception of music. She describes in detail how the students' descriptions of the music represent their perception of it. Bamberger illustrates how differently students may perceive a rhythm by setting up an imaginary dialogue between two students: one who stresses the metric features of the rhythm, the other who emphasizes the functional aspects of the rhythmic structure. Through their exchange of ideas, both students gain a new dimension in the ways in which music may be heard. Bamberger urges teachers to utilize the differences in the students' descriptions as a tool for broadening the students' understanding of music.

Moreover, Bamberger encourages teachers to see *behind* what, at first, may seem wrong in the students' descriptions, and to seek instead "the logic" reflected in their descriptions. For Bamberger, hearing music is a process of instant perceptual problem solving, and hearing in a new way is learning to enrich one's own understanding of music, to perceive in a new way (see Bamberger, 1978, 1981, 1990, 1991, and Bamberger and Schön, 1991, for a description of these theories and their pedagogical applications, and Bamberger, 1986, for a discussion on the development of musically gifted children).

REFERENCES

Bamberger, J. (1978). Intuitive and formal musical knowing. In S. Madeja (Ed.), *The arts cognition and basic skills.* St. Louis: CEMREL.
Bamberger, J. (1981). Revisiting children's descriptions of simple rhythms: A function for reflection-in-action. In S. Strauss (Ed.), *U-Shaped behavioral growth.* New York: Academic Press.

Bamberger, J. (1986). Cognitive issues in the development of musically gifted children. In R. J. Sternberg & J. E. Davidson (Eds.), *New conceptions of giftedness*. ambridge: Cambridge University Press.

Bamberger, J. (1990). The laboratory for making things: Developing multiple representations of knowledge. In D. A. Schön (Ed.), *The reflective turn*. New York: Teachers College Press.

Bamberger, J. (1991). *The mind behind the musical ear*. Cambridge, MA: Harvard University Press.

Bamberger, J., & Schön, D. A. (1991). Learning as reflective conversation with materials. In F. Steier (Ed.), *Research and reflexivity*. London: Sage Publications.

Knowing How and Knowing About

I begin with a conversation that will most likely sound familiar to many readers and yet its very familiarity continues to puzzle me. It starts with an observation by the speaker that she enjoys listening to music and can make sense of most of what she hears. Upon questioning, she agrees that she can clap simple rhythms, recognize tunes she has heard before, even sing or whistle at least some of them. But she then hastens to add: "But of course, I don't know anything about music."

These remarks are so familiar that, like much that is commonplace, the puzzlements in them pass by unnoticed. But if, for some reason, they catch our attention and we turn back to reflect on them, we may be surprised by what we have heard. Wittgenstein puts it like this:

> The aspects of things that are most important for us are hidden because of their simplicity and familiarity. (One is unable to notice something—because it is always before one's eyes.) The real foundations of his enquiry do not strike a man at all. Unless THAT fact has at some time struck him. —And this means: we fail to be struck by what, once seen, is most striking and most powerful. (Wittgenstein, 1953: 50)

The puzzlement that catches my attention in the conversation is this: How can a person say that she can remember, enjoy, sing, and understand the music she hears everyday and still say that she "doesn't know anything about music"? Is it the difference between knowing how to do something in contrast to knowing about it? Or perhaps the distinction isn't in the "knowing" at all, but in the "it"— the music, itself. Could "music" stand for two different kinds of things—one kind that you sing, dance to, recognize, and enjoy; and another kind that you "know about"? Or could it be both: when you "know about music," the music itself changes?

The conversation raises, in a quite natural way, questions such as the following: What do we mean by "knowledge," or more specifically, what does it mean to know, to have, or to use musical knowledge? And even if we could come to some agreement about that, we are quickly led on to other questions: How does musical knowledge develop? What, for instance, is the difference between what you or I hear in listening to the same piece of music? Why do even professional musicians so often disagree in their "interpretations" of the same piece of music? And how do we ever come to hear in new ways?

Musicians are more likely to talk to one another about their "hearings" of a piece rather than about knowledge. In rehearsing a string quartet, for instance, the violist might say to the cellist, "How do you hear that last passage?" And the cellist might answer, "Well, the second phrase begins on the downbeat of bar 19." To which the violist might answer, "No wonder we aren't together, I hear the phrase beginning with an upbeat starting in the middle of the previous bar." Or among music theorists you might hear one saying of another's analysis of a piece, "Your hearing just doesn't make sense to me." What, then, is meant by a "hearing" and how can we characterize the differences among them; or, even better, try to elicit and account for the usually tacit underlying assumptions that give rise to these differences?

But what is the evidence for another's hearing? My evidence for such hearings are usually subjects' descriptions of them, albeit in several media of which verbal descriptions is one, drawings and the spatial ordering of pitch-playing objects another. While each of these modes of description has its special qualities and constraints giving each a differing potential for what it might be trying to "say," still they all raise a very knotty problem for the observer: since a hearing is by its nature a necessarily private, internal experience, an external description in whatever mode can provide only impoverished clues to a subject's momentary organizing of a melody or rhythm—that is, to his or her hearing. Further, descriptions are influenced in interesting and often very specific ways by the terms—the "units of description"—that the hearer has available. We need to ask, then, what are the relations, often reciprocal relations since terms also influence hearings, between these units of description and what I will call the hearer's "units of perception"? And since a hearing is, perhaps paradoxically, a silent affair, how can anyone know?

I have addressed some of these questions elsewhere[1] but here I want to focus attention on an argument that must necessarily precede them. My argument is that *a hearing is a performance*; what the hearer seems simply to find in the music is actually a process of instant perceptual problem solving—an active process of sense making something like that evoked by the comments of the painter Ben Shahn: "So one must say that painting is both creative and responsive. It is an intimately communicative affair between the painter and his painting, a conversation back and forth, the painting telling the painter even as it receives its shape and form" (Shahn, 1957: 49). Like a painting, a hearing, too, is both creative and responsive, a conversation back and forth between the music, as material, and the hearer as he or she shapes its meaning and form in some particular way.

Making Meaning

In arguing that a hearing is a process of instant perceptual problem solving, I obviously intend to suggest that what we casually call "the mind" is actively engaged in making meaning—that is, in organizing incoming sensory material. And I also want to suggest that this is an ongoing generative process—that we are actively doing this organizing in real time as the sound/time phenomena are occurring "out there." But I do not want to suggest that by "organizing" I mean some kind of "decoding" process, as if the incoming material has already been segmented, and these entities labeled or otherwise symbolically "encoded." Rather, it is exactly because sound/time phenomena do not come already structured, but rather *hold the potential for being structured* that different hearings are possible. As Israel Rosenfield has said, "we perceive the world without labels, and we can label it only when we have decided how its features should be organized" (Rosenfield, 1988: 187).

However, I find Rosenfield's word, "decided," somewhat problematic here, since even that suggests more of an overtly intentional action than I mean to imply with the notion of instant perceptual problem solving. In fact, I suspect, and have some evidence to show, that the processes through which we actively organize incoming pitch/time phenomena are closely linked with the very basic, sentient organizing of our bodies as we move through space and time. For example, it is the *sequence of actions* that we practice and internalize in the process of carrying out familiar activities—most particularly action-paths that we internalize in learning to perform a piece on an instrument—that become our most intimate ways of knowing that piece. I call these internalized action-paths "felt paths."[2]

Research Methodology and an Example

In searching for research questions that might effectively address some of these larger issues, I have found that the most compelling and also most productive questions emerge from puzzling events that occur in the course of my everyday work with students in the classroom, or in working on a composition in preparation for teaching or performing it. Once I recognize an issue, and when I find it impossible to turn a question or puzzle aside, I am led to the design of more formal experimental situations.

For instance, initial evidence that there are specific differences in the hearings of familiar rhythms emerged first in children's drawings of rhythms, draw-ings that "happened" quite spontaneously in response to a practical necessity: As part of a composition project, the children in a fourth-grade music class had invented a rhythm they called their "Class Piece." The Class Piece was created during a regular class period and was to be played by all the children as a central part of their composition. But with much work still to be done on the composi-tion, the children noticed that the class period was coming to an end. In re-sponse, one child suggested, "We had better put our rhythm on paper so we can remember it tomorrow." In the next 10 minutes, each of the children invented a way of "notating" the piece so he or she could remember it the next day. And, as is often the case with invention, there was an unexpected spin-off: While the drawings were indeed there the next day to help the children remember their Class Piece, subsequent analysis of the drawings suggested surprising but very specific differences among them.

The drawings fell into two types, which I tentatively labeled "figural" and "metric." The differences between the two types rested on the kinds of features and relations the children chose or were able to attend to: Those who made metric drawings, as the term suggests, focused their attention on *measuring* the relative duration of events. Thus, clapped events were classified with respect to "same relative duration"—for instance, all "longs" were drawn with one size shape (large) and all "shorts" were drawn with another size shape (small). Metric drawings, then, were based on a notational strategy that is similar to standard rhythm notation and thus could easily be mapped onto it. In contrast, figural drawings exposed for scrutiny functional aspects of musical structure that are not captured by standard music notation. These children focused their attention on the *grouping of performed events into phrases or figures*. The Class Piece, notated in standard rhythm notation along with prototypical examples of each type, is shown in Figure 5.1.

It was only after the distinction between figural and metric drawings had emerged from the spontaneous drawings of the fourth graders that I was able to design an experiment to test the robustness of that distinction. To do so, I asked 186 children between the ages of 4 and 12 to clap and draw five different rhythms, including the children's Class Piece. The data from this larger experi-ment confirmed the robustness of the initial distinction. In addition, it was possible to organize the wider range of drawings into a typology that included

FIGURE 5.1. The Class Piece.

developmental tendencies within the figural/metric distinction (see Bamberger, 1980, 1981, 1988, 1991).

But the robustness of the distinction produced another unanticipated result: In discussing the drawings with the children and later with musically untrained adults who were asked to perform a similar task, it turned out that when subjects were asked to play back a rhythm from another's drawing, each type of drawer found it difficult to make sense of the other's. Figural drawers usually found a metric drawing to be inscrutable or they would suggest that "it must be a different rhythm"; metric drawers typically found a figural drawing simply wrong. (See Hildebrandt & Bamberger, 1979.)

Puzzling over this consistent and somewhat troubling response, it was important to remember that differences in subjects' drawings were reflecting, or were at least clues to, differences in their spontaneous hearings. It was not so surprising, then, that if a description of a hearing ran counter to one's own hearing, it was quite natural to find it difficult to grasp and more difficult to believe.

A Paradox and a Proposal

Considering that metric drawings give priority to the same kinds of entities as standard rhythm notation (SRN), while figural drawings give priority to entities that are not represented at all by SRN, it was also not surprising that regular users of standard notation (including some, but not all, professional musicians) had difficulty making sense of these figural drawings. At the same time, it is paradoxical that figural drawings express the ability to hear just those structures that professional musicians put great value on in their actual practice, namely, the grouping together of melodic events to form meaningful gestures, motives, or what I have called figures. To do so is often associated with what we call a "musical hearing," specifically with the performer's ability to "shape a phrase." In short, figural drawings show evidence of a musical intelligence we value—the mind behind a "musical ear."

It should now be clear that while figural and metric drawings point to different *kinds* of entities, both figural and metric relations are inherent in and contribute to the structure and coherence of rhythms; indeed, it is the particular intersection of metric and figural groupings that gives a rhythm its unique coherence. (See Cooper & Meyer, 1960; Lerdahl & Jackendoff, 1983.) And yet, the evidence suggests that musicians give a different status to the two aspects of musical structure—the one, metric relations, are considered "objective," the ability to recognize and encode them being associated with what can be taught and with knowledge in the domain; the other, figural relations, are considered "subjective," associated with intuition and musicality, even with the magic of musical "talent," but not easily notated and more difficult to teach and learn.

But in the interest of coming to hear in new ways, it would seem that rather than pitting one kind of structure against the other, or giving each a specially favored status, what is required is to help individuals learn selectively, knowingly, and at will to shift focus among the possible features and relations that give a composition its unique coherence, and to coordinate these features in new ways. In short, we need to help individuals learn to make *multiple hearings* of even simple rhythms or melodies.

But the difficulty in doing so lies in the nature of the spontaneous hearings we make: a hearing, particularly of an apparent simple rhythm, is usually experienced all at once, and at the moment it is made, it seems immutable—how could it be heard otherwise? And assuming that these ineluctable hearings, like drawings of them, differ with respect to the features one chooses or is able to attend to, then to make a hearing other than one's own, may require a shift, perhaps even a fundamental restructuring of one's focus of attention—giving priority to different features, regrouping, making new boundaries that carve out new entities, and liberating from the meld features that were previously unnoticed, even inaccessible.

Making Multiple Hearings

How, then, can we help individuals to make multiple hearings? As a first step we need to ask: How can we help individuals *to become aware of their own hearings* of even a simple rhythm so as to recognize which of the possible aspects they are giving priority to in their instant perceptual problem solving? We can then go on to ask: How can we help them to shift their focus of attention so as to participate in and to experience a hearing that differs from their own?

In working with students in my MIT classes, I have found one way that seems to be effective in achieving these goals. These classes usually include students with varied music backgrounds and thus it is predictable that, when asked to notate a rhythm, some will make figural notations and others will make metric notations. It is also predictable that each type of student will defend his or her notation as "right," rejecting others as "wrong." My ploy is to bring the two types of students into direct confrontation with one another, the challenge being that each should try to "put on another's head"—that is, each should try to make sense of and to hear the rhythm in the way his or her counterpart does.

To illustrate this process and to help readers actually live through the sometimes confusing experience of coming to hear in a new way, I have created a dialogue between myself and two college students modeled after those that have actually taken place in these classes. I think of the two students as prototypical figural and metric types: One, whom I have called Met, hears rhythms *metrically*; the other, whom I have called Mot, hears rhythms *motivically* (or what I have been more generally calling a figural hearing). While the students initially hold firmly to their respective hearings, I encourage their confrontations and also try to mediate between them. Through this process, the two students eventually succeed in making sense of one another's hearings but only after struggling with and revealing some of the fundamental assumptions that each of them holds. And since my experience strongly suggests that one or the other of these hearings is that of the reader, it is my hope that in following these conversations, the reader, too, will come to hear in a new way. However, I am also quite aware that to do so may require just as much work on the part of the reader as it does for Met and Mot.

In Which Met and Mot Come to Understand
One Another's Hearings

The dialogue begins after I have asked each of the students to clap and draw the children's Class Piece. They have already looked at one another's drawings and are now in the midst of arguing about them. As shown in Figure 5.2, Mot makes a prototypical figural drawing, while Met makes a prototypical formal drawing. Met is a computer science major who is very forthright in his opinions. Met took clarinet lessons in elementary school and currently plays the guitar. Mot is a humanities major who has had no formal music training and is rather easily intimidated by Met.

MOT (to Met):	I don't see how you can say that my third little circle should be a big one or a long. With a big circle there, it doesn't look the way it feels when you clap it.
MET:	It just seems obvious to me that your third little circle has to be a big one—at least if the circles are supposed to stand for longs and shorts.
MOT:	Of course they are. . . .
MET:	O.K. But then it's very difficult for me to understand the rhythm the way you've drawn it.
JEANNE:	Let me try to help. What I think Mot is paying attention to, and what I see in her drawing, are the little motives or groups of claps inside each of the larger repeated rhythms.
MOT:	Yes, that's right. Inside of each larger repeated pattern there are two groups of claps—you can see them quite clearly with my two big circles and then three little ones. And in between the two larger patterns I sort of take a breath and start again. I could make the grouping even more clear with a drawing (Figure 5.3).
JEANNE:	That's good. Now could you clap the rhythm again and while

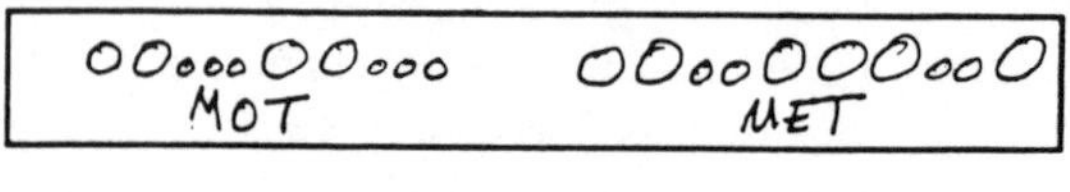

FIGURE 5.2. Mot's figural drawing and Met's metric drawing.

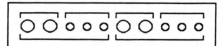

FIGURE 5.3. Mot's grouping structure for the Class Piece.

you are clapping say some numbers that seem to go along with your clapping?

MOT: Sure. It would be (*clapping the class piece*): 1 2 1-2-3, 1 2 1-2-3.

MET: But that's wrong again!

JEANNE: Please try to be a little patient, Met. Now, Mot, would you put the numbers you just said under the circles in your drawing so that we can see just what you mean? (*Mot adds numbers to her drawing; see Figure 5.4*).

JEANNE: O.K. Now try something else. Can you clap just the rhythm for the tune "Twinkle, twinkle, little star; How I wonder what you are" and, while you're clapping, say some numbers that seem to go along with your clapping?

MOT: (*clapping and counting*):

```
 1    2    3   4  5  6   7          1  2  3   4   5   6  7
(Twin-kle twin-kle lit-tle star,    How I won-der what you are.)
```

MET: Oh my!

JEANNE: All right, Met, so how would you count it?

MET: It's obvious. (*Met claps and counts*):

```
 1    2    3   4  1  2   3   4   1   2   3   4   1    2   3   4
(Twin-kle twin-kle lit-tle star,    How I won-der what you are.     )
```

JEANNE: Does that make any sense to you, Mot?

MOT: Not really. I especially don't understand why Met keeps counting up to 4 and then starting over again with 1.

JEANNE: Well, let's leave that problem for the moment. Could you draw a picture of the rhythm of Twinkle like you did for the Class Piece, Mot, and then put in numbers just like you said them when you were clapping?

MOT: I think so. (*She draws and numbers her graphics; Figure 5.5*).

MET: Now you're getting some place! Did you notice that you left a space between the two phrases, I mean between the words "star" and "How I"?

MOT: Of course. That's where you sort of inhale, take a breath. Like I

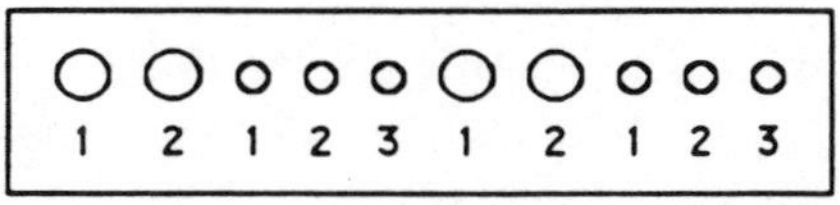

O O o o o O O o o o
1 2 1 2 3 1 2 1 2 3

FIGURE 5.4. Mot adds numbers to her drawing of the Class Piece.

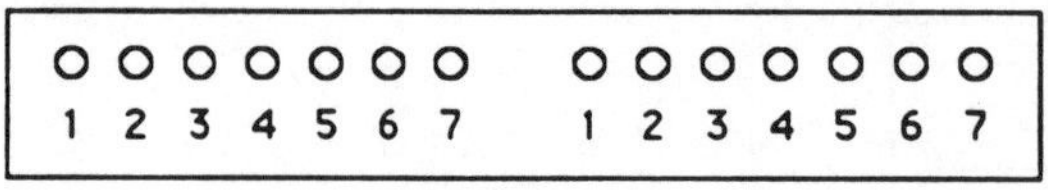

FIGURE 5.5. Mot adds numbers to her drawing of "Twinkle, Twinkle, Little Star."

said about the Class Piece, you take a breath and then start again.

MET: Exactly. But you have to *count that breath*, too—that stop before you start again.

MOT: What do you mean?

MET: Well if I count up the way you were counting up, then it would be like this: (*Met writes his numbers above Mot's drawing; Figure 5.6*).

MOT: That's interesting! You mean it's like there's a ghost beat there (*she points to the space where Met has written an "8"*). You don't actually sing or clap the ghost beat, but it's there anyhow.

MET: A ghost beat; I really like that. You see, time never stops, and the beats keep right on going, too, so you have to keep right on counting, right through the breath, even though you're not making any clap there.

MOT: Why don't we actually put the ghost beat in—the one you call "8." (*Mot draws her ghost beat; Figure 5.7*).

MET: You got it.

MOT: And now I see how you got your "8." Where I counted up to 7 and stopped, you counted up to 8 because you counted the ghost beat, too. So the ghost beat is the stop which sort of isn't a stop after all. But still, it is a stop, you know. I'm getting confused again.

JEANNE: But confusions need to be nurtured, too; they are often the necessary first step to learning anything new. Mot, would you mind clapping the Class Piece, again? And this time pay attention especially to the breath you talked about between the two larger figures.

MOT
(*clapping the
class piece
again*): Hmm. Yes, it seems like there's a space there, too; I mean between the two larger figures. Or I guess you could call it a space-of-time. How come I didn't notice that space before?

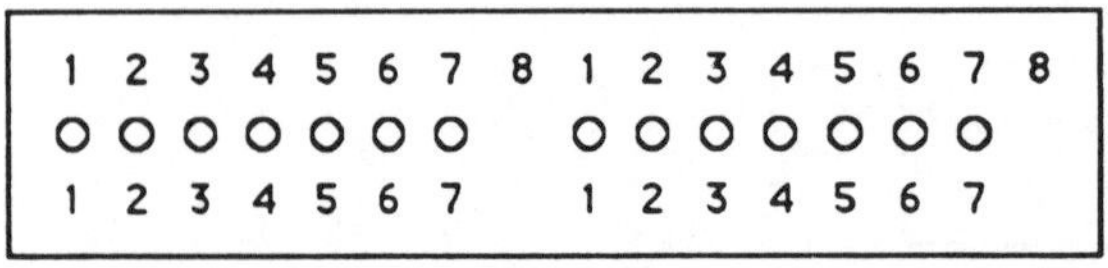

FIGURE 5.6. Met's numbering for "Twinkle, Twinkle, Little Star."

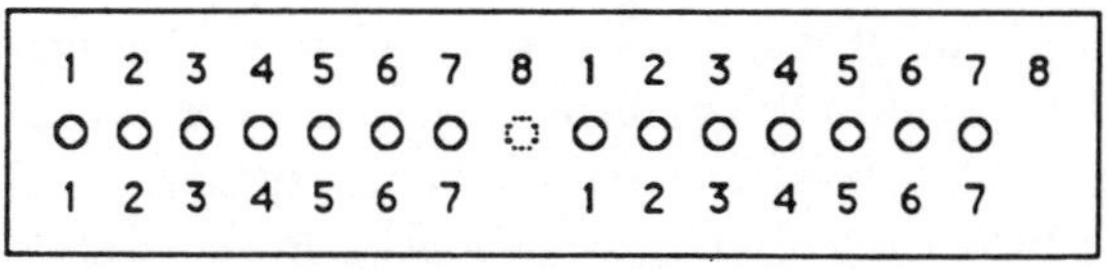

FIGURE 5.7. Mot's "ghost beat" in "Twinkle, Twinkle, Little Star."

JEANNE: Well, what do you think?

MOT: I seem to come to a boundary. I mean, when I clap the rhythm it's like I'm going along heading for a goal. For instance, I'm going along the path inside the inner fast figure till I come to the goal; and then I'm just inside the next figure, going along that one. I never paid attention to what was going on in between the two larger figures. In fact, there really wasn't any in between; I was simply in one figure and then I was in the other. The rhythm of Twinkle made me realize there is an in between. I sort of get it, but I don't.

JEANNE: That's quite understandable; it's hard to pay attention to all the different things that are going on: the claps you're making as you move along anticipating the goal or boundary; then arriving but also going across the boundary crossing. I think the way you talked about being inside one figure, moving along the path to the goal and then inside the next one, really captures what it feels like when you're actually clapping a rhythm.

MET: Sounds pretty strange to me. The rhythm is just there. . . .

MOT: Wait, I just realized something else.

MET: What's that?

MOT: I could put a ghost beat into my picture of our rhythm, too. (*Draws the Class Piece adding a "ghost beat" between the two larger figures; Figure 5.8*).

MET: That's great!

JEANNE: Do you think you could clap the Class Piece and actually clap the ghost beat, too, Mot?

MOT: I can try. (*Claps the Class Piece and includes the "ghost beat" as in Figure 5.8*) It seems like you almost expect that ghost beat to be there, but instead there's nothing.

MET: There isn't nothing. If there were nothing, you would clap it wrong. In fact, that's interesting—you clap it right, but you draw it wrong. Think about it this way: The *breath* you were talking about exactly takes up the space, I mean time, of your ghost beat.

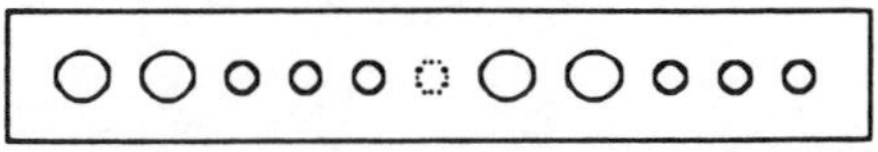

FIGURE 5.8. Mot's "ghost beat" in the Class Piece.

JEANNE: Good point, Met. And that suggests another question: Mot, how many faster claps would you say there are for each slower one?

MOT: Well, I think the little ones go twice as fast as the big ones. So I guess there are two for one. In fact, you could say there is a ghost beat inside of every big circle, too.

JEANNE: Could you explain that a little more?

MOT: It's hard to explain. . . . It seems like there's always a silence, a space, between every clap sound and I think the time of the actual clap sounds is always the same. So it must be the space-of-time between clap sounds that makes the difference between longs and shorts. Gosh this is getting so detailed!

JEANNE: But getting down into the details is useful, provided you can integrate what you've learned down there into the larger design when you climb back up again.

MET: Anyhow, what we are calling the length of a clap is really the clap sound and the gap before the next clap sound.

MOT: Yes, the length of the clap is really a package that includes both the clap and the gap. But when you're actually clapping, you don't think about that at all. With the first two claps you set a natural pace, and then you double it . . . or halve it. . . . Which is it, anyhow?

MET: When you start the faster claps, you double the speed but halve the time from one clap to the next.

MOT: This is beginning to sound like physics, not music.

MET: Not really. But now it should be obvious that if there is a clap and a ghost beat inside of every big circle like you said, then your fifth short clap, together with your ghost beat, will make up one longer clap. So the fifth clap that you've drawn as a little circle together with the gap is a slow clap so it should be a big circle— it's just the same as the slow sixth clap. (*He draws; Figure 5.9*).

MOT: But now that just doesn't look right. I can't see the larger re-peated patterns any more. And besides, the fifth clap isn't just like the sixth clap. The fifth clap is an *ending*, the sixth clap is a *beginning*, it starts the repetition, and that's not the same at all!

MET: Well, that's all beside the point.

JEANNE: No, Met, that is the point! You see, Mot is saying something very important. It's true that both the fifth clap and the sixth clap are the same if what you're paying attention to is simply measur-ing the time from one clap to the next. But that's not all there is to rhythms. Did you notice, for instance, that Mot talked about "beginnings" and "endings"?

MET: I did, but . . .

JEANNE: What do you make of that?

MET: Well, I guess you can't have a beginning and an ending without

FIGURE 5.9. The fifth clap together with the "ghost beat."

something happening that makes a start and stop. So Mot's first little circle or faster clap *starts off a new thing*—what you would call a new figure; and the last of her little circles (that fifth clap, again) ends the figure, or more like stops it.

MOT: Yes, and that's exactly why your big circle for the fifth clap gets me so upset. If you draw the fifth clap as a big circle, it makes the fifth clap look like the beginning of a three-clap slower figure when really the fifth clap is the ending of the previous faster figure.

MET: But we're not talking about how things *look*. I think we're getting off the track; we're supposed to be talking about time and motion, not about how things look standing still in space. Now I'm getting confused.

JEANNE: That's a beginning, too, Met. In fact, what you just said is the beginning of a real philosophical insight, so just hang onto your confusion for a bit. What do you think makes an event function as the beginning or the ending of a figure?

MOT: I've been wondering that, too. It seems like the function of a clap—whether you hear it as beginning or ending a motive—depends on where it happens—what comes before and after it. For instance, when I start clapping the rhythm, I sort of set the normal pace with the first two claps. So when I start going faster with the third clap, or really when I go from the third to the fourth clap, it feels like the beginning of something new. That new pace sets off the new figure.

MET: And I suppose the next one, the fifth clap that we keep arguing about, stops that run of claps. You get going at this new faster pace and when you get to the fifth clap it's longer than what you expect.

MOT: Well, I'd say it's because what you expect doesn't happen.

MET: I don't get it.

MOT: I mean, you're going along faster, and then you're stopped short because nothing happens. All right, I know, Met, we've been through this before; it's the gap, the ghost beat that's there but you don't actually play it. But that silent ghost beat is more like a comma at the end of a clause. So I guess another reason I made a small circle for the fifth clap is because I was drawing the claps I actually made and not the silent punctuation mark. After all, when we're reading out loud, we don't say commas either; we just make a little pause and that helps you to group the words so they make sense. Anyhow, just because the fifth clap has the same time as the sixth clap that comes next, they're still not the same.

JEANNE: Now, let's see if I've got it straight. What I hear you saying, Mot, is that even if two events have the same time value, they can still be different depending on where they happen. To use your example, if there's a change to a faster pace, that will set off a new little figure. Then you are moving along inside the new figure at that faster pace, expecting that pace to keep going. But when that pace changes because there is a silence where you might expect another event to occur if the faster pace continued, the new figure is brought to a halt. And that's what makes the boundary.

MOT: That's right.

JEANNE: But Met wants to make things simpler.

MET: Exactly. Since the fifth clap and the gap after it together make a long, it's a long event. What's the problem?

MOT: But if you only pay attention to how *long* an event lasts, never mind where or when, then you'll miss the boundaries altogether. And you will also miss the functional differences between beginning and ending events.

MET: That's funny. I never thought of it before: In a rhythm "where" and "when" mean the same thing.

MOT: That's true. Anyhow, a long after a run of shorts just isn't the same as a long after a long.

MET: Wait a minute, are you trying to tell me that the same two claps can be both the same and different at the same time?

MOT: Yes, depending on where they happen and what you're paying attention to.

JEANNE: Well put, Mot. And that turns out to be very important when you're performing a real piece of music. For instance, even though two notes have the same time value—let's say they both look like this in standard music notation (*she draws ♩ ♪*), you might very well play them differently exactly in order to express a beginning in contrast to an ending of a motive or a phrase. And the difference might involve, among other things, just how long you sustain a note. That is, inside the same sound-silence package, what we usually call the same notated duration, there can be a different relation between the sound and the silence. But when you're really playing a piece, you don't think about it at that level of detail; if you did, you'd feel paralyzed. It all becomes part of expressing the meaning of the piece, including its motives and phrases.

But the funny thing is, that while conventional music nota-

tion in its barest form is very good at showing you the time value
of events in relation to one another, it really doesn't tell you
anything about beginnings and endings of phrases or figures.
That's why violinists, for instance, spend so much time and
thought experimenting with bowings and fingerings, and clari-
netists worry so much about where to take a breath—they're
trying to find the best way to project these important differences
between notes that look the same on the page. For instance, in
some of Bach's suites for violin solo, practically all the note
values are the same. Can you imagine what that would sound
like if the violinist wasn't paying attention to the differences in
the functions of events that otherwise look the same timewise?
Composers, or sometimes editors in the case of Bach, try to help
by adding various kinds of so-called expressive markings—slurs,
or staccato marks like these (*she draws; Figure 5.10*).

But still, if you strictly follow the rule "what you see is what
you get," you'll hear a pretty boring and very unmusical performance. I remember Louis Krasner, the violinist who commis-
sioned the Berg Violin Concerto, saying to a student, "Just forget
the score and play the music." But to get back to where we were,
yes, two events can be both the same and different depending on
the context and on what you're paying attention to.

MET: That reminds me of a picture I saw in a book on vision, once.
When you look at it, you see this same shape in two different
ways depending on what's next to it (Figure 5.11). At first it
seems like you have no choice—you see two different shapes, a
diamond and a square. But if you really pay attention to the
geometric properties—just stare at the angles and the sides of
one shape at a time—of course you can see that they're the
same. So, yes, you could say they're both the same and different
depending on what you're paying attention to.

MOT: That's a great example, Met.

MET: But you know, we keep shifting back and forth between time and
space, and that makes me think of something else. Talking about
performers and experimenting, let's try one. You, Mot, pull this
piece of paper slowly across the table. While you're doing that,
I'll move my pencil up and down in one place, tapping out the
rhythm over your moving paper.

(*Mot and Met make the experiment. It leaves this trace;
Figure 5.12*).

FIGURE 5.10. Slurs as expressive markings.

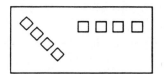

FIGURE 5.11. The same shape can look different.

MOT: That looks fine. You can see the repeated big patterns and the little inner figures, too. How come that works?

MET: Well, because we really made time become space. The trace left behind shows how continuous time or motion—the paper moving across the table—was marked off by my taps. That's the way the old piano rolls worked, and the first mechanized looms, too. First the paper was punched out as someone played—much like we just marked off the moving paper. Then, whenever the sensing mechanism moved across a hole in the paper piano roll, a piano key would be activated. So spatial relations turn into time relations or rhythms.

MOT: I guess I understand, but I keep getting confused between the dots and the spaces between the dots.

MET: Well, just reverse the process. Run your hand at a steady pace over the dots we made and every time you come to a dot make a click or something (*Mot tries it.*)

MOT: It works, all right. And I can really see the faster inner figures, too; the run of three faster claps stands out because there's a bigger space on either side of it—that's really a space-of-time, of course. In fact, what you see is the change of pace that actually generates the boundaries of figures.

MET: And putting it that way helps me to understand your drawing better, Mot, and to hear what you mean by figures, too.

MOT: Well, I'm glad of that. But what about the last clap—you could just go on forever.

MET: As a matter of fact, that's been bothering me all along. You can't know how long the last clap is because it always takes two to tango. I mean, seriously, you always need two claps to mark a time interval. It's your beginning and ending problem, in a way, but on a smaller scale: a beginning by itself, one mark or one clap, like you said, can go on forever; you need another one to stop it. But then, of course, you wouldn't know how long that one was.

JEANNE: This is getting pretty metaphysical. I really liked your experiment, Met, and I especially like the trace it left behind. It's a new notation that I think might have real possibilities.

FIGURE 5.12. The trace left by Met's experiment.

MET: By the way, you said I'd made some kind of philosophical insight back there. Aren't you going to tell me what it was?

JEANNE: Actually, the two of you sort of acted it all out just now. It was about the problems we make for ourselves when we try to describe actions moving through time. We make descriptions of moving things on paper in order to make them stand still, but then we end up with all these issues and confusions about time and space—like the ones that you've both noticed as we've been going along. When you learn how to make motion stand still like you've just been doing through your drawings of rhythms, you gain real power because then you can see, all at one time, what we necessarily experience as fleeting, evanescent, gone.

For instance, it was only after Mot had made her drawing of Twinkle that she was able to invent her ghost beat. Once the rhythm was held still in paper-space, then she could see the bigger space between the two phrases. And once seen, she could also recognize it as really a space-of-time. Only then could she catch on to what Met was saying, even if not totally agreeing with him. Making these static, spatial descriptions solves the problems of time and motion that Heraclitus might have put this way: "You can never put your foot in the same river once."

The trouble is, we are able to find ways of making actions and motion stand still on paper through the invention of a notation system, and that is very useful, even sometimes profound. But once it is made and deeply internalized through continuous use, we come to believe in the notation so thoroughly that we actually experience whatever it is—clapping, wheels turning, drummers drumming—through the lens of the notation, itself. So we go from Heraclitus's problem to taking literally what-you-see-is-what-you've-got.

MET: This has all been more interesting than I thought it was going to be at the beginning. And I think I do understand, now, what you were showing in your drawing, Mot.

MOT: Thank goodness. Things got better once you calmed down, Met. And I have to say I learned a lot, too. In spite of your unpleasantness at the beginning, and in spite of feeling like my head was swirling around some of the time, you helped me get at things I probably would never have gotten to by myself.

Comments on our Dialogue

While Met and Mot begin their conversation in what seems like irreconcilable conflict, by the end they have clearly come to a resolution of their sometimes contentious disputes. But interestingly, they have done so without either of them giving up the hearings expressed in their initial drawings. Instead, by actively confronting one another, each helped the other to notice features and relations of the rhythm that had been essentially inaccessible at the outset. In short, each has succeeded in making the hearing of the other but without either of them giving up his or her own.

And in the course of this educational resolution of their figural/formal disputes, Mot also answers a question that has remained quietly waiting beneath all the discussion of figural grouping: What are the temporal relationships that *generate the boundaries* of figures that figural drawings describe? Through Met's experiment—Mot pulling the paper while Met taps out the rhythm with his pencil—Mot is able to see that "the run of three faster claps stands out because there's a bigger space on either side of it—that's really a space-of-time, of course." In other words, it is a *change of pace* that generates the boundaries of figures. And in summarizing her comments, I point out that if there is a change from a slower pace to a faster pace, it will set off a new little figure; and within that faster pace if there is an event of longer duration, that will bring the new figure to a halt, thus creating a boundary.

Such contrasts in the prevailing rate of events can suffice in accounting for figural boundary making within these musically minimal examples—in particular, where events differ only with respect to their time values. But an account that may suffice for brief rhythms played on a nonpitch instrument (claps) and where there is not even any change in loudness will hardly suffice at the moment we consider "real compositions" such as a Beethoven piano sonata movement or a movement from a Bach partita with their much richer network of intersecting, sometimes conflicting, dimensions. Indeed, the issue of what generates grouping boundaries, and how hearings may differ with respect to the groupings heard, is a vexing and fascinating topic to which a number of music theorists have given their attention in recent years. (See Cooper and Meyer, 1960; Lerdahl and Jackendoff, 1983; Bamberger, forthcoming.) And yet, musically impoverished examples such as the Class Piece are useful because they can help to make clear just what kinds of questions we need to ask, what kinds of clues we need to look for, and how seemingly irreconcilable conflicts among disparate hearings might be resolved.

Conclusions

In the dialogue between Met, Mot, and myself, I have shown an instance of just how such clues to hearings can emerge, and how, through recognizing them, hearings can develop and change as each participant brings into existence features and relations that were inaccessible at the outset. For example, Mot's initial drawing provides clues that her attention is focused on the grouping of adjacent events as these form figures. And despite Met's objections, she seems unable to recognize, or is at least inattentive to, the shared proportional time values of some events. Met, recognizing these clues, helps Mot to hear that "time keeps on going" and that she needs to count the time "in between" clapped events, as well. This leads Mot to invent her "ghost beat," which, in turn, helps her to bring into existence, so to speak, an entity that had simply not existed for her before. And once seen, this new entity also helps Mot to understand why Met insists that the disputed fifth clap in the Class Piece should be a big circle instead of a small one—even though she doesn't like "the way it looks."

Met's initial drawing shows us clues to his singular focus on the measured time properties of events—all events that share the same event time are for him simply the same. Despite Mot's repeated attempts, she is at first unable to help Met shift his focus so as to hear her figures. But as she recognizes a critical aspect of her own hearing, Mot is able finally to help Met, too. Pointing out that even though two events may share the same time value, their *function* can change depending on the context in which they are embedded, Met is finally able to hear and appreciate the significance of the figural groupings within the rhythm. And in doing so, he too brings into existence an aspect of rhythms that had not existed for him before.

Through this process of reflective confrontation, then, new features emerge, making it possible for both students to include in their hearings new aspects of even these trivial rhythms. And it is this "liberation" of new features that eventually enables Met and Mot to resolve their disputes. With each having access to the preferred features of the other's hearing, they are able to agree that two events can be both the same and different *depending on what you are paying attention to*: Specifically, even though two events may be the same in that they *share the same event time* (e.g., claps 5 and 6), they can still be different with respect to their *figural function*—"where and when they happen" and what role they play as the rhythm unfolds in performance. Thus claps 5 and 6 are indeed the same with respect to their time values, but they still differ in their functions—one an ending, the other a beginning.

This, then, is an example of individuals coming to hear in new ways. Through the work of the two students, I have tried to illustrate that to make a new hearing we must confront those intimate, silent conversations back and forth through which we make and shape the meaning and form we seem simply and immutably to find in the musical phenomena "out there." I have also tried to show that one way to do that is to confront and perturb the hearings of others so as to become aware of *possible* aspects of a rhythm. For in that way we learn to recognize just those aspects to which we are currently giving privileged attention in making our own hearings. Experimenting with one another's hearings, then, we can learn to shift focus at will among the possible features and relations that give a rhythm, or even a moment in a complex composition, its unique coherence.

And through this process, knowing how and knowing about develop a new, *reciprocal* relation to one another in contrast to the adversary relationship I proposed at the outset: Interrogating what it is you know how to *do* becomes the means for learning to know *about* the music you can sing, clap, or dance to. Thus, instead of knowing about being distanced in and through the privileged languages of others, knowing about becomes a useful way of informing what is most intimate and most familiar. Together, then, knowing how and knowing about, in reflective interaction with one another, help us to hear in new ways, at the same time giving us the power to choose selectively and knowingly among the multiple possible hearings that we are able to make—depending on where, when, and what we want to use them for.

ACKNOWLEDGMENTS

This chapter includes versions of material covered more completely in my book *The Mind Behind the Musical Ear*, Harvard University Press, Cambridge, 1991.

NOTES

1. See Bamberger, 1991.
2. For more on the importance of sequential actions see Bartlett (1932), Lashley (1951), Gardner (1973), and Bamberger (1991).

REFERENCES

Bamberger, J. (1980). Cognitive structuring in the apprehension and description of simple rhythms. *Archives de Psychology, XLVLII*, 171–99.

Bamberger, J. (1981). Revisiting children's descriptions of simple rhythms: A function for reflection-in-action. In S. Strauss (Ed.), *U-shaped behavioral growth*. New York: Academic Press.

Bamberger, J. (1986). Cognitive issues in the development of musically gifted children. In R. J. Sternberg & J. E. Davidson (Eds.), *New conceptions of giftedness*. Cambridge, England: Cambridge University Press.

Bamberger, J. (1988). Les structurations cognitives de l'apprehension et de la notation de rhythmes simples. In Hermine Sinclair (Ed.), *Notations*. Paris: Presses Universitaires de France.

Bamberger, J. (1991). *The mind behind the musical ear*. Cambridge: Harvard University Press.

Bamberger, J. (forthcoming). *Parables of mind and music making*. New York: Schirmer Books.

Bartlett, F. C. (1932). *Remembering*. Cambridge: Cambridge University Press.

Cooper, G., & Meyer, L. B. (1960). *The rhythmic structure of music*. Chicago: University of Chicago Press.

Gardner, H. (1973). *The arts and human development*. New York: Wiley.

Hildebrandt, C., & Bamberger, J. (1979). Claps and gaps. Unpublished manuscript.

Lashley, K. S. (1951). The problem of serial order in behavior. In L. P. Jeffress (Ed.), *Cerebral mechanisms in behavior: The Hixon symposium*. New York: Wiley.

Lerdahl, F., & Jackendoff, R. (1983). *A generative theory of tonal music*. Cambridge: MIT Press.

Rosenfield, I. (1988). *The invention of memory*. New York: Basic Books.

Shahn, B. (1957). *The shape of content*. Cambridge: Harvard University Press.

Wittgenstein, L. (1953). *Philosophical investigations* (G. E. M. Anscombe, Trans.). New York: Macmillan.

6

Music Performance: Expression and the Development of Excellence

JOHN A. SLOBODA

Introduction

Music performance is a skill. As with any skill, there are two main psychological questions: What is the skilled performer like (the nature of skill) and how did the skilled performer get to be skilled (the acquisition of skill)? In the last two decades psychologists have given these questions intensive study (e.g., Anderson, 1981; Chi, Glaser, & Farr, 1988; Ericsson & Smith, 1991).

From studying a very wide range of skills (e.g., chess, sport, medical diagnosis, mathematics), a number of general conclusions have emerged. First, skill almost always depends on the ability of the performer to detect pattern and structure in the material, and to conceive the activity in terms of these patterns. Second, the level of skill is almost entirely dependent on the amount of relevant practice undertaken. In other words, learning to detect patterns and structures takes time, so the more time you have spent on a skill, the better you are at it. Third, as skills become practiced and fluent, they tend also to become "automatic"; that is, the details of how they are executed disappear from the conscious awareness of the performer. Fourth, because patterns and structures tend to be specific to a particular domain, there is little transfer between skills. A person can become very good at one skill (e.g., chess) while remaining very poor at another (piano performance). Partly because of this, some skills seem to be independent of general intelligence, and the psychological literature contains numerous examples of people with low general IQ who nonetheless excel at particular cognitive tasks (e.g., Ceci, 1990; Howe, 1989).

All these conclusions are true of music as well. The present chapter concentrates on the evidence for the first three of the above conclusions. For discussion of the fourth conclusion, including some fascinating studies of musical skill in the absence of high general intellect, the reader is referred to Howe (1991) and Miller (1989).

The chapter concentrates on a key aspect of music performance, that is, the ability to play notated solo compositions expressively. For a discussion of wider aspects of performance, including improvisation, ensemble playing, sight-reading, and performance anxiety, the reader is referred to Sloboda (1982, 1985, 1988).

The final prefatory comment concerns the status of music performance research. Although such research has a long history, it has, in recent decades, been eclipsed by studies of musical perception. This partly reflects a fact of our culture, that many more people engage in music passively (through listening) than they do actively (through performance). But it may also reflect the fact that experimental science likes to control situations in a rather tight way. It is much easier to do this when constructing computer-generated musical sounds than when confronted with a free-performance situation. Nonetheless, in the past decade, performance studies have reestablished themselves as able to meet the rigors of experimental science while addressing questions of theoretical and practical importance in fairly realistic settings.

REFERENCES

Anderson, J. R. (Ed.) (1981). *Cognitive skills and their acquisition.* Hillsdale, NJ: Erlbaum.

Ceci, S. J. (1990). *On intelligence . . . more or less: A bioecological treatise on intellectual development.* Englewood Cliffs, NJ: Prentice-Hall.

Chi, M. T. H., Glaser, R., & Farr, M. J. (Eds.) (1988). *The nature of expertise.* Hillsdale, NJ: Erlbaum.

Ericsson, K. A., & Smith, J. (1991). *Toward a general theory of expertise: Prospects and limits.* Cambridge: Cambridge University Press.

Howe, M. J. A. (1989). *Fragments of genius: The strange feats of idiots savants.* London: Routledge.

Howe, M. J. A. (1991). *The origins of exceptional abilities.* Oxford: Blackwell.

Miller, L. K. (1989). *Musical savants: Exceptional skill in the mentally retarded.* Hillsdale, NJ: Erlbaum.

Sloboda, J. A. (1982). Music performance. In D. Deutsch (Ed.), *The psychology of music.* New York: Academic Press.

Sloboda, J. A. (1985). *The musical mind: The cognitive psychology of music.* London: Oxford University Press.

Sloboda, J. A. (Ed.) (1988). *Generative processes in music: The psychology of performance, improvisation, and composition.* London: Oxford University Press.

Expressive Performance

The Rationality of Expression

Technical mastery of a difficult composition is undoubtedly an impressive achievement. We can admire such qualities as rapidity of playing, evenness of touch and timing, and large-scale accurate memory. Yet these things, necessary as they are to musical performance, are insufficient to justify the huge effort that goes into producing top-class performers. If that was all there was to performance, we might as well program scores into a computer, have them performed on instruments via a digital interface, record "perfect" performances once and for all, and close our conservatories!

It is well known, however, that computer renditions of familiar compositions sound dull and lifeless, no matter how fast or accurate they are. Human performances gain their lasting interest and appeal from the fact that they go beyond the information contained in the printed score. It was one of the earliest discoveries of the scientific studies of music performance (see Seashore, 1938) that musicians rarely play two apparently identical notes (from the point of view of the notated score) in the same way. Timing, loudness, tone quality, and intonation can be substantially varied, even within the same measure. Such variations together constitute what we usually call "expression." Variations in expression are what make one note-perfect performance different from another note-perfect performance. They explain why we bother to hear different people play the same piece. They explain why it is worth training successive generations of performers to repeat the same classical repertoire over and over. New and insightful interpretations are always possible.

Most musicians would agree that assigning expressive features to a performance (i.e., deciding on an interpretation of a composition) is a rational enterprise. That is to say, we agree that it matters which notes we vary and how. We can compare different interpretations and offer reasons why we feel one interpretation to be more appropriate or pleasing than another. This is not to say that there is only one acceptable interpretation of a piece of music. There may be an indefinite number. Rather, it is saying that there are criteria by means of which most musicians could come to a judgment that certain possible interpretations are not appropriate to the composition. Expression is not some kind of random or arbitrary variation that we apply to a performance. The structures in the music constrain the expression. Performance and pedagogical traditions constrain the expression. Dialogues between performers, teachers, judges, and critics formulate and make explicit these constraints and apply them to particular pieces and particular performances.

There is, however, a difference between saying, on the one hand, that an activity is rational and, on the other hand, that it is a matter of explicit conscious awareness to the performer during performance. On any particular occasion, a performer may be unaware of the exact nature of all the expressive variations that are being used, or may be aware only of some rather high-level description of the nature of the expression (e.g., "jerky") rather than the precise means by which this expressive quality is being produced. This has been demonstrated in several experimental studies. For example, Gabrielsson (1974, 1988) asked performers to produce absolutely strict rhythms, as notated, yet they produced performances that consistently deviated from strictness by making some notes shorter than their notated values, other notes longer. It appears that some types of expressive variations have become so automatic for some performers that they are not usually aware of them. Psychological investigations of performance expression cannot, therefore, proceed purely from verbal accounts given by performers of what they do. We actually have to measure performance parameters with a high degree of accuracy. The development of sophisticated computer-instrument links (e.g., the MIDI interface) has made such studies relatively easy, and the last 15 years has seen a steady growth in performance studies.

Quite a lot of the experimental research on performance has been devoted to showing that expressive variations are, indeed, rational, related to musical structure, and have a clear effect on perception. Such research is, however, nowhere near providing a complete explanation for, or prediction of, every expressive parameter of a performance. Musicians who are afraid that this kind of study will rob them of their art have really grossly overestimated the power of contemporary scientific investigations. Attempts to synthesize expressive performance by the computer application of expressive rules (e.g., Sundberg, 1988) are still rather primitive and pose no strong threat to real performers!

Experimental Studies of Expression in Performance

The first step in establishing the rationality of expressive performance is to demonstrate that expressive variations are *intentional*. There are two kinds of variation present in performance which we would not consider as intentional. The first we could call "noise." Every human performer has variations that reflect such limiting factors as muscular control or time estimation. These limits will create small random fluctuations. Hopefully, practice and experience will reduce the magnitude of these variations, but there will always be a residual "jitter." Because of the random nature of noise we would not expect it to show itself in identical ways in two performances. Therefore, the way to find out what is noise and what is not is to ask a person to repeat the same passage of music with exactly the same interpretation, several times over. Only those expressive variations which show up each time can be counted as intentional.

A number of studies of musical performances by professionals have shown a remarkable consistency in successive performances of the same piece (Seashore, 1938; Shaffer, 1981, 1984; Shaffer, Clarke, & Todd, 1985). For instance, Shaffer (1984) compared three performances by the pianist Penelope Blackie of a

Chopin étude, two of which were given a year after the first. Beat duration is plotted in Figure 6.1, which shows a remarkable consistency, not only in the location of major slowings (measures 20, 28, 53, and 57), but also in the distribution of beat durations within a measure (for instance, in measure 30 the first beat is always longer than the second).

The second kind of "unintentional" performance variation comes about be-

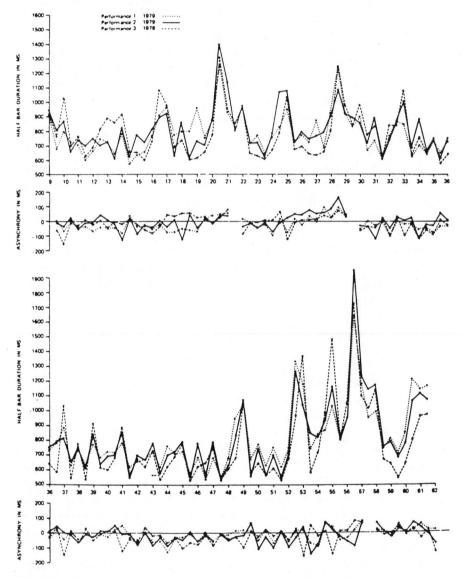

FIGURE 6.1. Beat duration in three performances of a Chopin Etude by the same pianist (Shaffer, 1984).

cause of some technical difficulty. Suppose, for example, that a pianist slowed the performance prior to every large intervallic leap. We would soon suspect that the sheer distance between two notes was the unintended cause of the delay, and would advise the pianist to go away and do some more practice. The most convincing way of showing that this kind of problem is absent is to find instances where exactly the same set of notes is played in two quite different expressive ways. If we can find such instances, then neither expressive pattern can be due to a technical difficulty. Sloboda (1983, 1985) used this method in a study where pianists were asked to provide five consecutive performances at sight of a set of simple melodies. Unknown to the performers, each melody was paired with a "twin" produced by shifting the bar-lines one note along the original melody, leaving the actual notes, their speed, and the fingers with which they were to be played exactly the same. An example of such a pair is shown in Figure 6.2.

Because the members of a pair were always separated by other melodies, no performer realized that the notes were identical. Despite being identical in all respects other than metrical location, the two melodies were played quite differently by all performers. Furthermore, these differences related very closely to the metrical structure. For instance, performers tended to make the first note of a measure significantly louder, longer, and more legato than the notes on either side. These differences were, therefore, truly intentional, even though the details of them may not have been fully available to the conscious awareness of each performer.

The results of this research help to elucidate the reason why a shared language of expressive "rules" does not lead to uniformity in performance. Each pianist's performance of a given melody in this study was quite different from every other pianist's performance although all used the same basic expressive strategies. This is because each pianist varied the extent, degree, and precise location of the variations available. Some pianists made more use of duration parameters, others of loudness. Some made large variations, others made more subtle ones. Some marked every measure, others marked only selected measures, and so on. Even within a fairly tightly defined "rational" expressive system, the potential for individual variation is still immense. There are many "free" parameters, even within a constrained system. We may suppose that the way which different performers "fill in" these free parameters is what is responsible for their unmistakable individual style that permeates all their performances (Sloboda, 1985). Connoisseurs of particular genres can often tell within a few measures of a recording who the performer is.

FIGURE 6.2. A sample pair of same-note melodies used in Sloboda's (1983) study.

The Effectiveness of Expressive Performance

It is one thing to show that measurable and intentional expressive variations are present. It is quite another to show that these variations are *effective*. What, in the context of music performance, do we mean by effective? First, differences in expression must be *detectable* by listeners; second, they must be *interpretable*. The first condition is there to ensure that expressive variations are large enough to make a difference to listeners; the second, to ensure that the variations mean something to the listener, at either an intellectual, aesthetic, or affective level.

Psychological studies of expressive musical communication have tended to remain at the level of intellectual judgment. So, for instance, Sloboda (1983) showed that listeners had some ability to correctly judge which member of a twinned pair of melodies a particular performance was representing. Different performers, however, had differing levels of success in conveying meter. This seemed to relate to performance experience. The most experienced pianist in the sample had 40 years of professional playing, and he was the most effective in conveying meter to a panel of listeners. The least experienced player had only (!) been playing for 12 years, and was the least effective communicator of meter. The most effective communicator was both more consistent and more exaggerated in the use of expressive devices. The least effective communicator showed some inconsistencies, with some expressive variations going against the "rules" extracted from the majority of the performances.

Meter is only one small part of what an expressive performance might communicate. Palmer (1988, 1989) in an extended series of studies showed that pianists asked to exaggerate or accentuate a melody tended to make the melody notes precede other notes which were notated as simultaneous. When asked to exaggerate or highlight a particular phrasing, they tended to increase rubato at intended phrase boundaries (similar results have been obtained by Todd, 1985) and increase legato playing within the phrase. In one experiment, pianists were asked to play the same piece in three different ways—as they normally do and then two exaggerated performances which accentuated different melodies or phrasings. Listeners tended to be able to accurately judge which performance was intended. Palmer also showed that it was, indeed, the timing variations that communicated the intended interpretation to the listeners. She resynthesized the performances by computer in such a way that all timing variations were eliminated while the loudness variations of the original were retained. Listeners were poor at identifying expressive intention from these resynthesized performances.

Davidson (1991, 1993) has recently shown that not all of the expressive intent of a performance is necessarily contained within the sound parameters. Her studies demonstrated that the body movements made by performers while playing contribute to the expressivity of the performance as judged by observers.

Movements of wrist, torso, and head tend to be systematic and related to specific structural features of the music. It is as if such body movements draw the observer's attention to particular parts of the music, enhancing their salience. Even when performers are asked to play the music "deadpan" (i.e., without expression), small but detectable body movements still occur. These are of exactly the same type as the movements observed when the performer is asked to play expressively and occur at the same points in the music. Just as in the Gabrielsson (1974) study discussed earlier, these movements seem to have become automatic. Davidson's results raise some interesting questions about the context of musical performance. Do they help explain why live performances are often so much more engaging than recorded ones? Does our society's increasing dependence on audio recordings of music mean that a whole dimension of musical expressivity is being downplayed or abandoned?

Summary

It has become increasingly clear from performance studies of the type described here that expressive variations in music are not simply a matter of arbitrary convention. They actually help listeners assign a structural interpretation to a passage of music that is the one intended by the performer. Many theorists (notably Lerdahl & Jackendoff, 1983; see Chapter 3) believe that an important part of what it is to have understood a piece of music is to have assigned to it a structural description in which related notes are grouped together, and in which different events are assigned different importance or prominence. Lerdahl and Jackendoff propose that this description is arrived at by assessing various cues in the music and then trying to achieve an interpretation that is consistent with them. In some musical passages, all the different cues (rhythm, harmony, articulation) are consistent, and so strongly suggest one structural description. In other cases, there are several possible descriptions, and the performer's role may well be to add expressive cues that will incline the listener toward one or another interpretation. These cues follow from general principles of musical perception. For instance, all other things being equal, notes that are longer than their neighbors will be heard as more prominent. Therefore, if a performer wishes to disambiguate a metrically ambiguous passage, he or she will tend to lengthen the first note of a metrical unit.

The Development of Excellence in Performance

Talent Versus Learning

There can be few questions which are of more intrinsic interest and pressing practical concern than the question of how music performers acquire high levels of expressive skill. Why is it that musicians differ in their level of expressivity? It has been common to discuss differences between musicians as differences in "talent" or "musicality." Yet, on their own, these words are simply redescriptions of the phenomenon to be explained. How *is* it that one person is more "musical" than another? The implicit assumption behind such language is that these differences are inborn or innate. Yet there is remarkably little evidence to support such an assumption. Studies by behavior geneticists (see Coon & Carey, 1989) suggest that the impact of environmental variables on musical achievement is unusually high when normal methods of estimating heritability (i.e., twin studies) are used. The validity of such twin studies has, of course, been widely questioned in any case (Ceci, 1990; Rose, Lewontin, & Kamin, 1984).

An alternative perspective, and one which follows rather naturally from the view that expressive performance is a rational activity closely related to the performer's understanding of the musical structure, is that such performance is a cognitive skill that is learned. If this latter perspective is correct, then to call someone exceptionally talented is to assert no more than the fact that such a person has had a certain sort of exceptional life, in which crucial and statistically unusual experiences occurred, allowing the development of skill beyond the norm. As I have argued elsewhere (Sloboda, 1990), exceptionality cannot be observed by its inherent qualities, as it were from within the person. A person is only exceptional in a certain cultural or historical context by virtue of doing better than most other people. For instance, the normal reading ability of a contemporary high-school graduate would have been considered totally exceptional 500 years ago.

Few people would consider it plausible to explain the general increase in reading efficiency by a massive increase in innate ability for reading over the last 500 years. Rather, we would look to broad social changes which turned exceptional experiences into common ones. As intensive exposure to the products of literacy and literacy education became more and more normal, it became possible for increasing numbers of people to undergo the set of experiences that resulted in the level of attainment we consider normal today.

What are the general characteristics of the lives of those people who have attained exceptional levels of musical skill by today's standards? To answer this question, researchers have recently begun to examine elite groups of musicians at various stages of their careers: students at special music schools, conservatory students, successful professionals, and competition winners.

The Role of Practice

Ericsson, Krampe, and Tesch-Romer (1991) recently conducted an extensive study of the practicing history of 40 violinists. Thirty of these were students at the Music Academy of West Berlin; 10 "best" students nominated by their professors as having the potential for careers as international soloists; 10 "good" violinists from the same department; and 10 "teachers" studying the violin in a department (education) with lower performance admission standards. All these groups were matched for age and sex. The fourth group ("professionals") comprised 10 middle-aged violinists from two symphony orchestras in West Berlin with international reputation.

Each participant undertook extensive interviews, was asked to keep a daily diary of activities for a week, and was asked to estimate the number of hours of practice on the violin each week for each year since he or she had started to play the violin. Figure 6.3 shows the accumulated hours of practice for each group at each age up to 20. The "best" and "professional" violinists show a very similar curve, which suggests that the professors' classification was accurate. By age 20, they had accumulated an average of over 10,000 hours of practicing, compared to some 8,000 for the "good" students, and some 5,000 for the "teachers." Indeed, the "best" violinists had accumulated by the age of 15 the same amount of practice as the "teachers" had by age 20. Even as young as 10, there is a distinct difference between the "best" players and the others.

The reliability of the estimated figures was checked by comparing estimated figures for the current year to the actual figures recorded in the diaries. The concordance was quite high. At the time of the study the "best" students were averaging 30 hours per week of practice, the "good" students 25, and the "teachers" only 10.

Ericsson, Tesch-Romer, and Krampe (1990) point out that accumulated skill through practice has "many of the properties associated often attributed to inherent characteristics such as talent. If, for example, two individuals of the same age differ dramatically in accumulated practice time . . . there is no way for the less trained individual to catch up with the more experienced person, if both maintain the same weekly schedule."

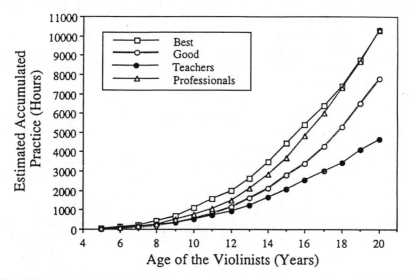

FIGURE 6.3. Accumulated hours of practice in four groups of violinists (Ericsson, Krampe, & Tesch-Romer, 1991).

Where, as in the case of music, access to the highest levels of teaching and coaching is based on competitive hurdles to be overcome in a narrow age window (typically 18 to 20), then clearly the successful musicians will be those who managed to accumulate as much practice as possible by this age. There is now considerable evidence that the highest levels of musical achievement are normally attained by individuals who began systematic study of an instrument before the age of 10 and maintained regular and increasing amounts of practice through the years of adolescence. In Ericsson et al.'s (1991) study, the mean age of the first violin lesson was 7 years. In a study of 21 international pianists in the United States, Sosniak (1985, 1990) found that the mean age of the first lesson was 6. A study by Sloboda and Howe (1991) on 42 adolescent students of a specialist English music school also revealed a mean starting age of 6 (range 3 to 10).

Of course, sheer amount of practice is a rather crude measure from a psychological point of view. The nature of learning will depend on what is done during practice as well as how much of it is done. Surprisingly, there is almost no reliable scientific information on how musicians practice. Gruson (1988) is the only researcher to date who has compared the practicing strategies of expert and novice instrumentalists. She found that experienced musicians showed much more sensitivity to structural units in the music (by, for instance, taking such units in isolation for repeated practice). Novices tended to indulge in more playing through of a whole piece, and repeating individual wrong notes, rather than repeating the sections in which they were embedded. A detailed case study of an individual professional pianist (Miklaszewski, 1989) confirms the importance of identifying structural "fragments" for detailed work. Clearly, since expressive performance is closely related to the detailed structure of a composition, practice that shows awareness of structural factors is more likely to lead to the development of an appropriate expressive repertoire.

Although amount of practice may be a conveniently simple predictor of "talent," it is far from simple to explain how large amounts of practice are initiated and sustained over a long period of a person's life. Ericsson et al. (1990: 113) expresses the problem succinctly:

> Practice activities, which involve careful analysis of one's performance, deliberate fine-tuning and acquisition of new procedures through massive repetition, are of a very different nature from spontaneously enjoyable activities within the domain. Examples of such spontaneously enjoyable activities are the play of children and the "flow state" which is defined by Csikszentmihalyi (1975) as the optimal match between the individual's skill level and the demands of the chosen field, with the individual feeling fully consumed by the activity. In contrast, practice requires deliberate control and effort, which most people, especially children, find unpleasant, particularly as it is extended over longer periods of time.

The issues here are basically ones of motivation and reward. Why do some children start music lessons and then continue effortful involvement through many years, when the "typical" child abandons effort after a few months or years?

Early Biographical Precursors of Excellence

One prevalent "myth" concerning exceptional musicians is that they typically demonstrated very early signs of their exceptionality by, for instance, early accurate singing, early reproduction of melodies on an instrument, exceptional concentration on music, or spontaneous early requests to begin lessons. Evidence from neither Sosniak (1985, 1990) nor Sloboda and Howe (1991) unequivocally confirms this view. Although parents of some children reported such things, the majority of children showed no special or outstanding ability or interest in music significantly before the start of lessons. In Sloboda and Howe's study, most children began instrumental lessons for reasons other than their own choice. In some cases it was a normal part of the school routine; in others the parents had decided it was a good thing for all their children to do, regardless of "ability." Sosniak discovered that it was sometimes not until five or six years after the start of formal instruction that her top pianists began to show the signs that led teachers to believe that a professional career was possible. When they started lessons, all of her sample were perceived as normal and unexceptional.

Sloboda (1989) has provided evidence to suggest that where the motivation for beginning lessons comes from the child, it is more likely to arise from some intense and pleasurable experience of music listening rather than from performance accomplishment. Such experiences motivated their recipients to wish to be able to reproduce these experiences through performance. The study, which asked adults to recall music-related events from their childhoods, suggested that early performance-related activities were very often negatively, rather than positively, motivating, being perceived as sources of anxiety, humiliation, or even physical abuse. It is possible to account for many apparent cases of "unmusicality" through early negative reinforcement, usually administered by a schoolteacher, which inhibited further engagement or effort in music performance.

Even when instrumental learning is not inhibited by negative reinforcement, it is clear that many young people become unhelpfully focused on "playing the right notes," and are so anxious about their own performance that they cease to enjoy the music or become emotionally engaged in it for its own sake. In these contexts it may become rather difficult to learn to play expressively. The tuition in expressive performance given by a teacher will fail to generalize unless a student can experience *why* that expressive device is appropriate through his or her own listening responses. If a young person has never experienced the emotional delight of, say, an enharmonic change, then he or she won't grasp, from the inside, why a slight slowing before the change may heighten the aesthetic effect. The teacher's performance instruction will seem arbitrary, rather than something which is immediately understood and assimilated for use in analogous situations.

Recent data on emotional responses to music (Sloboda, 1991a, 1991b) demonstrate that intense physical concomitants of emotional responses to music (such as tears or shivers down the spine) are linked to specific structures in the music, such as appogiaturas or enharmonic changes. If a child rarely has the opportunity to experience music in the kind of relaxed settings that promote these intense responses, then he or she will never be able to apply appropriate performance expression to such events other than something learned mechanically. The amount of expressive detail in a single performance is so great that it would be very difficult and time consuming to learn it "from scratch" for each piece. Good performers must be able to apply general rules of expression which make intuitive sense to them. Intense, involved, and enjoyable listening experiences are the key to the acquisition of this intuitive "sensibility."

The Early Years of Instrumental Learning

The general conclusion that emerges from the various biographical studies mentioned is that, for those children who later achieve performance excellence, the earliest years of instrumental learning are characterized by an atmosphere of pleasure and enjoyment. In this respect, the first teacher seems to have been crucial. In both Sosniak's (1985) and Sloboda and Howe's (1991) studies, respondents tended to describe their first teachers with such adjectives as warm, friendly, fun, loving, and encouraging. Lessons were enjoyable events to be looked forward to, and it seemed to be the quality of the teacher-pupil relationship, rather than the technical excellence of the teacher, which counted for most. In Sosniak's study first teachers were very often characterized as the "nice old lady down the road."

Two findings from Sloboda and Howe's study extend this "pleasure principle" to the home environment. Their sample contained both outstanding and average students from a specialist music school. It was discovered that the outstanding students generally had parents who were not themselves performing musicians. Average students were more likely to have come from families where one or both parents earned their living as a musician. Second, the outstanding students had accumulated significantly less practice than the average students prior to entry at the specialist. Table 6.1 shows accumulated practice for each group by instrument. It is necessary to present the results by instrument, because an unexpected finding of the study was the fact that most students had studied at least two instruments. The first instrument learned was not necessarily the one on which the student currently excelled. Table 6.1 makes it clear that the differential practice effect shows most strongly for the first instrument studied.

A tentative interpretation of these findings, supported by the more qualitative aspects of the data (see Howe & Sloboda, 1991a, 1991b), is that children of nonmusicians are more likely to be praised for their early accomplishments so that they acquire an early sense of themselves as "musician" and "special." Parents tend to be supportive but nondirective, allowing their children freedom

TABLE 6.1 Accumulated Hours of
Practice as a Function of Ability

	Ability	
Instrument	Exceptional	Average
First	454	1,095
Second	320	422
Third	217	62
All	1,012	1,580

Source: Adapted from Sloboda and Howe, 1991.

to decide whether to do formal practice or more free improvisatory musical play. Musician parents, in contrast, tend to view their children's accomplishments in the light of known standards to be attained. They are less likely to praise early achievements and are more likely to impose a rather rigid or structured practice regime. Such children may become technically adept, but fail to find their own musical motivation and creativity. Staff at specialist music schools are only too aware of the possibility of "adolescent rebellion" among such children, who belatedly realize that they are fulfilling their parents' ambitions rather than their own.

The Transition to Commitment

Practice cannot always be enjoyable, and at some stage in an instrumental career, a young person must make the decision to invest in practice activities beyond what is immediately rewarding. Transitions to new teachers or schools appear to be a vital component of this process. Almost all respondents in the various studies discussed reported a progression through a series of teachers who imposed increasingly demanding requirements on their pupils. Terms like "stretching" or "challenging" tended to be used much more when describing later teachers. Many students at music school came to see their teachers as role models or "heroes." The desire to be like the teacher, or like another eminent performer, is apparent in the motivation of many young performers.

As adolescence approaches, the existence of a reference group for whom high musical achievement is the norm becomes more important. One clear reason why many children drop out of instrumental learning is that their efforts are not valued by their peers (Howe & Sloboda, 1991c). In many environments, including schools, musical achievement is met with indifference, or even mockery. This seems to be particularly so for boys, because other boys brand musical activities as "unmasculine." Specialist music schools can provide a haven for young musicians where, for the first time in their lives, their activities are accepted as normal by their peers (Sloboda & Howe, 1990). Those who do not go to such schools typically find similar support in specialist music groups such as orchestras.

Because there are so many pressures on children to do other things than devote time to instrumental learning, parents play a crucial role. Despite misgivings about the "ambitious parent," the studies of Sosniak (1985), Manturszewska (1990), and Sloboda and Howe (1991) all confirm the vital importance of a high level of parental support and encouragement. Almost all parents of successful musicians devoted large amounts of time, effort, and money to their children's musical activities. In Sloboda and Howe's (1991) study, the vast majority of parents had regular meetings with instrumental teachers and provided specific incentives to undertake practice. In a large minority of cases this actually involved being present throughout a practice period, helping the child to structure the practice activity. Research currently underway intends to specify the precise differences in parental behavior between successful and unsuccessful musicians.

Conclusions

This part of the chapter has outlined a picture of exceptional achievement as resulting, not from some unique or rare characteristic of an individual, but from a series of events and experiences that stimulate a statistically rare learning trajectory. Following from, but extending, a framework devised by Ericsson et al. (1990), a three-stage developmental framework may be proposed. In the first stage musical engagement is sustained primarily through pleasure: aesthetic/sensual pleasure in the experience of musical sound; pleasure in rewarding relationships; pleasure in praised achievements. Many nonmusicians seem never to have experienced this stage at the appropriate point in childhood. Some average musicians may also have experienced this stage inadequately, leading to "proficiency without spark." In the studies examined here, this first stage typically encompasses the first three to four years of instrumental study.

In the second stage, musical learning is sustained primarily through a constructed environment in which practice levels may be increased and sustained. This involves some external regulation of activity by parents and teachers, often in the context of specialist environments with like-minded peers. Specific achievement targets (such as examinations) often become prominent motivators. This stage typically coincides with the period of secondary schooling and ends when the individual decides on his or her long-term goals for music, whether to give up serious effort, to remain at an amateur level of proficiency, or to progress to professional levels.

In the third stage, the impetus for musical learning becomes fully internalized to the maturing individual, who will sustain and direct his or her own practice activities independently. Typically, in the highest group of performers, practice activity now predominates over all other forms of life activity. The role of the teacher moves toward that of mentor and guide rather than director. This stage typically begins in the late teens or early twenties and continues to the point where a professional career is established.

There are, of course, further stages in the life-span of a professional musician (see Manturszewska, 1990), but there is not space in this chapter to describe them. It is more important to point out that the stages described are relative to a particular culture, that of the Western classical music profession. Little serious study has been made of the development of the popular or jazz musician (although see Sloboda, 1991c, for a discussion of the untutored development of Louis Armstrong). What is clear from case studies of jazz musicians and idiots savants (see Miller, 1989; Sloboda, Hermelin, & O'Connor, 1985) is that high levels of intrinsic motivation can sustain learning in the absence of formal tuition provided certain environmental conditions appertain (Sloboda, 1991c).

Finally, it is necessary to point out that there exist many cultures, especially traditional non-Western cultures, where the spread of musical accomplishment in the population is much more even than it is in modern Western culture. In such cultures, participation in musical activity is often more rooted in the whole life and work of society, rather than being something separate (e.g., Blacking, 1976). In the long view, it may turn out to be modern Western society that is unusual in its capacity to inhibit musical development in all but a small minority. Rather than looking within a small number of individuals for signs of genetic superiority in "musicality," we may need to look more closely at the way our culture operates to inhibit the majority of people from becoming the fully expressive musical performers that they could be.

REFERENCES

Blacking, J. (1976). *How musical is man?* London: Faber.

Ceci, S. J. (1990). *On intelligence . . . more or less: A bioecological treatise on intellectual development.* Englewood Cliffs, NJ: Prentice-Hall.

Coon, H., & Carey, G. (1989). Genetic and environmental determinants of musical ability in twins. *Behavior Genetics, 19,* 183–93.

Csikszentmihalyi, M. (1975). *Beyond boredom and anxiety.* San Francisco: Jossey-Bass.

Davidson, J. W. (1991). *The perception of expressive movements in music performance.* Unpublished doctoral dissertation, City University, London.

Davidson, J. W. (1993). Visual perception of performance manner in the movement of solo musicians. *Psychology of Music, 21,2,* in press.

Ericsson, K. A., Krampe, R. T., & Tesch-Romer, C. (1991). *The role of deliberate practice in the acquisition of expert performance* (Tech Rep. No. 91-06). Boulder, CO: Institute of Cognitive Sciences, University of Colorado at Boulder.

Ericsson, K. A., Tesch-Romer, C., & Krampe, R. T. (1990). The role of practice and motivation in the acquisition of expert-level performance in real life. In M. J. A. Howe (Ed.), *Encouraging the development of exceptional skills and talents.* Leicester: British Psychological Society.

Gabrielsson, A. (1974). Performance of rhythm patterns. *Scandinavian Journal of Psychology, 15,* 63–72.

Gabrielsson, A. (1988). Timing in music performance and its relations to music experience. In J. A. Sloboda (Ed.), *Generative processes in music: The psychology of performance, improvisation, and composition*. London: Oxford University Press.

Gruson, L. (1988). Rehearsal skill and musical competence: Does practice make perfect? In J. A. Sloboda (Ed.), *Generative processes in music: The psychology of performance, improvisation, and composition*. London: Oxford University Press.

Howe, M. J. A., & Sloboda, J. A. (1991a). Young musicians' accounts of significant influences in their early lives. 1. The family and the musical background. *British Journal of Music Education, 8*, 39–52.

Howe, M. J. A., & Sloboda, J. A. (1991b). Young musicians' accounts of significant influences in their early lives. 2. Teachers, practicing and performance. *British Journal of Music Education, 8*, 53–63.

Howe, M. J. A., & Sloboda, J. A. (1991c). Problems experienced by young musicians as a result of the failure of other children to value musical accomplishments. *Gifted Education, 8*, 102–11.

Lerdahl, F., & Jackendoff, R. (1983). *A generative theory of tonal music*. Cambridge, MA: MIT Press.

Manturszewska, M. (1990). A biographical study of the life-span development of professional musicians. *Psychology of Music, 18*, 112–39.

Miklaszewski, K. (1989). A case study of a pianist preparing a musical performance. *Psychology of Music, 17*, 95–109.

Miller, L. K. (1989). *Musical savants: Exceptional skill in the mentally retarded*. Hillsdale, NJ: Erlbaum.

Palmer, C. (1988). *Timing in skilled music performance*. Unpublished doctoral dissertation, Cornell University, Ithaca, NY.

Palmer, C. (1989). Mapping musical thought to musical performance. *Journal of Experimental Psychology: Human Perception and Performance, 15*, 331–46.

Rose, S., Lewontin, R. C., & Kamin, L. J. (1984). *Not in our genes: Biology, ideology, and human nature*. London: Penguin Books.

Seashore, C. E. (1938). *The psychology of music*. New York: McGraw-Hill.

Shaffer, L. H. (1981). Performances of Chopin, Bach, and Bartok: Studies in motor programming. *Cognitive Psychology, 13*, 326–76.

Shaffer, L. H. (1984). Timing in solo and duet piano performances. *Quarterly Journal of Experimental Psychology, 36A*, 577–95.

Shaffer, L. H., Clarke, E., & Todd, N. P. (1985). Meter and rhythm in piano playing. *Cognition, 20*, 61–77.

Sloboda, J. A. (1983). The communication of musical metre in piano performance. *Quarterly Journal of Experimental Psychology, 35A*, 377–96.

Sloboda, J. A. (1985). Expressive skill in two pianists: Style and effectiveness in music performance. *Canadian Journal of Psychology, 39*, 273–93.

Sloboda, J. A. (1989). Music as a language. In F. Wilson & F. Roehmann (Eds.), *Music and child development*. St. Louis: MMB.

Sloboda, J. A. (1990). Musical excellence: How does it develop? In M. J. A. Howe (Ed.), *Encouraging the development of exceptional skills and talents*. Leicester: British Psychological Society.

Sloboda, J. A. (1991a). Music structure and emotional response: Some empirical findings. *Psychology of Music, 19*, 110–20.

Sloboda, J. A. (1991b). Empirical studies of emotional response to music. In M. Riess Jones & S. Holleran (Eds.), *Cognitive bases of musical communication*. Washington, DC: American Psychological Association.

Sloboda, J. A. (1991c). Musical expertise. In K. A. Ericsson & J. Smith (Eds.), *Toward a general theory of expertise: Prospects and limits*. Cambridge: Cambridge University Press.

Sloboda, J. A., Hermelin, B., & O'Connor, N. (1985). An exceptional musical memory. *Music Perception, 3*, 155–70.

Sloboda, J. A., & Howe, M. J. A. (1990). Reasons for choosing specialist music schooling: An interview study. *Journal of the Music Masters and Mistresses Association, 25*, 17–20.

Sloboda, J.A., & Howe, M. J. A. (1991). Biographical precursors of musical excellence: An interview study. *Psychology of Music, 19*, 3–21.

Sosniak, L. A. (1985). Learning to be a concert pianist. In B. S. Bloom (Ed.), *Developing talent in young people*. New York: Ballantine Books.

Sosniak, L. A. (1990). The tortoise, the hare, and the development of talent. In M. J. A. Howe (Ed.), *Encouraging the development of exceptional skills and talents*. Leicester: British Psychological Society.

Sundberg, J. (1988). Computer synthesis of music performance. In J. A. Sloboda (Ed.), *Generative processes in music: The psychology of performance, improvisation, and composition*. London: Oxford University Press.

Todd, N. P. (1985). A model of expressive timing in tonal music. *Music Perception, 3*, 33–58.

The Perception
of Melody, Tonality, Rhythm
and Timing

7

Melodic Contour in Hearing and Remembering Melodies

W. JAY DOWLING

Introduction

In recent years, research on the perception of melody has received much attention. Frequently, the melody is the musical element we most easily recognize, reproduce, and remember because it is perceptually the most salient. A melody is a sequence of single pitches organized as an aesthetic musical whole. In trying to explain how some sets of notes are heard as integrated melodic wholes, psychologists have invoked Gestalt principles (see discussions in Deutsch, 1982a; Dowling & Harwood, 1986; Sloboda, 1985). These are principles of perception that were originally formulated to investigate the perception of visual stimuli (Wertheimer, 1923; see Arnheim, 1969, for application of Gestalt principles to the perception of visual art). Some of the most important of these principles are based on laws that govern proximity, good continuation, and similarity, as illustrated in Figure 1.

If we consider a melody as a line, it is easy to see how principles of perception may be successfully applied in researching melodic patterns. Indeed, in music performance and music teaching there is an emphasis on the "direction," the "shape" of the melodic line. We often speak of a melody and its accompaniment as the "foreground" and the "background." All these are visual analogies that are very pertinent musically.

A melodic contour is a sequence of single pitches that resembles the original intervallic pattern of a melody. The importance of the melodic contour, or shape, is such that it is nearly impossible to recognize a familiar tune if its pitches are played in random octaves on the keyboard: that is, if the original melodic line is broken as illustrated in Figure 2.

The more the pitches of the melody are played randomly among several octaves, the more difficult it is to recognize the melody. Such randomness violates the Gestalt principles of good continuation and proximity. Our recognition of this familiar melody increases as more pitches are played within the

a.

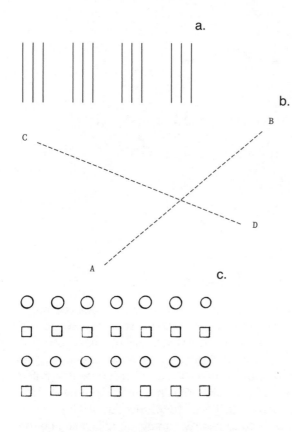

b.

c.

FIGURE 1. Gestalt principles. (A) *Proximity.* We tend to group nearer elements together rather than spacing them apart; therefore, we tend to perceive this diagram as four sets of three lines each rather than a set of 12 lines. (B) *Good continuation.* We tend to perceive that the set of dots starting from point A goes to point B rather than going to point C or D. (C) *Similarity.* We tend to perceive the above as rows of similar elements—namely, rows of squares or circles—rather than perceive columns combining both squares and circles.

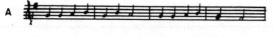

FIGURE 2. From Dowling & Hollombe (1977). Copyright © 1991 by The Psychonomic Society, Inc. Used by permission.

174

Bouree

from Suite No. 3 in C for Unaccompanied Cello   J. S. Bach

FIGURE 3. J. S. Bach, Bourée, from Suite No. 3 in C for unaccompanied cello.

same octave, or within an overall order of ascending or descending octaves—
that is, as the distorted version begins to resemble more and more the original
version. These findings, which are based on earlier studies by Diana Deutsch
(1972, 1973), encouraged much research on the importance that pitch height
(the location of a pitch on a piano keyboard) and pitch chroma (the position of
a pitch within a scale) have in the perception of melodies.

To perceive a melody, we must perceive a coherence within the sequence of
pitches that make up the melody. We group sounds according to various
perceptual and cognitive organizational mechanisms. Some of the musical
characteristics that may influence our perception of a melody are its contour,
timbre, rhythm, intensity, and tempo (Deutsch, 1982a,b). Bregman (summarized in Bregman, 1990; see also Bregman & Campbell, 1971) has shown
experimentally that when we hear rapid sequences of tones varying widely in
frequency, we organize the sounds into perceptual streams of narrower range
to create a psychological coherence. Musically speaking, in hearing the beginning of the Bourree from the Suite for Violoncello No. 3 in C major by J. S. Bach,
although only one instrument is playing, we segregate the sounds perceptually
as if we were hearing two lines: a higher and a lower one (Figure 3).

Polyphonic compositions are excellent examples of how perceptual principles are applied when listening to music. For instance, the practice of avoiding
part-crossing in writing polyphonic compositions reflects the composer's sensitivity to avoiding potential perceptual confusion on the part of the listener
(Huron, 1991).

We may not necessarily recognize, reproduce, or remember a melody
exactly as we heard it. Instead, we may recognize, reproduce, or remember a
melodic contour that approximates the original melody. In this chapter, W. Jay
Dowling discusses the perception of the melodic contour and describes some
of the features that make it perceptually relevant. He demonstrates how we
perceive the difference between the overall contour of a melody and the
specific intervals that make up the contour. He explains the interaction between contour and tonality and describes the results of several experiments
that look at the contour of tonal and atonal melodies and transpositions to
closely or remotely related keys.

REFERENCES

Arnheim, R. (1969). *Art and visual perception.* Berkeley: University of California Press.

Bregman, A. S. (1990). *Auditory scene analysis: The perceptual organization of sound.* Cambridge, MA: MIT Press.

Bregman, A. S., & Campbell, J. (1971). Primary auditory steam segregation and perceptual order in rapid sequences of tones. *Journal of Experimental Psychology, 89,* 244–49.

Deutsch, D. (1972). Octave generalization and tune recognition. *Perception and Psychophysics, 11*(6), 411–12.

Deutsch, D. (1973). Octave generalization of specific interference effects in memory for tonal pitch. *Perception and Psychophysics, 13,* 273–75.

Deutsch, D. (1982a). Grouping mechanisms in music. In D. Deutsch (Ed.), *Psychology of music.* Orlando, FL: Academic Press.

Deutsch, D. (1982b). The processing of pitch combinations. In D. Deutsch (Ed.), *Psychology of music.* Orlando, FL: Academic Press.

Dowling, J. W., & Harwood, D. L. (1986). *Music cognition.* Orlando, FL: Academic Press.

Dowling, J. W., & Hollombe, A. W. (1977). The perception of melodies distorted by splitting into several octaves: Effects of increasing proximity and melodic contour. *Perception and Psychophysics, 21*(1), 60–64.

Huron, D. (1991). The avoidance of part-crossing in polyphonic music: Perceptual evidence and musical practice. *Music Perception, 9*(1), 93–104.

Sloboda, J. A. (1985). *The musical mind.* Oxford: Oxford University Press.

Wertheimer, M. (1923). Untersuchung zur Lehre von der Gestalt II. *Psychologische Forschung, 4,* 301–50.

What Is Melodic Contour?

Melodic contour—the overall pattern of intervals that make up a melody—is a feature of music that stands out distinctively for the listener on first hearing, and indeed composers use this feature in the construction of pieces of music, making use of the aesthetic tension that results by repeating a contour with altered intervals. A striking example is provided by the first movement of Beethoven's Fifth Symphony, which is built out of a brief melodic motif presented twice in succession at the outset (Figure 7.1). That motif and its sequences share contour (indicated under the score) but differ in the size of the interval between the two pitches: four semitones between G and E-flat in the first presentation and three semitones between F and D in the second. Throughout the movement,

FIGURE 7.1. The opening measures of Beethoven's Fifth Symphony. Contour and interval sizes are indicated under the score by 0 for unison and − with the interval size in semitones (half steps) for a descending interval. Ascending intervals would be indicated by +.

FIGURE 7.2. Bach's Fugue in C Minor from Book I of *The Well-Tempered Clavier.* Occurrences of the subject in the three voices. (Schott/Universal Edition, ed. Walther Dehnhard.)

TABLE 7.1 Interval Patterns in Semitones for Presentation of the Three Voices in Bach's Fugue in C Minor from *The Well-Tempered Clavier*, vol. 1, BWV 847

Occurrence/ measure		Intervals
1	1	−1 +1 −5 +1 +4 −1 +1 +2 −7 +5 −1 +1 +2 −9 +2 +1 −1 −2 −2
b	3	−1 +1 −7 +3 +4 −1 +1 +2 −7 +5 −1 +1 +2 −9 +2 +1 −1 −2 −2
c	7	like a

Beethoven repeats this motif over and over, using virtually all the possible intervals between the two pitches, in each case preserving the contour. The repeated contour provides unity to the piece, while the small intervallic changes with each repetition provide interest.

There are many examples of the use of a repeated contour with changes in intervallic detail. One can be found in Bach's Fugue in C minor from volume 1 of *The Well-Tempered Clavier* (Figure 7.2). The initial pitch contour [− + − +] at a in the subject is repeated not only in recurrences of the whole subject (at b and c) but also as a simple thematic kernel throughout the fugue. If we compare the recurrences of the initial melodic contour a, we see that while b preserves the contour pattern, it does not preserve the pattern of exact interval sizes in semitones. This is because of the difference between "tonal answers" and "real" answers in a fugue—tonal answers modify the interval pattern so that they can remain in the same key, while exact answers preserve the melodic pattern at another pitch level. Table 7.1 lists the pattern of intervals for the three appearances of the initial contour. Here Bach has treated contour as a feature of the melody that can be transported into other contexts and given different intervals while still preserving its identity. In fact, melodic contours recur in fugues with each return of the subject, but only sometimes does the subject repeat the initial melodic interval pattern exactly.

The Importance of Melodic Contour: Experimental Evidence

The importance of melodic contour in melodies we hear for the first time is borne out by experiments that test the recognition memory of subjects. In such experiments the listener hears a novel melody—never before encountered—on each trial, and then has the task of recognizing a transposition of that melody. Sample trials from a typical experiment are shown in Figure 7.3. On some trials the test melody will in fact be an exact transposition of the initial melody, in which case the listener's response should be, "Yes, that is the melody I just heard." (Figure 7.3B is a transposition of Figure 7.3A.) On other trials, however, the test melody will be different, and the listener should say, "No, that is not the

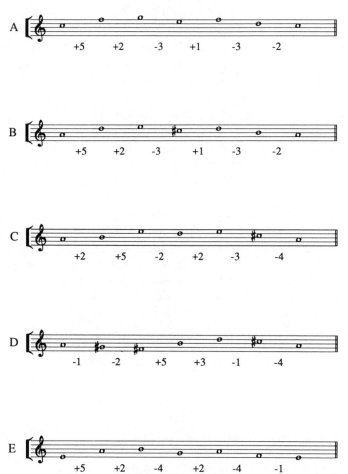

FIGURE 7.3. Typical melodies used in recognition memory experiments: (A) a novel melody in the key of C major presented on a trial; (B) an exact transposition of that melody to the key of A major; (C) a same-contour imitation of the initial melody, with different interval sizes; (D) a test melody with a different contour; (E) an imitation produced by moving the original melody along the C major scale, preserving diatonic but not semitone intervals. The contour and interval sizes are shown below each score.

same as the first melody." When the test melody is different, it might have a totally different contour (as in Figure 7.3D), in which case it will be easy for the listener to reject it. The most difficult type of melody recognition test will be an imitation of the original melody that shares its overall contour but differs in interval sizes (as in Figures 7.3C and 7.3E). Contour similarity will pull the listener in the direction of saying "Yes," while the intervallic differences, which are not always easy to notice on first hearing, prevent such a melody from being an exact transposition.

The results of a number of experiments show that listeners usually find it easy to respond positively to all comparison melodies that share contour, and respond negatively to melodies with different contours. Listeners find it much more difficult to distinguish exact transpositions from same-contour imitations. Dowling and Fujitani (1971) found this to be true using nontonal melodies; Dowling (1978) found it true using tonal melodies.

The confusion of transpositions with same-contour imitations is especially strong when the two melodies are in the same or in closely related keys (Bartlett & Dowling, 1980). That is, two melodies that share both contour and scale are easily confused, even if they differ in pattern of intervals. This confusion diminishes as the scales are made less similar by increasing key distance around the circle of fifths.

What psychological principles underlie the importance of contour in human memory? We now proceed to a description of the psychological features of melodies. The evidence suggests that contour similarity is especially important for recently encountered novel melodic phrases that are about five notes long. Contour is less important as melodies are remembered for longer periods of time, as they become more familiar, and when they are longer than five notes. Contour is more important for younger children under the age of 5 than for older ones, since before the interval patterns of tonal scales in a culture's music must be learned and incorporated into the listener's pitch, analyzing procedures and contour represents the main organizing principle for pitches in melodies (Dowling & Harwood, 1986).

The Role of Tonality

Features of Melodies

In addition to contour and interval sizes, a set of pitches also serves as a set of features to describe a melody. With that set of pitches comes the feature of its "key," or "tonality" (at least for tonal melodies). Key or tonality is the organization of the tones and chords of a piece of music in relation to a tonic. Contour and intervals remain invariant when a melody is transposed but the key changes—now it is based on a different tonality (as between C major and A major going from Figure 7.3A to 7.3B). All these features are psychologically relevant. Listeners are often led to treat an imitation as a transposition when contour and key remain similar to the original (Bartlett & Dowling, 1980). This tendency to confuse imitations and transpositions is especially strong when the key remains the same, and the imitation has simply been moved along the original scale (as in Figure 7.3E), preserving only some of the intervals (Dowling, 1978).

Key is an important feature in other ways. Watkins (1985) has shown that listeners experienced in Western music find a melody easier to recognize when its pitch set remains within a diatonic musical scheme. Furthermore, the key is not just a static set of notes; it is a framework that assigns tonal functions to the various pitches in hierarchical relations to one another (Krumhansl, 1990). The tonic pitch is the most important, and other pitches tend to gravitate toward the tonic as a center of stability. Melodies such as those in Figure 7.3A to 7.3D begin and end with the tonic, moving from a stable point out into the rest of the scale and then returning to the stable tonic. The seventh scale degree (or "leading tone") for example, tends to pull upward toward the tonic. Francès (1958/1988) showed that when the leading tone was mistuned downward, contrary to that tendency, the mistuning was much more noticeable than when it was mistuned the same amount in the direction of the tendency.

A key defines a set of more or less expected pitches within the range of possibilities. When a melody follows those expectations, it is easier to follow and to remember. Watkins (1985) contributed additional evidence for the importance of key and the tonal hierarchy by showing that melodies whose pitches are chosen from a relatively small region around the circle of fifths are easier to recognize than melodies that involve large leaps around the circle of fifths.

A feature of melodies that should be mentioned here because of its importance is rhythm. In all the examples mentioned so far, not only melodic contour but the rhythmic pattern of the melody has been preserved. Changing the rhythm would produce a markedly different melody (Monahan, 1984). However, consideration of rhythm is beyond the scope of this chapter.

A variety of features can be used to describe a melody. In addition to contour, there are the interval pattern, pitch set, and the key. All of these have been shown to have some importance to the way in which melodies are first perceived and then remembered. But which of those patterns is most fundamental in our memory for melodies? Since interval patterns most obviously remain constant through transposition, a good case can be made that they are the most fundamental. Nevertheless, I believe that melodies are remembered as ordered sets of pitches. The pitch framework provided by the scale temporarily fixes a set of pitches as landmarks in terms of which the pitches of the melody are organized and understood.

From a psychological point of view, the scale framework itself is best understood as a set of pitches, rather than as a set of intervals, as I have argued at greater length elsewhere (Dowling, 1991a). The dynamic tendencies of pitches to gravitate toward points of stability in a tonal context, as described above in the experiment by Francès (1958/1988), are characteristic of sets of pitches, not of intervals. Furthermore, intervals, far from being psychologically more fundamental than pitches, are themselves most easily grasped with reference to pitch patterns of familiar melodies. Imagine the case of a music student faced with the task of singing the interval "ascending minor seventh" (Figure 7.4A). Abstracted from a context of melody and key, this is a very difficult task. However, if the student should happen to recall that a familiar melody (such as "Somewhere" from Bernstein's *West Side Story*; Figure 7.4B) begins with an ascending minor

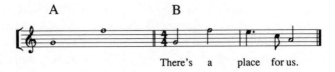

FIGURE 7.4. The interval of an ascending minor seventh (10 semitones); (B) the same interval embedded in the start of the song "Somewhere" from Leonard Bernstein's *West Side Story*.

seventh, the task is easily solved. Students learn to sing difficult intervals most easily with reference to the pitch patterns of familiar songs in which they occur.

Another line of evidence arises from multidimensional scaling studies which suggest that intervals in a melodic context are generally heard, not as intervals per se, but rather in terms of their position within the scale (Balzano & Liesch, 1982). Still more evidence comes from studies involving cued recognition, in which the listener hears a familiar tune and then is asked to discern it even when it is presented in a confusing way designed to preserve the pitch classes of its notes while destroying their interval relationships. Listeners are able to recognize tunes even when their intervals (but not their pitches) are obscured by scrambling their notes into different octaves (Dowling, 1984a) or interleaving distractor tones temporally among their notes (Dowling, 1973a). All of this strongly suggests that the psychological representation of the tonal framework is in terms of pitches, and not the logically equivalent representation in terms of intervals.

Memory for Melodic Contour

Several factors affect listeners' memory for melodic contour relative to memory for other features of melodies such as intervallic detail. Those factors include the delay between first hearing a melody and when it is tested, the familiarity of the melody to be remembered, its length, and the age and experience of the listeners. I will treat each of these factors in turn.

Short versus Long Delays in Recognition Memory

Contour is a strong determinant of transposition recognition when the comparison follows the introduction of a new melody by an unfilled delay of a few seconds. Contour becomes less important, however, after a delay of 30 or 40 seconds, while interval sizes become more important (Dowling & Bartlett, 1981; DeWitt & Crowder, 1986). One reason contour decreases in importance over time in relation to intervals is a decrease in the confusion due to scale relations, as already noted. After a short delay the scale of the initial melody is still fresh in memory, and perception of the comparison melody is affected by it. When the comparison is in a relatively close key (as in the experiments just cited), confusion between exact transpositions and same-contour imitations results. Following a delay filled with other material the scale of the initial melody becomes less salient, and false recognitions of same-contour imitations decline. According to this explanation, the shift over time of the relative importance of contour and intervals should disappear with atonal melodies, since confusions due to key similarity should no longer operate. And that is exactly what happens (Dowling, 1991b). Atonal melodies are more difficult to recognize than tonal ones after both long and short delays, and (as with tonal melodies) discriminating contour differences is easier than discriminating interval differences. However, the relative difficulty of those two discriminations does not shift over time as it does for tonal melodies.

A second reason that has been put forward for the decline in importance of contour with longer delays is that contour can serve as a much better retrieval cue when the initial melody and its comparison are close together in time and there are fewer alternatives to choose from (Dowling & Bartlett, 1981). However, when the comparison comes after a delay filled with alternative possible choices lying between it and the initial melody, the relative importance of contour declines. (This would be like a series of trials with melodies such as in Figure 7.3, but with numerous items like 7.3D intervening between 7.3A and 7.3B.) We cannot rule out the possibility that more precise information than contour (namely, interval sizes) may be needed to differentiate among the numerous melodies we store in our memory. One could argue that such an effect ought to operate as well with atonal as with tonal melodies. Moreover, Dowling (1991b) failed to find any decline in the usefulness of contour information between short and long delays in that experiment.

Nevertheless, it is clear that with the passage of time the contours of tonal melodies become relatively less important to recognition and specific intervals become relatively more important. The end result of this shift can be seen in the great importance of intervals in memory for overlearned melodies in long-term memory storage.

Familiar versus Unfamiliar Melodies

Contour is highly salient in memory for novel melodies. In contrast, the exact interval patterns of familiar melodies are very well remembered. Dowling and Fujitani (1971) found that listeners rarely confused same-contour imitations with familiar versions of tunes such as "Twinkle, Twinkle, Little Star" and "Yankee Doodle." In fact, when asked to respond positively to the imitations, listeners succeeded about 60% of the time. Listeners' knowledge of the intervals of familiar tunes is so precise that Attneave and Olson (1971) were able to use memory for the intervals of the call signal of NBC, an American television network (G-E-C; intervals +9 semitones, −4 semitones) as the basis for a pitch-scaling task. This accuracy with familiar melodies is true of musically inexperienced as well as experienced listeners.

Melody Length

The familiar versus unfamiliar melody results were obtained with five-note-long melodies (Dowling & Fujitani, 1971; Dowling, 1978; Bartlett & Dowling, 1980) and seven-note-long melodies (Dowling & Bartlett, 1981; Dowling, 1991b). Edworthy (1985) has shown, however, that contour is not nearly so easy to remember with longer tonal melodies of 11 or 13 or 15 notes. Part of this result must be due to complexity, and Cuddy, Cohen, and Mewhort (1981) have shown that contour complexity affects memory. Part of the result may, as Edworthy suggests, also be due to the fact that a longer melody provides time for the listener to achieve a firmer grasp of the key. Edworthy's task was quite difficult, requiring the listener to notice particular details in the contour rather than make a global same-different judgment. However, it is plausible that contour should decline in importance with melody length, since inevitably the number of possible contours (hence the amount of contour information conveyed) increases with length.

The way longer melodies are remembered should be a fruitful area for research. Longer melodies must break down into phrases that should be to some extent remembered independently. We know that phrases are in fact remembered as units. Dowling (1973b) constructed melodies using four five-note phrases to form the rhythmic pattern [. . . ._ . . . ._ . . . ._ . . . ._]. Each phrase had a different pitch contour. After hearing such a melody, listeners were given test patterns that replicated whole phrases from the longer melody [. . . ._] or that cut across phrase boundaries [. ._ . .]. Memory performance was much better with the whole phrases (about 70% correct) than with the ends of one phrase and the beginnings of another (about 60% correct). We also know something of the way melodies are parsed into phrases on the basis of rhythmic grouping, changes in melodic contour, melodic leaps, patterns of repetition, and so forth (Jones, 1987). The relationship between memory for phrases and memory for whole melodies poses a particularly interesting question for future research.

The Role of Development

Infants are sensitive to changes in melodic contour long before they begin to speak or sing (Trehub, Bull, & Thorpe, 1984). As soon as children begin to speak they also begin to sing. That singing generally takes two forms: vocal play exploring the limits in pitch and loudness and rapidity of what their voice can do, and the creation of spontaneous songs (McKernon, 1979; Dowling, 1982, 1984b, 1988; Dowling & Harwood, 1986). Spontaneous songs at the age of one or two years are characterized by a more or less regular beat on which the speech rhythms of the words of the song and the use of discrete levels of pitch are overlaid. The pitches are not those of the adult scale and the pitch levels are continually in flux. Nevertheless the steadiness of the metrical pattern (the beat) and the use of discrete, sustained pitch levels for vowels distinguishes singing from speech at this age. What the child controls at this age in terms of pitch is not the exact frequency or pitch of the tone, but the pattern of ups and downs— the contour.

Children sing spontaneously created songs beginning around the age of one. Such songs divide naturally into phrases that are characterized by melodic-rhythmic contours. The melodic contour patterns recur within the structure of the song. Sometimes contour patterns are copied from nursery tunes the child has heard, but typically they are made up by the child. Sometimes a contour will repeat over and over with the same words, whether nonsense ("Sippah, suppah. Sippah, suppah. . . .") or relatively meaningful ("Come a duck on my house. Come a duck on my house. . . ."). Sometimes one contour shape will alternate with another in a regular pattern throughout the song. Often the song ends with a "coda" constructed from new contour material. As the child gets older, some of the songs come to approximate nursery tune models more and more closely, but even then those songs are not literal reproductions of adult models, but are versions that have been regularized according to the child's own musical syntax (Dowling, 1984b). Children's spontaneous singing through the preschool years involves principally a manipulation of musical materials encoded as rhythmic and melodic contours.

By the age of five children's pitch levels are beginning to approximate adult categories, and some children younger than that can distinguish between tonal versions of familiar melodies that conform to adult pitch categories for the diatonic scale and atonal versions that do not (Trehub, Morongiello, & Thorpe, 1985), especially if they are rated by adult judges as being able to sing "in tune" (Dowling, 1988). Also, by five, children are able to stay within the scale of a single key in singing a familiar tune (Davidson, McKernon, & Gardner, 1981). By the age of eight, children notice changes of mode from major to minor (Imberty, 1969), are better at noticing pitch alterations in tonal (vs. atonal) melodies (Zenatti, 1969), and are beginning to acquire a sophisticated scheme for the hierarchical organization of pitches in a tonality (Krumhansl & Keil, 1982).

These shifts in relative importance of the various melodic features with changes in age and experience can be seen in the results of Andrews and Dowling (1991). Their listeners across a variety of ages were asked to identify familiar melodies in versions that either exactly reproduced their familiar pitch intervals or were changed in pitch while preserving contour. The changed versions either remained within the same key ("tonal") or did not remain within any key ("atonal"). Andrews and Dowling found a regular developmental progression of reliance on different melodic features. Five- and six-year-olds identified the melodies equally well in all forms, changed as well as original versions. Seven- and eight-year-olds tended to identify principally tonal melodies, original and changed. Nine- and 10-year-olds performed much better with original version of the melodies than with either tonal or atonal changed melodies. With these highly familiar melodies, adults performed about equally well on all versions.

Contour and Gestalt Principles

One result that has gradually emerged from experiments in which listeners have judged melodic contour in a variety of contexts is that a melody is very much an integrated whole, a Gestalt. Contour is not an entirely separable feature of a melody in Garner's (1974) sense. Contour interacts with both tonality and rhythmic pattern in perception and memory. This is not what I initially thought when I began to investigate this area. In 1978 (Dowling, 1978) I suggested that contour and scale (the embodiment of the features of tonality) might be processed and remembered independently of one another. Thus a melody could be created by generating a contour and hanging it on a scale. Scale similarity might cause confusions in short-term recognition tasks, but only with interval, not contour, recognition. That is, changes in the scale should not affect recognition of the pattern of ups and downs.

Recent studies have shown, however, that tonal context affects memory for contour. Bartlett and Dowling (1988) had listeners judge sameness of contour in pairs of seven-note melodies in which one member of the pair was tonal and the other atonal. The contour change was produced by making the lowest pitch in the melody the highest, or vice versa. There were always the same number of specific pitch differences between members of a pair. Listeners were better at discriminating contour changes when the pairs were presented in atonal-tonal order than the reverse. And in a study already cited (Dowling, 1991b), I had listeners attempt to discriminate transpositions from same-contour imitations and different-contour test melodies (like those in Figure 7.3) either immediately or after a delay of about 40 seconds filled with other melodies. The melodies were strongly tonal, weakly tonal, or atonal. Strongly tonal melodies began and ended on the tonic (like Figure 7.3A to 7.3D), and weakly tonal melodies began and ended on pitches other than the tonic (like Figure 7.3E). Listeners' performance is shown in Figure 7.5. At short delays discriminating transpositions from different-contour lures was uniformly easier than discriminating them from same-contour lures for both tonal and atonal melodies (Figure 7.5). With increasing delay this difference tended to disappear for the tonal melodies, but not for the atonal. Furthermore, the tendency to falsely recognize different-contour lures was markedly affected by tonality, being lowest for strongly tonal melodies. Thus listeners' ability to reject a different-contour test item depended on tonal context, and not just on its difference of contour.

Contours are interrelated in memory with tonal and rhythmic context. The parsing of a contour into phrases and the assignment of melodic accents depend

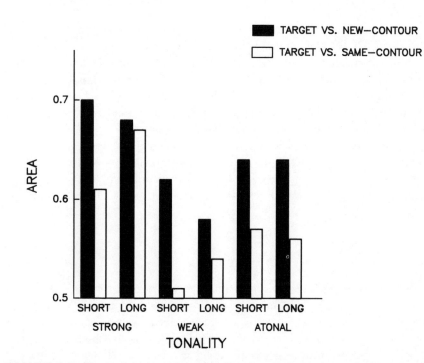

FIGURE 7.5. The interaction of tonality (Strongly Tonal, Weakly Tonal, Atonal) by delay (Short and Long) by test comparison (Targets vs. Different—or Same-Contour Lures). Performance distinguishing between exactly transposed targets and different-contour lures is shown by solid bars; that for targets versus same-contour lures is shown by open bars (after Dowling, 1991b).

FIGURE 7.6. The opening phrases of a version of the folksong "Barbara Allen" and the sextet from Donizetti's *Lucia di Lamermoor* (after Kolinski, 1969, Fig. 17). Note the identical pattern of pitches with different rhythm, which in effect makes it a different melody.

187

not only on note durations, but also on accents arising from contour inflections (Jones, 1987; Drake, Dowling, & Palmer, 1991). Kolinski (1969) vividly demonstrated the interrelatedness of pitch and rhythmic patterns by showing that, if the rhythm and the number of a repeated pitch were altered, a variant of "Barbara Allen" would become the tune from the Sextet from Donizetti's *Lucia di Lammermoor* (see Figure 7.6). The very same pitch pattern (and contour) can become an entirely different tune with a change of rhythm.

It would have been simpler for psychology if melodies had divided neatly into contours, rhythms, and pitch sets, but it would probably have been a loss to music. The ways in which musical material is transformed by shifts of context provide an important source of complexity which contributes to its richness as art.

Summary

In this chapter I discussed melodic contour in relation to other features of melodies in the pitch and time domains. An important feature of melodic contour is the distinction between pitches as interval patterns and pitches as patterns within a tonality. Evidence was cited suggesting that both representations are necessary in music cognition. Along with evidence showing the importance of contour in melody recognition and production, I presented evidence showing the limits of that importance. Contour is most important in memory for novel melodies tested after brief delays, and less so after longer delays and with familiar melodies. While contour dominates much of the preschool child's music behavior, adults are able to use contour more flexibly when the task demands it. Finally, I noted that melodic contour does not function entirely independently of the other features of melodies, but rather is part of the integrated melodic Gestalt.

REFERENCES

Andrews, M. W., & Dowling, W. J. (1991). The development of perception of interleaved melodies and control of auditory attention. *Music Perception*, 8, 349–68.

Attneave, F., & Olson, R. K. (1971). Pitch as medium: A new approach to psychophysical scaling. *American Journal of Psychology*, 84, 147–66.

Balzano, G. J., & Liesch, B. W. (1982). The role of chroma and scalestep in the recognition of musical intervals in and out of context. *Psychomusicology*, 2, 3–31.

Bartlett, J. C., & Dowling, W. J. (1980). Recognition of transposed melodies: A key-distance effect in developmental perspective. *Journal of Experimental Psychology: Human Perception and Performance*, 6, 501–15.

Bartlett, J. C., & Dowling, W. J. (1988). Scale structure and similarity of melodies. *Music Perception*, 5, 285–314.

Cuddy, L. L., Cohen, A. J., & Mewhort, D. J. K. (1981). Perception of structure in short melodic sequences. *Journal of Experimental Psychology: Human Perception and Performance*, 7, 869–83.

Davidson, L., McKernon, P., & Gardner, H. (1981). The acquisition of song: A developmental approach. In *Documentary report of the Ann Arbor symposium* (pp. 301–15). Reston, VA: Music Educators National Conference.

DeWitt, L. A., & Crowder, R. G. (1986). Recognition of novel melodies after brief delays. *Music Perception, 3,* 259–74.

Dowling, W. J. (1973a). The perception of interleaved melodies. *Cognitive Psychology, 5,* 322–37.

Dowling, W. J. (1973b). Rhythmic groups and subjective chunks in memory for melodies. *Perception and Psychophysics, 14,* 37–40.

Dowling, W. J. (1978). Scale and contour: Two components of a theory of memory for melodies. *Psychological Review, 85,* 341–54.

Dowling, W. J. (1982). Melodic information processing and its development. In D. Deutsch (Ed.), *The psychology of music* (pp. 413–29). New York: Academic Press.

Dowling, W. J. (1984a). Musical experience and tonal scales in the recognition of octave-scrambled melodies. *Psychomusicology, 4,* 13–32.

Dowling, W. J. (1984b). Development of musical schemata in children's spontaneous singing. In W. R. Crozier & A. J. Chapman (Eds.), *Cognitive processes in the perception of art* (pp. 145–63). Amsterdam: North-Holland.

Dowling, W. J. (1988). Tonal structure and children's early learning of music. In J. Sloboda (Ed.), *Generative processes in music* (pp. 113–28). Oxford: Oxford University Press.

Dowling, W. J. (1991a). Pitch structure. In P. Howell, R. West, & I. Cross (Eds.), *Representing musical structure* (pp. 33–57). London: Academic Press.

Dowling, W. J. (1991b). Tonal strength and melody recognition after long and short delays. *Perception and Psychophysics, 50,* 305–13.

Dowling, W. J., & Bartlett, J. C. (1981). The importance of interval information in long-term memory for melodies. *Psychomusicology, 1,* 30–49.

Dowling, W. J., & Fujitani, D. S. (1971). Contour, interval, and pitch recognition in memory for melodies. *Journal of the Acoustical Society of America, 49,* 524–31.

Dowling, W. J., & Harwood, D. L. (1986). *Music cognition.* New York: Academic Press.

Dowling, W. J., & Hollombe, A. W. (1977). The perception of melodies distorted by splitting into several octaves: Effects of increasing proximity and melodic contour. *Perception and Psychophysics, 21,* 60–64.

Drake, C., Dowling, W. J., & Palmer, C. (1991). Accent structures in the reproduction of simple tunes by children and adult pianists. *Music Perception, 8,* 315–34.

Edworthy, J. (1985). Melodic contour and musical structure. In P. Howell, I. Cross, & R. West (Eds.), *Musical structure and cognition* (pp. 169–88). London: Academic Press.

Francès, R. (1958). *La perception de la musique.* Translated by W. J. Dowling. Hillsdale, N. J.: Earlbaum, 1988.

Garner, W. R. (1974). *The processing of information and structure.* New York: Wiley.

Imberty, M. (1969). *L'acquisition des structures tonales chez l'enfant.* Paris: Klincksieck.

Jones, M. R. (1987). Dynamic pattern structure in music: Recent theory and research. *Perception and Psychophysics, 41,* 621–34.

Kolinski, M. (1969). "Barbara Allen": Tonal versus melodic structure, part II. *Ethnomusicology, 13,* 1–73.

Krumhansl, C. L. (1990). *Cognitive foundations of musical pitch.* New York: Oxford University Press.

Krumhansl, C. L., & Keil, F. C. (1982). Acquisition of the hierarchy of tonal functions within a diatonic context. *Journal of Experimental Psychology: Human Perception and Performance, 5*, 579–94.

McKernon, P. E. (1979). The development of first songs in young children. *New Directions for Child Development, 3*, 43–58.

Monahan, C. B. (1984). *Parallels between pitch and time: The determinants of musical space*. Unpublished doctoral dissertation, University of California at Los Angeles, Los Angeles.

Povel, D.-J., & Essens, P. (1985). Perception of temporal patterns. *Music Perception, 2*, 411–40.

Trehub, S. E., Bull, D., & Thorpe, L. A. (1984). Infants' perception of melodies: The role of melodic contour. *Child Development, 55*, 821–30.

Trehub, S. E., Morongiello, B. A., & Thorpe, L. A. (1985). Children's perception of familiar melodies: The role of intervals. *Psychomusicology, 5*, 39–48.

Watkins, A. J. (1985). Scale, key, and contour in the discrimination of tuned and mistuned approximations to melody. *Perception and Psychophysics, 37*, 275–85.

Zenatti, A. (1969). Le developpement génétique de la perception musicale. *Monographies Françaises de Psychologie, 17*.

8

Describing
the Mental Representation
of Tonality in Music

DAVID BUTLER AND HELEN BROWN

Introduction

The research of Hermann von Helmholtz (1885/1954) on the combinations of musical sounds and the qualities of musical tones has influenced most subsequent investigations of the perception of consonance and tonality. Helmholtz believed that to study auditory events carefully they should be broken down into their most elementary units, and that certain pitch relationships are musically significant because of the physical properties of the tones themselves.

During the last decade, research in the perception of tonality has figured prominently in the psychology of music. The scholarly work of Carol Krumhansl described in *Cognitive Foundations of Musical Pitch* (1990) has been very significant (see also Krumhansl, 1991; for summaries of her earlier work see Krumhansl, 1983, 1985). Krumhansl's research has offered empirical validity to aspects of music theory such as the prominence that specific tones assume within a scale, and the relationships between the keys in the circle of fifths. Often she utilized geometric models to describe her results. Most of Krumhansl's experiments investigated tonality using what she called "the probe-tone technique." This technique required subjects to listen to a musical context that could be an ascending or descending diatonic scale, a chord, a chord progression, or a brief excerpt from a musical composition. The musical context was followed by the presentation of a tone (called "the probe tone") which was randomly chosen from among the 12 pitches. Subjects are asked to rate on a scale from 1 to 7 (1 = very bad to 7 = very good) how well the probe tone fit in the previously heard musical context.

In one of her early experiments (Krumhansl & Shepard, 1979) Krumhansl investigated how subjects perceived tonality using as the musical context an incomplete ascending or descending C major scale played without the final tonic and followed by the probe tone. She found that the results of subjects with a formal musical background conformed to the qualitative predictions of music theory: these subjects perceived the tonic, the dominant, and the mediant tone of the scale as the tones best fitting the given musical context.

Krumhansl's probe-tone ratings have also been applied in investigating the perception of North Indian (Castellano, Bharucha, & Krumhansl, 1984) and Balinese music (Kessler, Hansen, & Shepard, 1984), demonstrating that the probe-tone technique could also be successfully used to investigate the tonal hierarchies of these non-Western musical styles.

The research conducted by Butler, Brown, and Bharucha has provided valuable information that emphasizes other aspects of the perception of tonality. In this chapter, Butler and Brown describe the importance of the temporal element in perceiving tonality. They look at how single pitches and combinations of pitches are organized over time and show that it is the order in which pitches are played, not just the pitches themselves, that influences which key the listener perceives a piece to be in (see Brown, 1988; Brown & Butler, 1981; Butler, 1989, 1991). Butler and Brown believe that the scale per se does not adequately describe the relationships that listeners actually hear in the music; instead, they propose that the intervals of the scale indicate the tonality to the listeners.

Specifically, Butler and Brown demonstrate that within a major scale, the minor second and the tritone provide distinctive cues in perceiving tonality. Butler and Brown call the minor second and the tritone "rare" intervals because within a major scale the interval of a minor second occurs only twice (between the third and fourth scale degrees, and between the seventh scale degree and the tonic) and the tritone occurs only once (between the fourth and seventh scale degrees); thus they are heard less frequently than the other intervals. Butler and Brown propose that the infrequency with which these intervals occur within the major scale gives the listener distinctive cues for perceiving which tonality a piece is in.

REFERENCES

Brown, H. (1988). The interplay of set content and temporal context in a functional theory of tonality perception. *Music Perception, 5,* 219–50.

Brown, H., & Butler, D. (1981). Diatonic trichords as minimal tonal cue-cells.:I2 In Theory Only, 5(6,7), 37–55.

Butler, D. (1989). Describing the perception of tonality in music: A proposal for a theory of intervallic revalry. *Music Perception, 6,* 219–41.

Butler, D. (1991). *The musician's guide to perception and cognition.* New York: Schirmer Books.

Castellano, M., Bharucha, J., & Krumhansl, L. C. (1984). Tonal hierarchies in the music of North India. *Journal of Experimental Psychology: General, 113,* 394–412.

Helmholtz, H. L. F. (1954). *On the sensations of tone as a physiological basis for the theory of music* (A. J. Ellis, Ed. and Trans.). New York: Dover. (Original work published 1885)

Kessler, E., Hansen, C., & Shepard, R. N. (1984). Tonal schemata in the perception of music in Bali and the West. *Music Perception, 2,* 131–65.

Krumhansl, C. L. (1983). Perceptual structures for tonal music. *Music Perception, 1,* 28–62.

Krumhansl, C. L. (1985). Perceiving tonal structure in music. *American Scientist, 73,* 371–78.

Krumhansl, C. L. (1990). *Cognitive foundations of musical pitch.* New York: Oxford University Press.

Krumhansl, C. L. (1991). Music psychology: Tonal structures in perception and memory. *Annual Review of Psychology, 42,* 277–303.

Krumhansl, C., & Shepard, R. N. (1979). Quantification of the hierarchy of tonal functions within a diatonic context. *Journal of Experimental Psychology: Human Perception and Performance, 5,* 579–94.

During the past three centuries, listeners in our Western musical culture have learned to expect certain underlying conventions in ways tones are combined to form meaningful patterns. A few of these conventional combinations are related to acoustical and sensory characteristics of tones, but most tonal patterns can change from one musical culture to another and from one style to another within a culture. Our purpose in this chapter is to examine these tonal patterns as perceptual objects and as cognitive processes. A goal of this discussion is to impress on the reader the importance of temporal relations in the comprehension of pitch relationships in tonal music—the importance of the manner in which pitches provide context for one another as the music unfolds before the listener.

Nature presents us with choices of smoother- or rougher-sounding combinations of tones and these combinations might have important connotations within one musical style, or throughout an entire musical culture; yet, musical cultures are sometimes very different. Our own musical culture includes highly varied approaches to combining pitches and even to contriving pitch-sets from which pitches may be combined; as the same concert, for example, you can hear a minimalistic work that might contain only five or six pitch classes, followed immediately by a microtonal work containing two dozen or more tones within the octave. Within these extremes, several well-worn, well-understood stylistic norms have been tremendously important in shaping Western music for the past three centuries or so. Another way of saying this is that composers and listeners have formed an unspoken pact, a fairly sophisticated set of ground rules, regarding how pitches are to be organized to form normal-sounding patterns. This set of conventions is known as· *tonality*, which undergirds the learned system of "keyness" that to some extent governs how melodies and chords are organized throughout the duration of a tonal musical composition. In this chapter, we describe these conventions of organization and then review experimental studies that have described listeners' recognition of these conventions.

Pitch Relationships

It is necessary to make a few distinctions about the ways that the term "pitch" might be used.[1] Pitch may refer to nothing more than a loose registral differentiation, the difference between "high" and "low." Sounds with little or no discernible pitch—clicks, thumps—can nonetheless be described as having a higher or lower pitch. The definitions of pitch relating more directly to this discussion are two levels more specific than this, however. The first level of specificity refers to the pitch material from which tonality is built. There are 12 equal logarithmic divisions of the octave; these equal divisions produce the equal-tempered 12-tone set, variously called the *chromatic set*, the *chromatic scale* (if the tones are arranged in scalar order), or the *equal-tempered twelfth-octave collection*. Distances among tones in this 12-tone set can be described neutrally using modulo-12 (clockface) numbers: 0 stands for C, B-sharp, D double-flat, and its other enharmonic spellings in all possible octave registers; 1 stands for the next-higher semitone, and so on through 11, which stands for B and its enharmonics. The system therefore refers not to single, specific pitches, but rather to 12 *pitch classes*. The neutrality of these pitch-class numbers is appropriate for discussions of pitch relations beyond the scope of the Western tonal tradition, but discussions of tonal pitch relations cannot remain neutral. The second level of specificity pertains to tonal context. Intervals can sometimes be considered nothing more than gaps between pitches. The term "interval class" is conventionally applied to these neutral spans of pitch space: the intervals E–F and D-double-sharp– G-double-flat both belong to interval-class (ic) 1, for example, because each spans one semitone. Interval-class labels, however, are not precise enough to describe pitch relationships in tonal music. For example, the three-semitone gap between pitch classes 0 and 3 has no distinctive tonal meaning, but when 0 becomes the specific pitch middle C, and 3 becomes the E-flat a minor third above it, that particular three-semitone gap will be found in different harmonic and tonal contexts than it would if 0 were C and 3 were the D-sharp an augmented second above it. When discussions involve pitch sets derived from specific tonal contexts, spelling definitely counts.

This discussion implies that the pitch set comes close to describing a pitch pattern found in a piece of music already composed. This is not just academic fussiness; rather, it is one of the more important musical observations in this chapter. Although some accounts describe scales as the basis of music, historically the music comes first, and the scales come later. Scales are theorists' attempts to describe the pitch materials in music that already exists.[2] The scale is a handy index of the pitch contents of some piece or pieces of music, but the scale's simplicity comes at a hefty price. The scale is a highly simplistic construction that fails to describe much of what is most important about pitch relationships in tonal music. First, there is no guarantee that all notes in the scale may be used in a composition, and there is definitely no guarantee whatever that the scale fully represents all notes that may be encountered within the music. Second, the scale says nothing at all about how the notes within the piece of music are to be arranged throughout the composition—how they are to unfold as the composition is heard.

A listener who has become familiar with the tonal idiom tacitly gains an underlying sense of *key level*, and within that a sense of *harmonic level*, in a piece of tonal music as it unfolds across time. This is one of the strongest perceptual binding forces—that is, features through which we perceive coherence—in tonal music (see, for example, Krumhansl, 1979; Brown & Butler, 1981; Deutsch, 1982; Krumhansl & Kessler, 1982; Brown, 1988; Butler, 1989). Although we may never have been formally trained to do it (see, for example, Moog, 1976; Shuter-Dyson & Gabriel, 1981; Hargreaves, 1986; Serafine, 1988), most of us seem to pick up some skill—some of us have a little, others a lot—at hearing tonal music as arranged around the context of a perceptually central pitch (e.g., Brown & Butler, 1981; Butler, 1983, 1989; Butler & Brown, 1984; Brown, 1988).

Harmonic Context

The term "harmony" has acquired several meanings. One colloquial definition is roughly equivalent to "good-sounding accompaniment" as, for example, when two people might sing in two-part harmony. Harmony also is often equated with *chord*. On a more abstract musical level, harmony is often used to mean harmonic level, something bigger than a single chord. Music analysts may speak, for example, of a lengthy segment of a composition existing on a single harmonic level, even though it may be represented in some compositions by a sequence of several (or several dozen) chords. Although this chapter does not contain a discourse on harmony on this level of abstraction, it is important to recognize that harmony can carry any or all of these connotations. At both the simplest and the most abstract levels, we can refer to harmony without dealing directly with chords.

Chords, however, are what first come to mind when we speak of harmony. To some extent, chords are similar to the harmonic partials of a complex tone. In fact, many music theorists have argued that chords in Western harmonic practice are (or ought always be) patterned after the harmonic series; some theorists have gone so far as to call the harmonic series the "chord of nature" (e.g., Catel, 1801). Although it has become a mainstay in some theories of tonal music, this resemblance between *harmonic* partials of complex tones and musical *harmony* is restricted in three important ways. First, the harmonic partials of complex tones are ideally positioned at exact integer relations ($1:2:3: . . . :n$) to one another, but this isn't always true in real musical sound; the partials of some "harmonic" complex tones (such as tones produced by the piano) are actually slightly inharmonic. Second, virtually all fixed-pitch instruments are tuned so that the octave is divided into 12 equal logarithmic increments, and this equal-tempered tuning system produces no intervals other than the octave that match exactly with the intervals between the partials of a complex tone. Third, chords can be built of intervals other than thirds, although chords built in thirds and containing perfect fifths are considered inherently consonant in many accounts of tonal relationships. But tastes change. Only a brief millennium ago, for example, a major triad was considered a clashing discord by many writers: the two outer tones (the fifth) would have been thought acceptable, but the middle tone (the third) was considered a clangorous dissonance. Twentieth-century composers such as Debussy and Hindemith have made consonant sonorities of chords built in fourths and seconds.

There is another aspect of consonance and dissonance beyond the sensory response that two tones may sound either smooth or rough in the presence of one another. In most accounts, dissonance (a "rough-sounding" combination such as a second, a seventh, a tritone, or any chord containing one or more of these intervals) is regarded as a point of musical instability, of musical tension: the listener is expected to respond to dissonant combinations of tones with the feeling that they do not project the sense that the music has "arrived" at a convincing point of repose, a good stopping point. Alternatively, consonant combinations of tones ("smooth-sounding" intervals such as thirds, perfect fourths, fifths, and octaves, or chords limited to them) are presented in these accounts of music as points of stability, good stopping points. Historical and speculative music theory, as well as empirical evidence (e.g., Cazden, 1980; Brown, 1988), offer convincing counterexamples to this point of view. To illustrate, you might try playing a chord containing the pitches C_3-B_3-E_4-A_4-D_5 (Figure 8.1a); although it contains sensory dissonances in the form of several minor and major seconds (or their octave complements or compounds), the chord forms a perfectly acceptable ending chord in some tonal styles, particularly the big-band and jazz styles of the 1940s and later. Conversely, a major triad built on the dominant scale degree may sound perfectly smooth and agreeable (Cazden used the term "euphonous"), and yet be interpreted by a listener as an unstable, unfinished point within a tonal composition. Because sensory consonance and dissonance are not necessarily equivalent to perceived stability and instability, there is growing acceptance of the use of such terms as "systemic" or "musical" consonance and dissonance to refer to perceived instability (nonfinality) and stability (finality), and "sensory" consonance or dissonance when referring to the smoothness or roughness of the

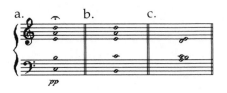

FIGURE 8.1. (a): Simultaneity containing several sensory dissonances forming a stable harmony in some styles. (b) and (c): Simultaneities discussed in note 3, p. 210 containing the same pitch classes but in varied registral arrangements.

combination's sound.[3] Moreover, dissonance means something more than tension and consonance means more than release. Meyer (1956; see esp. pp. 35–42), for example, has argued persuasively that musical events—which may be single tones, chords, entire phrases, or even entire sections of compositions—have "embodied meanings": they point to, or make us expect, other musical events. For example, an expert musical listener, upon interpreting a chord as a dominant harmony, will likely be able to know more than simply that the chord is unstable or tension-arousing; in addition, the listener will quite firmly anticipate that the dominant seventh chord will lead directly (or seldom with more than a perfunctory delay) to a tonic harmony. The essential two points in all of this are that there is a resemblance between acoustical and musical harmony, and that there is a relationship between sensory and musical consonance and dissonance, but the relationships are neither as rigid nor as extensive as they are sometimes portrayed.

Key Context

Earlier, the term "tonality" was characterized as "keyness": a system of pitch relationships governing how we interpret music to be situated "in" a key, and how we interpret what that key is. Tonality can actually be considered a bigger and more abstract concept than key, however, and in fact even bigger and more abstract than a single *style* of music (Brody, 1985). Tonality is perhaps best considered as an idiom—similar to a dialect, or similar perhaps even to an entire grammatical system. Within the tonal idiom, one can point to a number of different Western musical styles including late Baroque, Classical, Romantic, and some twentieth-century art-music styles, and also including most of the Western popular and folk styles of the last three centuries.

   One perceptual feature shared by all these styles is that music written in any of them will give the enculturated listener some sense that the music has a home base, a central and most-important pitch. This pitch stands for the *key* (sometimes called *key level*) of the piece. It is common to speak of the key as the more-general scheme of pitch relationships within a piece of music, and of the mode—major or minor—as the more specialized set of relationships within that key level. For example, Mozart's Symphony No. 40 is in the key of G minor, which is a brief way of saying that its most-important focal pitch is G and the pitch relationships in the minor scale come closer to describing the music than do the pitch relationships in the major scale. Even though the symphony is said to be in the key of G minor, at various points the listener hears a fair amount of music in B-flat major, one movement in E-flat major (in which the key migrates to B-flat major and then returns), and other sections in even other keys (such as G major and F-sharp minor). In trying simply to describe the perceptual object, then, we must recognize that tonal music is complex enough that the concept of key exists on more than a single level. Returning to the Mozart example, G minor is a global description of the primary key level of the entire four-movement composition, but the listener hears a succession of keys within different parts of each movement of the composition. As complicated as this sort of listening activity seems, both musical and psychological theorists concur (e.g., Brown & Butler, 1981; Browne, 1981; Deutsch & Feroe, 1981; Deutsch, 1982; Boltz, 1989) that musical listeners do interpret tones according to the context of the single key governing the music.

Depending on the experience of the listener and on the specific piece, the perceptual clarity of this central pitch class will vary. Yet (as stated earlier) listeners who can successfully hear musical pitch patterns within the mental context of a key do not necessarily have to have gone through a great deal of formal training in music. Nor do they necessarily have to be able to read musical notation, or have a working knowledge of scales or chords or key relationships. It is not customary to distribute scores to audience members at concerts, nor is it common for the performer(s) to play a tone, a scale, or a chord, as a point of reference with which to prime the audience before each composition is performed. How, then, do we get a mental grip on the music—that is, how do listeners recognize that the music is tonal, and simultaneously recognize the key in that piece of tonal music, given nothing more than an aural presentation of the music itself? Obviously, the code must be located within and among the pitch patterns in the music, rather than inside some abstract construct such as a chord, a scale, or some other set of pitches.

Most accounts of this code have to do with the traditional notion that the *tonic* or keynote is the reference point in any key, it is somehow invested with the most stability of any of the tones in any key, and that all other tones in the set relate to the tonic in varying ways, and to varying degrees. Until recently there has been comparatively little experimental research conducted to explore how we recognize these tonal relationships. So how do we recognize tonic as tonic, dominant as dominant, and so on? In the next section, we examine studies undertaken in the attempt to answer these questions.

Research on Key Identification

Major Mode

One testable model of this recognition was proposed by Richmond Browne (1981). Browne began with a well-known property of the major pitch set (Babbitt, 1960), which is that each interval class occurs at least once in the set and each class occurs a unique number of times. This is shown in Figure 8.2, represented by the C major set. Although the intervals in Figure 8.2 are notated specifically out of necessity, they are merely a single representation of all possible enharmonic spellings, octave complements, and octave compounds of those intervals.

It should be emphasized that there is an important difference between *scale* and *pitch set:* while pitch sets are not necessarily ordered or grouped in any certain way, scales are conventionally ordered within an octave span, and also ordered so that they form a ladder-like arrangement. The order of tones in any scale is a matter of convention and convenience, but it does not impose any necessary order on the pitches as they may be used in a piece of music.

Although the tones in Figure 8.2 are arranged as scales, the intervallic properties of the major pitch set go beyond the obvious pattern of whole steps and semitones that we see in the scale. For example, consider the intervals formed by tones not adjacent in the scale. Some intervals span three semitones, some span four, and so on. Browne (1981) recognized that the major diatonic set stands out from other pitch-class sets because every interval class is present somewhere in the set—none is omitted. Each occurs a unique number of times. There are two semitones in the set (see Figure 8.2a); no other interval is present that exact number of times. Each interval class is pointed out in each succeeding line within Figure 8.2: two members of interval class (ic) 1 (i.e., semitones, Figure 8.2a) and five members of ic2 (Figure 8.2b); four members of ic3 (Figure 8.2c) and three members of ic4 (Figure 8.2d); six members of ic5 (Figure 8.2e) and

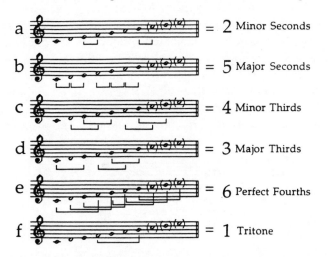

FIGURE 8.2. The various intervals comprising in the C major set (shown in scalar order in this figure). Beginning with the smallest interval other than the unison, there are (a) two intervals of one semitone (interval class or ic1); (b) five intervals comprising a two-semitone span (ic2); (c) four three-semitone spans (ic3); (d) three four-semitone spans (ic4); (e) six five-semitone spans (ic5); and (f) one six-semitone span (ic6).

only one member of ic6 (Figure 8.1f). Octave complements and compounds are assumed within interval classes.

Browne pointed out that while some intervals are abundant, others such as the semitones and the tritone occur infrequently within the major diatonic set. These rarer intervals (a term indicating relative rarity in the set, but not necessarily rare in actual tonal music), Browne reasoned, ought to serve better as perceptual cues that listeners can use to gain a sense of key in music they hear. A series of experiments has produced evidence bearing out Browne's prediction.

In the first study (Brown & Butler, 1981) listeners heard a minimal amount of pitch information, in melodic trichords, from which they made determinations of key center. Choices were limited to the major mode and excluded chromatic interpretations (these will be discussed later). After hearing only three tones in each pattern, listeners were asked to hum, whistle, sing, or otherwise produce a direct judgment of key center. Examples of these three-tone stimulus patterns are shown in Figure 8.3.

Although the pattern in Figure 8.3a looks quite similar to that in Figure 8.3e, the small change of pitch (one semitone) in the third note of the pattern produces a very different intervallic configuration, as can be verified by reviewing Figure 8.2. The rarest interval to be found among the three tones F-G-C in Figure 8.3e is the two-semitone span between F and G. The tones G and C fall within interval class 5, as shown in Figure 8.3e. This means that the intervals between the notes in Figure 8.3 are quite common in the diatonic set. One way of demonstrating this is that we can find that same pattern of ic2 combined with ic5 at five different starting points in the C major scale, as may be seen in Figure 8.4a. Another demonstration (Figure 8.4b–f) is that we can find the specific notes F, G, and C at various points in five different major scales. But the tritone (Fig. 8.3a) occurs just once in the major set; thus there is only one correct major-mode key interpretation for the pitches shown in Figure 8.3a.

When a listener is required to identify appropriate key centers for sequential combinations of tones such as those illustrated in Figure 8.3a and 8.3e, the listener may reasonably expect two things to be true. First, since a rare-interval pattern such as that in Figure 8.3a could fit into only one major pitch set, it

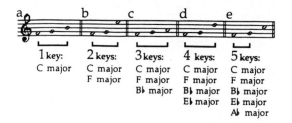

FIGURE 8.3. Transcribed examples of trichordal patterns representative of stimuli used by Brown and Butler (1981). The rarest intervals in each trichordal pattern narrowed its tonal field such that pattern (a) could fit into one major pitch set, pattern (b) into two, and so on.

FIGURE 8.4. (a) Five places within the C Major scale where one can find the intervallic combination of ic2 and ic5. (b–f) Conversely, the five scales containing ic2 and ic5 represented by the tones F, G, and C.

ought to be much easier to identify an appropriate tonal center for a pattern such as that in Figure 8.3e, to which one could respond with five different and equally appropriate key centers. Second, although there would be more potential right answers to a pattern such as Figure 8.3e illustrates, listeners' responses might well be spread out among the several appropriate alternatives. Both expectations were borne out in the results reported by Brown and Butler (1981), who asked musicians to sing, whistle, or hum the most appropriate tonal centers for three-tone patterns such as those illustrated in Figure 8.3. Although overall accuracy in key identifications for the common-interval combinations (as represented by Figure 8.3e) were a few percentage points higher than for the rare-interval combinations (as represented by Figure 8.3a), listeners were fully twice as likely to agree on a key center for the rare-interval combinations as for the combinations containing only common intervals.

The stimulus patterns drawing the strongest responses (in both accuracy and confidence levels) were not necessarily the patterns adhering to any scalar order, so it was suspected that the patterns carried implied harmonic messages—in other words, that listeners mentally supplied something like a chordal accompaniment as a perceptual framework for these tiny melodic patterns. If this were true, the impact of the varying of time orders of tones on listeners' responses could be explained in terms of common harmonic practices in Western tonal music: it is much more common in typical harmonic successions for the subdominant harmony to precede the dominant than to follow it. If the fourth scale degree were interpreted as representative of the subdominant harmony, and the seventh scale degree (the leading tone) as representative of the dominant, listeners could be expected to feel that they were on firmer tonal harmonic ground hearing the four-to-seven order of presentation.

Another result of this test was that variations in the order of presentation of tones made a difference in the accuracy levels of responses to the patterns containing rare intervals. For instance, listeners concurred more on the choice of tonal center when they heard the pattern shown in Figure 8.3a than when they heard its reverse. The clearest sense of key center seemed to arise when scale step 7 was heard after scale step 4; whenever the temporal order of these two steps was reversed (regardless of the placement of the third tone in the pattern), response accuracy and confidence levels both dropped.

The second study (Butler, 1983) dealt directly with chordal successions. The test explored this question of temporal order by presenting, as paired dyads, four members of the major diatonic set: scale members 3, 4, 7, and 8(1). The critical variable was the time order in which the tones were presented. In the first of two stimulus categories, set members 4 and 7 were always heard simultaneously, as were scale members 8(1) and 3; these combinations are shown in Figure 8.5a. The 4-7 combination comprises the tritone, the rarest interval in the set; it also is the clearest, most unequivocal presentation of dominant harmony that can be made with a dyad. (Scale members 4 and 7 were combined to imply the dominant harmony in this test, in contrast to the earlier study in which scale degrees 4 and 7 were presented separately, perhaps implying different chords.) The 8(1)-3 combination is the clearest representation of tonic harmony that can be produced with two tones, and—as Figure 8.5a shows—the 4-7 combination can proceed to these two tones by semitone succession. Patterns such as these were presented both to expert musicians and to musical novices, and it was found that as long as the simultaneities clearly represented the dominant and tonic harmonies, as they do in Figure 8.5a, both experts and novices concurred strongly in their choices of the key that each of these patterns represented. On the other hand, both experts and novices were much less accurate in their identification of the key that patterns such as those in Figure 8.5b represented—this even though exactly the same set members were heard, and even though the intervals separating the simultaneities were still semitones. The critical difference apparently was that the simultaneities no longer clearly represented an unequivocal dominant-tonic or tonic-dominant harmonic succession. It seemed clear from this result that pitch relations alone were not sufficient to convey a sense of key to musical listeners; the clarity came when those pitch relations were presented in a temporal order that allowed listeners to interpret those tones within a meaningful harmonic context that the listener tacitly provided.

Subsequent experimental studies have added interesting detail to what we know about the effects of temporality on the perception of pitch relations in tonal (and posttonal) music. Brown (1985, 1987, 1988) demonstrated that when well-known musical excerpts are distilled by deleting repeated pitches, the source pitch set can be ordered so that listeners identify the melody's original key as the key of the new pattern, but when those same pitches are ordered another way, listeners are just as convinced that the pitches belong to a second key. When the pitches are reordered in a third way to induce tonal confusion in listeners, listeners are indeed much less likely to agree on the key for that pattern.

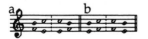

FIGURE 8.5. Transcribed examples of three-tone patterns representative of stimuli used by Butler (1983). Tones were arranged temporally either so that (a) the tritone was presented as a simultaneity, or so that (b) the tritone was presented asynchronously, within different vertical dyads.

Figure 8.6 is an example from Brown's (1988) study. Listeners were 86% accurate in identifying D as the tonal center of an excerpt (see Figure 8.6a) from the third movement of Schubert's Sonata in D Major, D.664, in which tonic and dominant seventh chords are arpeggiated over a tonic pedal. The remaining 14% mistook F-sharp, the last tone heard in the melody, as tonic. When the excerpt (which comprises the diatonic set of D major, missing only the submediant) was reduced to one instance of each within an octave of its component pitches and was ordered to promote identification of the original key (shown in Figure 8.6b), agreement on D as tonic increased to 95%. The pitches were also ordered and presented with the intent of eliciting the choice of G major as the key (Figure 8.6c). While 41% responded to the diatonic set, identifying D as the tonal center, 45% chose G, a key that no listener thought was implied by the musical excerpt or by the ordering of pitches shown in Figure 8.6b. When the sequence was arranged so that rare intervals did not imply clear harmonic progressions in any key (Figure 8.6d), choices of key were indeed more diffuse: Forty-five percent of the listeners chose D, but tonic identifications were scattered among seven other pitches, three of which were not in the tonal pattern (as indicated by whole notes). Responses to the pitch set as ordered in Figure 8.6c and 8.6d indicate that reversal of the single tritone from its optimal 4-7 ordering (the ordering that clearly suggested its major tonic in the pattern shown in Figure 8.6b) greatly diminishes the power of even the rarest interval to suggest a key.

This effect can also be observed in melodic patterns comprising the tones found in a single major triad. In a recent study by Brown, Butler, and Jones (in progress), listeners heard short contextual patterns such as those shown in Figure 8.7, and then rated all members of the chromatic set (which followed the

FIGURE 8.6. (a) Excerpt from Schubert, Sonata D. 664, movement III, containing at least one of each interval in the diatonic set and containing no conflicting rare intervals; (b) pitches extracted from the Schubert excerpt and ordered serially to promote identification of D as tonal center; (c) the same pitches reordered to promote G as tonic; (d) the same pitches reordered to be tonally ambiguous. Levels of identification as tonal center for each pattern are given in percentages; whole notes in (d) show out-of-pattern pitches identified as tonic. (NR means no response.) (After Brown, 1988.)

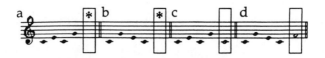

FIGURE 8.7. Tones of a C major triad arranged in two temporal orders (a,b) that preceded all members of the chromatic set (presented at the points indicated by the asterisks). (c) The tone with the highest rating for well-fittedness for the first pattern; (d) the tone rated as best-fitting for the second pattern.

patterns at the point indicated at the asterisk in Figure 8.7a,b); ratings were based on the listeners' estimates of how well each tone fit with the pattern preceding it. Listeners rated the root of the triad as the most appropriate completion when the triad was arranged to reinforce that choice (see Figure 8.7c). When the same contextual tones were rearranged (as is shown in Figure 8.7b,d) to undo the rhythmic regularity of C4 within the contextual pattern, the highest rating indicated an interpretation of the contextual pattern as a dominant chord, with the test tone implying resolution to tonic (Figure 8.7d).

Minor Mode

Our discussion until this point has been limited to tonal harmony in the major mode. This is an important limitation. The perceptibility of other important aspects of tonal harmony has received relatively little experimental investigation thus far. We next consider the topics of minor mode and chromaticism and their relationships with tonality.

One likely reason that most research in tonal harmony has concentrated on the major mode is that it is so much simpler to discuss than the minor mode is. The harmonic form of the minor scale is most relevant to the topic of harmony and tonality because this form has both a leading tone below the tonic and an "upper leading tone" above the dominant. There are three semitones and one augmented second among the adjacent scale members in harmonic minor; this is shown in Figure 8.8.

As Figure 8.8 illustrates, the minor diatonic set has very different intervallic properties from the major set. There are two of the rarest interval class in this set, and only five of the most common. The tritone in major mode is likely to sound unique because it is; the two tritones in minor, however, are obviously not unique. They are inherently more ambiguous in regard to placement in the

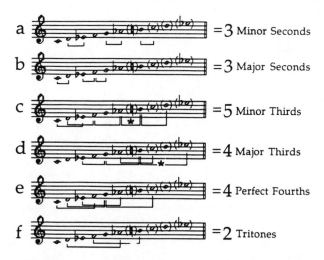

FIGURE 8.8. The various intervals found among tones in the C minor diatonic set (shown in scalar order in this figure). Beginning with the smallest interval other than the unison, there are (a) three members of ic1; (b) three also from ic2; (c) five members of ic3; (d) four members of ic4; (e) four members of ic5; and (f) two tritones (ic6).

pitch set, because any tritone we hear in a piece of music in the minor mode has two potential diatonic points of reference.

There are unique intervals within the six categories shown in Figure 8.8, however. Notice that in Figure 8.8c there are five intervals within interval class 3. Four of these are notated as minor thirds, while one, marked with an asterisk, is notated as an augmented second. Similarly in Figure 8.8d, there are four intervals within ic4: three are notated as major thirds, while the fourth interval is notated as a diminished fourth. Within a musical context (see Figure 8.9) sufficient to clarify the identities of the augmented second and the diminished fourth, it is logical that these rare intervals both assist listeners as they ascertain their tonal whereabouts in music in minor mode. Butler's (1992) data show that this is the case; listeners who heard brief melodic patterns resembling those in Figure 8.9 exhibited almost the level of agreement on minor-mode tonal center as they did for analogous patterns made up of the rarer intervals in the major diatonic set.

Chromaticism

Chromaticism has been equated with randomness or atonality in some perceptual studies (e.g., Taylor, 1976; Krumhansl, 1990). Notice, however, in the second melodic sequence derived from the Schubert excerpt above (Figure 8.6c), in which pitches were arranged to elicit tonic responses of G major, that listeners who did interpret it in that key understood C-sharp to be the leading tone of D,

FIGURE 8.9. (a) A melodic pattern that includes a diminished fourth between notes 1 and 3; (b) a melodic pattern that includes an augmented second between notes 1 and 3.

the dominant pitch, which follows it here. Listeners in Brown's (1988) study were able to interpret this C-sharp as a raised fourth scale step that harmonically intensifies the approach to the dominant. This melodic emphasis on a note other than tonic, achieved by chromatically raising the note below it, is known as *microtonicization*.[4] Listeners' responses indicate that, in direct judgments of tonal center, chromaticism is not an element of the tonal fabric that necessarily suggests randomness or atonality. Temporal arrangements and harmonic implications in experimental stimuli can be evaluated as reflective of cognitive processes that enable listeners to incorporate chromaticism into their interpretations of tonality in music. The discussion below draws from both analytic interpretations and experimental data to support this position.

Figure 8.10 contains an example of a set of stimuli (Brown, 1985) manipulated in a way similar to the Schubert excerpt discussed above, but the pitch set of this musical excerpt from Ives's *Concord Sonata* can be reduced neither to a diatonic set nor to any familiar scale. Its interval-class content includes one more minor second than the major diatonic set and one fewer tritone (that is, none). The musical excerpt (Figure 8.10a) consists of an arpeggiated E-flat major triad, in addition to these nonchord tones: F functioning as an appoggiatura on the downbeat, and D and F-sharp functioning as lower neighbors to the root and third of the triad. F-sharp, the chromatic tone that adds two minor seconds to the set, acts as a microtonicization of G both in the excerpt and in Figure 8.10b, the melodic sequence arranged to suggest the key of E-flat to listeners. In the latter context, an arpeggiation of the dominant triad (F–B-flat–D) resolving to the tonic note by the best rare interval available for E-flat, this chromatic pattern elicited unanimous agreement among listeners. In Figure 8.10c, although there is no A-flat and no rare interval for the key of A-flat major in this set, arpeggiation of its dominant triad (B-flat–E-flat–G) ends with its leading tone to suggest resolution to A-flat to listeners. This resulted in 60% agreement on that key while choices of E-flat as tonic dropped to 12%. Responses to the last ordering, shown in Figure 8.10d, clearly illustrate the features of a tonally ambiguous melodic pattern: Responses were scattered among 10 of the 12 possible tonics, with listeners exhibiting the most reliance on the first and last pitches.

With musical excerpts and their reduced melodic sequences that included from as few as three to as many as 10 of the 12 pitches of the chromatic set, results in these studies indicated consistently that virtually any set of pitches could be manipulated temporally either to suggest various tonal centers or to be tonally confusing. Even subsets of a single diatonic pitch set could not be assumed to suggest that key on the basis of nontemporal considerations. In other words, the results indicated that critical relationships among pitches in tonal

FIGURE 8.10. (a) Excerpt from Ives, Sonata No. 2 (Concord), "The Alcotts"; (b) pitches extracted from the Ives excerpt and ordered serially to promote the identification of E-flat as tonal center; (c) the same pitches reordered to promote A-flat as tonic; (d) same pitches reordered to be tonally ambiguous. Levels of identification as tonal center for each pattern are given in percentages; whole notes show out-of-pattern pitches identified as tonic. (NR means no response.) (After Brown, 1985.)

music do not arise solely from the pitch-set properties of those tones, but arise also to a great extent from their temporal context in the specific pattern being heard.

It is possible, though, for each pitch in a chromatic set to carry a unique meaning that suggests relationships to a tonal center. It takes more than the usual chromatic scale to illustrate this, because tonal music may have only 12 tones per octave, but it has more than 12 functional pitches per octave. In Mitchell's words:

> The ordering force of diatonicism becomes a dispersing force of the chromatic scale. Where each degree of the diatonic major scale is imbued with a single meaning, due to its characterizing interval set and its distance from a tonic degree, the tones of the chromatic scale have multiple meanings. (Mitchell, 1962: 8)

A representation of pitch classes called the "tonal chromatic collection," developed by Brown (1987, 1992), illustrates a distinction among the multiple meanings resulting from mixture and tonicization. According to Proctor (1977), these two processes are the sole sources of chromaticism in diatonic tonality. Although there can be abundant chromaticism in diatonic tonality, the asymmetry of the diatonic basis, with its unique pitch relationships, is preserved. This is distinguished from symmetrical structures in chromatic tonality (Proctor, 1977), where an equal-tempered 12-pitch-class collection is appropriate and where enharmonicism is a tonal, as well as a notational, phenomenon. An example of

o = key level
● = dominant of each key

FIGURE 8.11. Synopsis of key areas in Chopin's Prelude in E Major, op. 28, no. 9. (a) Each key level in the prelude is prefaced by its dominant; (b) ties indicate pitches in common among the tonic harmonies.

this symmetrical construction is found in Chopin's E major Prelude, op. 28, no. 9, where key relationships represent a symmetrical division of the octave into major thirds: E, C, A-flat/G-sharp, E. These relationships are shown schematically in Figure 8.11.

The process of chromaticism has also received experimental attention (see, e.g., Brown, 1988, 1992; Butler, 1980, 1988), and these studies indicate that the process involves much more than simply adding nondiatonic pitches to somehow dilute the strength of the prevailing tonality. Chromatic chords can lead skilled listeners to expect that some chords will form more appropriate resolutions than others and can thus be clear signals both of the key level and of unfolding harmonic events at the local level. Until much more experimental research has been carried out, however, it is impossible to say just how unequivocal these signals are, or to say just how many listeners can reliably pick them up.

Summary

Theoretical discussions of tonal harmony tend to begin with abstractions such as scales, idealized chords, and key signatures. It is important to remember, however, that listeners are forced to pick up information about tonal harmony from one or several tones at a time as the music unfolds perceptually across time. Leading theories of tonal harmony have been only partly successful in explaining how this information is picked up, however. There are two leading reasons for this limited success. First, some of the most influential theories assert (or imply) that musical harmony is intrinsically related to the harmonic frequency relations among partials of periodic tones (e.g., Helmholtz, 1863; Schenker, 1906; Schoenberg, 1911). One hazard of this assertion is that harmony could then be considered solely as a relationship of simultaneous sounds; musical harmony, on the other hand, comprises relationships among sounds that may be successive, or even sounds that may be temporally far removed from one another. Second, theories have emphasized abstractions such as scales and chordal prototypes (e.g., Forte, 1979; Piston, 1987), devoting comparatively little attention to the temporal aspects of harmony and tonality.

The discussion in this chapter, on the other hand, has proceeded on the assumption that the perception of tonal music is inherently temporal—that listeners discover harmonic relations within a key, and track harmonic successions hinting at or actually moving to other keys, as tonal music unfolds in time. This discussion has concentrated on the perception of two facets of musical harmony: first, how listeners recognize the key in which the harmonies reside, and second, how listeners recognize harmonic successions that may or may not be limited to the notes within a single diatonic system. These harmonic successions may be conveyed explicitly by chains of chords, or they may be implicit in a single line—in as few as a handful of tones. Riemann's theory of harmonic function includes this central assertion:

> There are only three kinds of tonal functions (significance within the key), namely, tonic, dominant, and subdominant. In the change of these functions lies the essence of modulation. (Riemann, 1895: 9)

If we are to learn how a listener can recognize any of these three fundamental harmonic functions, we must begin by asking how the listener recognizes the key forming the context for these functions. A number of studies reviewed in this chapter (e.g., Brown & Butler, 1981; Butler & Brown, 1984; Brown, 1988; Butler, 1989) have gathered evidence that listeners get their tonal bearings from the critical intervallic relationships, arranged in conventional patterns across time, that convey the harmonic message of dominant harmony progressing to tonic. If we then ask how a listener is to recognize the change of these functions wherein the essence of modulation lies, we find that the functions change when critical intervallic relationships are taken away from the primary dominant-tonic progression and transposed to some alternate progression. Riemann, in fact, stated that modulation—the change of harmonic functions—resulted from "leading-tone exchange" (*leittonwechsel*). A number of studies cited in this chapter have presented evidence that this leading-tone exchange is recognized when the rare intervals of the diatonic set are encountered in conventional temporal patterns: when one rare interval—the tritone—can indicate a dominant harmonic condition (either on the original dominant, or elsewhere in chromatic harmony), and when other rare intervals—the semitones—lead to the dominant's objective harmony (either the original tonic, or elsewhere in chromatic harmony, or in modulation). These leading-tone relations carry the essence of dominant-to-tonic harmonic progression. They can be fragmented and transposed to produce chromatic harmonic successions that are clearly tonal, or they can be subverted to deny tonality.

NOTES

1. While we assume that the reader has a solid working acquaintance with traditional musical terminology, some of this nomenclature is problematic because some of the most basic terms have been encumbered with too many meanings. Thus, we will give narrow operational definitions to the terms "pitch," "harmony," and "key," and will discuss their relationships to traditional Western tonality.

2. It is obviously true that most instruments in our musical culture are designed such that they will most readily produce tones separated by twelfth-octave pitch increments. This certainly does not mean that composers are limited to those choices of pitch materials, as compositions by Harry Partch, Easley Blackwood, and numerous others will attest. More germane to this discussion, scales possess no intrinsic properties that force—or even necessarily guide—composers' choices on how the members of the scale are to be arranged across the time-span of the composition.

3. What if the voicing of the chord C_3-B_3-E_4-A_4-D_5 were changed to B_3-C_4-E_4-A_4-D_5 (Figure 8.1b)? —or to A_3-B_3-C_4-D_4-E_4 (see Figure 8.1c)? It might well be that fewer listeners would accept the second voicing as pleasant, and fewer still the third. Although some readers might argue that this undermines Cazden's distinction between sensory and systemic dissonance, other readers could argue that it strengthens Cazden's argument: if the same pitch-classes (and thus the same interval classes) can give rise to different reactions of sensory dissonance, how can sensory consonance and dissonance be a sufficient basis for a rigorous and useful musical theory of consonance and dissonance?

4. The reader is invited to compare the process of microtonicization with Bharucha's (1984) perceptual study of melodic anchoring.

REFERENCES

Babbitt, M. (1960). Twelve-tone invariants as compositional determinants. *The Musical Quarterly, 46,* 246–59.

Bharucha, J. (1984). Anchoring effects in music: The resolution of dissonance. *Cognitive Psychology, 16,* 485–518.

Boltz, M. (1989). Perceiving the end: Effects of tonal relationships on melodic completion. *Journal of Experimental Psychology: Human Perception and Performance, 15,* 749–761.

Brody, M. (1985). Reply to Serafine and to Marantz on Serafine. *Cognition, 19,* 93–98.

Brown, H. (1985). *The effects of set content and temporal context of pitches on musicians' aural perception of tonality.* Unpublished, doctoral dissertation, Columbus, OH: The Ohio State University.

Brown, H. (1987, October). *Relationships between aural and visual analytic skills.* Paper presented to the College Music Society, New Orleans, LA.

Brown, H. (1988). The interplay of set content and temporal context in a functional theory of tonality perception. *Music Perception, 5,* 219–50.

Brown, H. (1992). Cognitive interpretations of functional chromaticism in tonal music. In M. R. Jones & S. Holleran (Eds.), *Cognitive bases of musical communication.* Washington, DC: American Psychological Association, 139–160.

Brown, H., & Butler, D. (1981). Diatonic trichords as minimal tonal cue-cells. *In Theory Only, 5*(6&7), 39–55.

Browne, R. (1981). Tonal implications of the diatonic set. *In Theory Only, 5*(6–7), 3–21.

Butler, D. (1980, August). *Some remarks on tonality cues and tonal stimuli.* Paper presented at the Third Workshop on Physical and Neuropsychological Foundations of Music, Ossiach, Austria.

Butler, D. (1983). The initial identification of tonal centers in music. In J. Sloboda & D. Rogers (Eds.), *Acquisition of symbolic skills.* New York: Plenum Press.

Butler, D. (1988). A study of event hierarchies in tonal and post-tonal music. *Psychology of Music*, *18*(1), 4–17.

Butler, D. (1989). Describing the perception of tonality in music: A proposal for a theory of intervallic rivalry. *Music Perception*, *6*, 219–41.

Butler, D. (1992). On pitch-set properties and perceptual attributes of the minor mode. In M. R. Jones & S. Holleran (Eds.), *Cognitive bases of musical communication*. Washington, DC: American Psychological Association, 161–69.

Butler, D., & Brown, H. (1984). Tonal function versus structure: Studies of the recognition of harmonic motion. *Music Perception*, *2*(1), 6–24.

Catel, C. S. (1801). *A treatise on harmony*. Novello's Theoretical Series, No. 5. London: J. A. Novello. (Original work published 1854)

Cazden, N. (1980). The definition of consonance and dissonance. *International Review of Aesthetics and Sociology of Music*, *11*, 123–68.

Deutsch, D. (1982). Grouping mechanisms in music. In D. Deutsch (Ed.), *The psychology of music*. New York: Academic Press.

Deutsch, D., & Feroe, J. (1981). The internal representation of pitch sequences in tonal music. *Psychological Review*, *88*, 503–22.

Forte, A. (1979). *Tonal harmony in concept and practice* (3rd ed). New York: Holt, Rinehart & Winston.

Hargreaves, D. (1986). *The developmental psychology of music*. Cambridge: Cambridge University Press.

Helmholtz, H. L. F. von. (1954). *On the sensations of tone as a physiological basis for the theory of music* (A. Ellis, Trans.). New York: Dover. (Original work published 1863)

Krumhansl, C. (1979). The psychological representation of musical pitch in a tonal context. *Cognitive Psychology*, *11*, 346–74.

Krumhansl, C. (1990, Spring). Tonal hierarchies and rare intervals in music cognition. *Music Perception*, *7*(3), 309–24.

Krumhansl, C., & Kessler, E. (1982). Tracing the dynamic changes in perceived tonal organization in a spatial representation of musical keys. *Psychological Review*, *89*, 334–68.

Meyer, L. B. (1956). *Emotion and meaning in music*. Chicago: University of Chicago Press.

Mitchell, W. (1962). The study of chromaticism. *Journal of Music Theory*, *6*, 2–31.

Moog, H. (1976). *The musical experience of the pre-school child* (C. Clarke, Trans.). London: Schott.

Piston, W. (1987). *Harmony*, (5th ed., rev. by M. DeVoto). New York: Norton.

Proctor, G. (1977). *Technical bases of nineteenth-century chromatic tonality: A study in chromaticism*. Unpublished doctoral dissertation, Princeton University, Princeton, NJ.

Riemann, H. (1895). *Harmony simplified; or, the theory of the tonal functions of chords* (H. Bewerunge, Trans.). London: Augener.

Schenker, H. (1906). *Neue musikalische Theorien und Phantasien. v. 1. Harmonielehre*. Vienna: Universal-Edition A.G. *Harmony* (E. M. Borgese, Trans.; O. Jonas, Ed.). Chicago: University of Chicago Press, 1954.

Schenker, H. (1979). *Free composition* (E. Oster, Trans.) New York: Longman, 1979. (Original work published 1935)

Schoenberg, A. (1911). *Harmonielehre*. Leipzig, Wien: Verlagseigentum der Universal-Edition. *Theory of harmony* (R. E. Carter, Trans.). Berkeley: University of California Press, 1978.

Serafine, M. (1988). *Music as cognition; The development of thought in sound*. New York: Columbia University Press.

Shuter-Dyson, R., & Gabriel, C. (1981). *The psychology of musical ability* (2nd ed.). London: Methuen.

Taylor, J. (1976). Perception of tonality in short melodies. *Journal of Research in Music Education*, 24(4), 197–208.

9

Tonality and Expectation

JAMSHED J. BHARUCHA

Introduction

Jamshed Bharucha's research has been highly influential in proposing that tonality gives rise to both expectations and aesthetic experiences (Bharucha, 1984). In this chapter Bharucha discusses how musical expectations are generated experimentally. He describes the relationship between tonal expectations, consonance, stability, and memory, and questions whether musical expectations are learned, innate, or based on the structure of the sounds themselves. His interest is in understanding the cognitive processes that underline tonal expectations and their acquisition. Bharucha points out that when listening to music listeners rejoice at what they already know; therefore, he asks, are they giving up the element of surprise or the element of familiarity? For Bharucha, tonal expectations are a compelling aspect of the aesthetic experience of listening to music. He divides expectations into two kinds: schematic expectations, which are culturally generic, automatic, and related to a general schema, and veridical expectations, which are related to the actual piece of music, to a specific memory.

Bharucha explains how he has used neural networks to account for certain findings about music perception. Neural networks are computer models that simulate brain-like systems based on fundamental principles of neural organization: they have been used to model human behavior. The application of neural networks to the perception of music is a promising and fast-growing area of research (see Bharucha, 1987 and 1991; Gjerdingen, 1989; Todd & Loy, 1991).

REFERENCES

Bharucha, J. J. (1984). Anchoring effects in music: the resolution of dissonance. *Cognitive Psychology, 16,* 485–518.

Bharucha, J. J. (1987a). MUSACT: A connectionist model of musical harmony. In *Ninth Annual Conference of the Cognitive Science Society* (pp. 508–17). Hillsdale, NJ: Erlbaum.

Bharucha, J. J. (1987b). Music cognition and perceptual facilitation. A connectionist framwork. *Music Perception, 5,* 1–30.

Bharucha, J. J. (1991). Tonality and learnability. In M. R. Jones & S. Holleran (Eds.), *Cognitive bases of musical communication.* Washington, DC: American Psychological Association.

Gjerdingen, R. O. (1989). Using connectionist models to explore complex musical patterns. *Computer Music Journal, 13*(3), 67–75.

Todd, P. M., & Loy, G. D. (Eds.) (1991). *Music and connectionism.* Cambridge, MA: MIT Press.

Why does a segment of music ending in a dominant chord generate strong expectations for the tonic to follow? What is the relationship between tonal expectations, consonance, stability, and memory? Are expectations of this kind learned, innate, or based on the structure of sound? If they are learned, how?

Some of these and related questions about tonality and expectation have been pondered through the ages by music theorists,[1] and today we benefit from a wealth of work on which to build. In this chapter I shall sketch an approach to these questions based on psychological experiments and computational modeling designed to explore the cognitive processes underlying tonal expectations,[2] their relationship to consonance, stability, and memory, and their acquisition.[3]

Tonal expectations are important to study for several reasons, including their role in the aesthetic experience of music, their role in the mental organization of music, their influence on consonance and dissonance, and their role in learning. The advantage of viewing these disparate phenomena in terms of expectation is that there is the promise that the processes that underlie expectations underlie aspects of these other phenomena as well.

The interested reader is directed to a substantial body of important work that will not be reviewed in this chapter, particularly work on the specific musical determinants of expectation (Meyer, 1956; Carlsen, Divenyi, & Taylor, 1970; Narmour, 1977, 1990; Carlsen, 1981; Schmuckler, 1989). The focus in this chapter will be on trying to understand the perceptual processes that underlie expectation. Toward this end, only a small set of specific musical expectations will be addressed—tonal harmonic expectations—by way of illustrating the potential of certain experimental and computational approaches. The reader is also directed to the work of Jones (1981a, 1981b) for a more overarching theoretical approach to understanding musical expectation.

Tonal Expectation and Aesthetics

Tonal expectations are a compelling aspect of our aesthetic experience of music. The deception of a deceptive cadence, the irresolution of a half cadence, and the finality of a final cadence are only the most obvious examples of tonal expectations at work in Western tonal music. Delayed resolution of tonal expectations is often a central distinguishing characteristic ascribed to late romantic composers such as Wagner. Tonal expectations can be found in other cultures as well. Some of the most dramatic moments of a performance of Indian classical music involve an eventual resolution to the tonal center after a prolonged yearning for it.

The most influential modern exponent of the role of expectation in musical aesthetics is Leonard Meyer (1956). According to a widely accepted view based largely on the work of Meyer, a piece of music in a familiar genre generates expectations, the subtle violation of which is emotionally important. There is considerable support in psychology for the relationship between expectancy violation and emotion (e.g., Mandler, 1984).[4]

Little, if any, work has been done by cognitive psychologists on the affective aspect of experiences associated with expectation. In contrast, a fair amount of research has been done on the processing of sound that leads up to (and is a prerequisite to) this affective experience. This chapter thus focuses exclusively on trying to understand these prerequisite processes, without taking a position on the nature or interpretation of the affective experience induced thereby.

The Puzzle of Expectations

There is a puzzle concerning the role of expectations in music that Dowling and Harwood (1986) call "Wittgenstein's paradox": The puzzle is that when we are familiar with a piece of music, there can be no more surprises. Hence if expectancy violation is aesthetically important, a piece would lose this quality as it becomes familiar.

Attempts to resolve this apparent paradox often postulate a mental structure, called a schema (Dowling & Harwood, 1986), that has assimilated the music of a genre over a lifetime of experience. The expectations produced by this system are generic in that they represent the most likely transitions in one's musical culture.[5] They are also automatic, in the sense that they cannot easily be suppressed. Even when a given piece has been heard often enough to be familiar, it cannot completely override the generic, automatic expectations. Surprises in a new piece thus continue to have a surprising quality because they are heard as surprises relative to these irrepressible expectations.

This line of reasoning seems necessary but cannot be sufficient. If the surprises in a new piece continue to be surprises even after repeated hearing, the piece would never sound familiar. Furthermore, a performer playing from a schematic representation would be unable to predict the next event, but would instead drift into the most generic progression; the performer would, for example, always follow a dominant chord with a tonic. Using this explanation, you either give up surprise or you give up familiarity.

Yet it clearly must be the case that an atypical transition in a familiar piece is both familiar and surprising. It is familiar in a sense and surprising in another. It is thus necessary to postulate two kinds of expectations, which may be called *schematic* and *veridical* (Bharucha, 1987a). Schematic expectations are the automatic, culturally generic expectations mentioned above. They must be generated by a system that has learned to expect the events that are the most likely. Veridical expectations are for the actual next event in a familiar piece, even though this next event may be schematically unexpected. They must be generated by a system that has learned that particular piece. Since schematic expectancies are acquired from hearing many individual pieces, the two kinds of expectancies will converge more often than not for pieces typical of one's musical culture. Sometimes they will diverge, however, creating the sense of violation of which Meyer wrote.

Expectation and Mental Representation

The existence of two kinds of expectations suggests (but doesn't require) the existence of two systems that generate them. These may be called a *schema* and a *memory*, which generate schematic and veridical expectancies, respectively. A schema is a term used by cognitive psychologists to refer to a mental representation of generic relationships. The memory, in contrast, would represent specific sequences of music in a way that enables them to be retrieved (recognized or recalled) individually. A schema enables one to recognize the style of a new piece; a memory enables one to recognize a particular piece.[6]

A schema generates expectations for events (such as chords) that *typically* follow. A schema thus embodies the information that would generate *typical* hierarchies of stability. These hierarchies, called *tonal hierarchies*, reflect the relative stability of tones or chords in given key-inducing contexts.

A memory, in contrast, generates expectations for events that *actually* follow in a particular familiar piece of music. A memory thus embodies the information that would enable a listener to recognize an error in a familiar piece, and that would enable a performer to play the correct note, however schematically unexpected.

Expected events are heard as more consonant and more stable than unexpected events, as will be seen below. Thus expectation, consonance, and stability covary with the musical context. If this is true, these terms refer to slightly different experiential aspects of the same underlying process.

The activation of a schema while listening means that, in addition to hearing the sounded pitch events (along with their temporal, timbral, and other qualities), schematic expectations are generated and are fulfilled or violated to varying degrees, with concomitant effects on stability. The schema thus imposes a cultural elaboration on the sounded events. Elaboration is widespread in perception and cognition (see Anderson, 1990). While reading a story, for example, inferences are drawn and familiar themes are triggered. These happen automatically, unavoidably, and constitute a mental elaboration of the text.

The representations postulated by Lerdahl and Jackendoff (1983) and by Deutsch and Feroe (1981) are essentially representations of mentally elaborated pieces of music. According to Lerdahl and Jackendoff, a piece of tonal music is represented as an inverted tree, of which the pitch-time events of the piece are at the terminal branches (see Figure 9.1). An inverted tree diagram shows levels of abstraction from the piece of music (eighth-note level, quarter-note level, etc.).

FIGURE 9.1. An inverted tree diagram shows levels of abstraction from the piece of music (eighth-note level, quarter-note level, etc.). A branch that terminates at a longer branch represents the subordination of an event to a more stable event. The most stable event (E in the last measure) is represented by the uninterrupted trunk of the tree. The increasing levels of abstraction are written out in musical notation below the score of the piece. (Reprinted from Lerdahl & Jackendoff, 1983. Copyright © 1983 by M.I.T. Press.)

A branch that terminates at a longer branch represents the subordination of an event to a more stable event. The most stable event (E in the last measure) is represented by the uninterrupted trunk of the tree.

A piece of music is thus represented simultaneously at various levels of abstraction. We may call this an *event hierarchy* (see Bharucha, 1984). An event hierarchy specifies how the events in a particular piece are organized hierarchically. An event hierarchy is a hierarchy of specific pitch-time events (e.g., a particular C in this piece dominates the D passing tone following it; see Figure 9.1). In contrast, a tonal hierarchy is a hierarchy of pitch classes (e.g., when the key of C major has been established, C's are in general more stable than D's). An event hierarchy is a mentally elaborated representation of the piece of music.

Lerdahl and Jackendoff specify a set of rules for determining which branches fuse into larger branches, and which of two fusing branches dominates the other. One of their rules determines which of two branches dominates based on which is more stable. How does the listener know which is more stable? This is precisely what the tonal hierarchy specifies. An event hierarchy thus presupposes a tonal hierarchy. The tonal hierarchy, generated continuously by the schema, is the cultural elaboration that is imposed on the music, thereby enabling it to be heard as an event hierarchy.

In the areas of visual perception and language, a debate has raged among cognitive psychologists as to whether events are stored in memory in the pristine form in which they occur or whether the elaboration is stored together with them. For example, are the inferences and themes that are automatically triggered while reading a story stored along with the words themselves? In the case of stories, there seems little doubt that aspects of the elaboration are stored; in fact, it's more likely that the reader will be able to recall the theme than the text of the story itself.

The evidence from cognitive domains other than music thus strongly suggests that a piece of music is remembered not just as a recording of the sound but in all its mentally elaborated glory.[7] Storing the entire event hierarchy would make it possible to retrieve selected levels. In this way, one could recall the piece at abstract levels of the tree without having to play it back in one's head, note by note. This possibility seems congruent with casual experience.

The following is a summary of experimental and computational work that supports aspects of the theoretical framework sketched here—in particular, schematic expectations, their relationship to consonance and stability, and an exploration of how they might be learned.

The Measurement of Schematic Expectations

Tonal expectations have been studied quite exhaustively, both theoretically (Narmour, 1977, 1990) and empirically (Carlsen, Divenyi, & Taylor, 1970; Carlsen, 1981; Schmuckler, 1989). The experiments discussed below employ a method called priming. They were designed to measure schematic expectations in such a way as to provide some insight into the underlying processes. They were also designed to be able to detect schematic expectancies in the minds of listeners with no formal musical training whatsoever.

In the priming task, listeners hear a musical sample (called the prime) followed by a chord (called the target chord). If the target is an expected chord, it should be processed more quickly than if it is an unexpected chord. Speed of processing is a widely accepted measure of expectancy in cognitive psychology. This is because expectation is thought to play a preparatory role. If something is expected, the perceptual system prepares for it; if that expected event occurs, the advance preparation results in faster processing. This is an adaptive strategy because it enables us to anticipate events in our environment.

In order to measure the speed with which the target is processed, it is essential to have the listener make some binary judgment about it and then press a button indicating the judgment. A computer records which button was pressed and the elapsed time from the onset of the target to the button press (called the reaction time). Since we are interested in the time it takes to process the target in a musically meaningful way (as opposed to the time to simply detect its presence), the binary judgment must be one that focuses the listener's attention on a musically relevant aspect of the target. The judgment we chose was an intonation judgment. On half the trials, the target was mistuned by flattening the fifth degree of the chord by approximately 1/4 of a semitone. The listener's task is therefore to press one designated button if the target is in-tune and another if it is out-of-tune.

In order to remove all subjectivity from the intonation judgment, the main experiment is preceded by a session in which target chords are presented in the absence of primes, and listeners are given feedback as to the correctness or incorrectness of their response. Thus the criterion for what counts as in-tune and what counts as out-of-tune is established objectively for all subjects. This last point is critical in order to study listeners who have had no formal musical training. When this group of listeners is studied in experiments, their responses often show very little clear structure with open-ended judgments (such as "rate the intonation on a scale from 1 to 7"), and the subjects express considerable uncertainty about what they are doing, because they are inexperienced at making such judgments. When the judgment is binary and there is a correct and incorrect answer, however, these subjects understand the task immediately and reveal clear patterns in their responses.

A binary true/false judgment is also useful for studying professional composers or theorists. This group tends to be understandably skeptical about the validity of making such simplistic judgments as are used in psychological experiments, and also finds that they can't help making the judgments based on their analytical knowledge. But when there are clearly defined correct and incorrect answers (and when they are persuaded by the experimenter that "correct" and "incorrect" do not imply value judgments), they abandon their theoretical qualms and seek to maximize the percent of trials they get correct (which is displayed at the end of the experiment).

Another reason for employing an intonation judgment is that it enables us to study how the perceived consonance of a chord is influenced on the basis of whether or not it was expected. To summarize, the priming task using an intonation judgment has two goals: (1) to measure expectation using reaction time, and (2) to study the effect of expectation on consonance. The task is designed so as to pursue these goals for musically untrained as well as trained listeners.

From trial to trial, the experimenter varies the degree to which the target chord is expected[8] given the prime. In the simplest such experiment (Bharucha & Stoeckig, 1986, experiments 2 and 3), the prime was a single chord, and the target was either most highly expected or most highly unexpected given the prime. Thus if the prime was C major, the target was either G major or F-sharp major, as shown in Figure 9.2 (all keys were used in the experiment).[9]

This yielded four types of trials: in-tune expected, out-of-tune expected, in-tune unexpected, and out-of-tune unexpected. The listeners only needed to concern themselves explicitly with whether or not the target was in-tune or out-of-tune.

The results were as follows. First, listeners were faster and more accurate, on average, to make intonation judgments for the expected chords than for the unexpected chords (see table). This demonstrates that the process underlying expectation is one of preparation or facilitation. It is as if a representation of the expected chord had been mentally activated even before the chord occurred, based on its being highly probable in the familiar tonal style.

The second central result was that listeners were faster and more likely to respond "in-tune" when the chord was expected than when it was unexpected, or, equivalently, they were faster and more likely to respond "out-of-tune" when the chord was unexpected than when it was expected. This indicates that expected chords sounded more consonant, or, equivalently, unexpected chords sounded more dissonant. This result shows starkly that there are at least two determinants of consonance. One is the relationship between simultaneous sounds. This in turn is based on the way sound interacts with the inner ear (see below) as well as learning. The second determinant is the relationship between

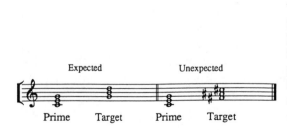

FIGURE 9.2. The design of the priming experiment (Bharucha & Stoeckig, 1986). The figure shows root position triads in close position only to illustrate the difference between expected and unexpected. The actual chords heard by the subjects were considerably more complex (see note 9).

Results of priming experiment
(in milliseconds)

	Expected	Unexpected
In-tune	788	982
Out-of-tune	864	803
Average	826	893

two sequential sounds. This, it is claimed here, is primarily learned and is mediated by expectations.

Both effects described above were observed for rank novices and professionals alike. The novices were novices only insofar as they had no formal training and no experience playing an instrument. But by virtue of having grown up in a particular culture (in this case, the United States), they have presumably learned what to expect from extended passive exposure.

It is important to note that expected events aren't necessarily preferred over unexpected events. This caution about expectation holds true of consonance and stability as well. If there is any relationship between expectation and its associated concepts, on the one hand, and preference, on the other, it takes the form of an inverted-U function (see Dowling & Harwood, 1986, for a discussion): A moderate amount of violation of expectations is generally preferred over always fulfilling expectations or always violating them.

Even this trend should be viewed with some caution. People who are immersed in experimenting with new musical forms may develop preferences based on phenomena other than expectation, consonance, and stability. Although a composer may have exposure to several genres, including some that are very different from tonal-harmonic music, and would thus develop a rather diverse set of schemata, it is almost impossible to escape exposure to tonal-harmonic music if one grows up in a Western society. Tonal-harmonic music pervades television, radio, supermarkets, and the dominant popular forms of music. Some of the subjects in the above priming experiment were composers who viewed the experiment with grave suspicion, seriously doubted they would show any evidence of schematic tonal expectations, and asserted their lack of preference for expected tonal events. Nevertheless, they showed the same pattern of results as novices. A person is in a sense a prisoner of the schematic expectations driven by the inadvertent learning of musical patterns that pervade the environment.

This means that it is difficult to suppress schematic expectations. Can this be demonstrated empirically? In one experiment, 80% of the trials contained highly unexpected chords and only 20% contained highly expected chords. Even over a session of 100 trials, the chords that were processed more quickly were those that were traditionally expected even though they were in the clear minority during the session (Bharucha & Stoeckig, 1989). Distorting the musical environment in this way was not sufficient to wipe out a lifetime of exposure.

In another experiment, each prime-target pair was played twice in succession. For example, in an "unexpected" trial, the subject would hear C-F-sharp-pause-C-F-sharp. The last chord was mistuned on half the trials, and subjects had to decide whether it was in-tune or out-of-tune. The last chord, F-sharp, is schematically unexpected (since it rarely follows C) but veridically expected (since it actually follows C and the subject knows the same pair will be repeated). Nevertheless, schematically expected chords are still processed more quickly than schematically unexpected chords (Bharucha & Stoeckig, 1989). These experiments thus provide some preliminary evidence that schematic expectations are very difficult to suppress.

Expectation and Tonal Hierarchies

There has been a more extensive study to date of tonal hierarchies than of expectations. Since one of the claims in this chapter is that the processes that underlie schematic expectations may also be responsible for tonal hierarchies, a summary of research on tonal hierarchies is relevant.

Tonal hierarchies have been studied most exhaustively by Krumhansl (1979, 1990; Krumhansl & Shepard, 1979). The term "tonal hierarchy" signifies the relative differences in stability of tonal elements. For example, when the key of C major has been strongly established during a piece of music, the diatonic tones (C, D, E, F, G, A, B) are more stable than the nondiatonic tones. If a different key is established, a different set of tones will be the stable diatonic set. Among the diatonic set in any given key, the tonic is the most stable, and the major third and perfect fifth are generally more stable than the remaining four.

Although this tonal hierarchy for tones in the context of an established key is well known from elementary music theory of the common practice period, Krumhansl sought to quantify this hierarchy. Among the many advantages of quantifying a tonal hierarchy are the following. First, although the tonal hierarchy is quite clear when a key is strongly and unambiguously established, it is less clear when a key is weakly established or when there is more than one established key (as in polytonality). A quantification of tonal hierarchies makes it possible to track the development of keys even in the latter case. For example, there has been considerable debate as to whether the opening passage of Stravinsky's *Petroushka* is simultaneously in C major and F-sharp major or, alternatively, in no key at all. By quantifying the tonal hierarchy in this passage, Krumhansl and Schmuckler (1986) were able to determine that indeed both keys, C major and F-sharp major, were established.

A second advantage (perhaps the more significant psychologically) of quantifying the tonal hierarchies is that it makes it possible to depict tonal relationships spatially. For example, the circle of fifths is a spatial depiction of the relationships between major keys (see Figure 9.3). A single spatial representation such as a circle captures, all at once, the many pairwise relationships between

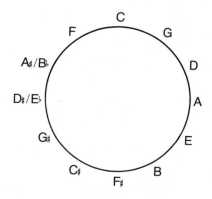

FIGURE 9.3. The circle of fifths.

the 12 possible major keys. Thus, instead of individually enumerating the relationship between all the keys (e.g., C is most closely related to G and F, less closely related to D and B-flat and so on, G is most closely related to D and C, less closely related to A and F, and so on, and so forth), a single diagram with the 12 keys labeled shows all the relationships simultaneously. The advantage is even more striking if minor keys are included. A single spatial representation that captures all these pairwise relationships at once provides a vivid insight into the psychological representation of tonality. That is not to say that the same spatial representation necessarily exists physically in the brain.[10] Rather, it means that the physical representation in the brain encodes the information that is contained in the spatial representation.[11]

At this point one might be inclined to ask why quantification of tonal hierarchies is an advance, since music theorists have a long tradition of tracking keys and employing spatial representations (the circle of fifths, in particular). The answer is that methods of quantification permit us to investigate tonal hierarchies in the minds of listeners other than theorists, who, after all, have extensive formal training and who, by the very nature of the enterprise, adopt a highly analytical stance toward listening.

The method Krumhansl has used most extensively to investigate tonal hierarchies is called the *probe tone technique,* originally developed with Roger Shepard (Krumhansl & Shepard, 1979). In this technique subjects hear a musical context followed by a probe tone. The musical context could be either a musical scale, a chord, a chord progression, or an actual sample of music. The *probe tone* is picked at random from the 12 chromatic pitch classes. The listener's task is to rate how well the probe tone fits within the musical context by rating it on a scale from 1 to 7. The context is then repeated and a different probe tone is presented. The context has been fully probed when all 12 chromatic pitch classes have been presented. This process may be repeated for the same listener and also repeated for many listeners, yielding several replications of each of the 12 probe tones. The ratings for each probe tone are averaged across the replications, yielding 12 numbers, one for each probe tone. This set of 12 numbers is called a *profile* (see Figure 9.4).

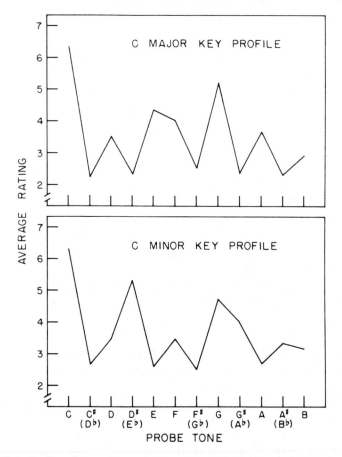

FIGURE 9.4. Profiles for major and minor keys. The rating for any given probe tone depicts the perceived stability of that tone in that key. The profiles are shown with respect to C major and minor for convenience only. (Reprinted from Krumhansl & Kessler, 1982. Copyright © 1982 by the American Psychological Association. Reprinted by permission.)

When the musical sample establishes a key strongly and unambiguously (e.g., a IV-V-I cadence), the profile shows the tonic being the most highly rated, followed by the other two tones of the tonic triad, followed by the remaining diatonic tones (Krumhansl, 1979, 1990). The profiles from samples with a strong and unambiguous key are averaged and the resulting profile is used as a standard profile for that key. The standard profiles for the 24 major and minor keys constitute the standards against which the profiles of samples with weaker or more ambiguous keys are assessed.

Krumhansl and Kessler (1982) showed how one can track the development of keys in a musical sample of interest. To do this, the profile obtained for that sample is correlated with each of the 24 standard profiles. The strength of the sample's correlation[12] with a key standard indicates the strength of that key in the sample as of the moment at which the probe was presented. By probing a piece of music at different points in time, the development and change of keys over time can be tracked.

To represent the relationships between keys spatially, the standard profiles for the 12 major and minor keys are themselves correlated with each other. The higher the correlation between two keys, the closer they are in the spatial representation. Thus C major is highly correlated with G major and F major, as well as with A minor and C minor, and therefore needs to be located close to them. In addition, it has a range of correlations with the other keys, which must therefore be located at corresponding distances. Simultaneously satisfying all these constraints is very difficult. This is accomplished by a computerized method called multidimensional scaling, developed by Shepard (1964). Krumhansl and Kessler (1982) found that the spatial representation that best satisfies these multiple constraints is a torus. A torus requires four dimensions, but for convenience can be imagined in three dimensions as a doughnut, with the proviso that the inner and outer perimeters of the doughnut be equal (which is why three dimensions don't suffice). This solution captures the circle of fifths for major keys and for minor keys, and puts the two together in such as way as to preserve the relative and parallel major-minor relationships. The relative positions of keys on the torus can be examined by cutting it and unfolding it into a flat sheet, as shown in Figure 9.5. A torus results from joining the top and bottom edges

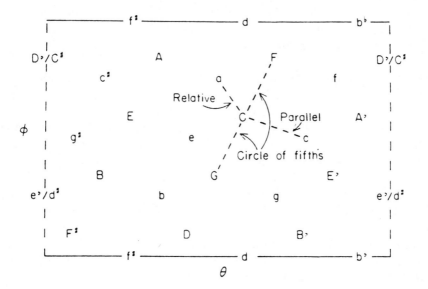

FIGURE 9.5. An equivalent two-dimensional map of the multidimensional scaling solution of the 24 major and minor keys. (Reprinted from Krumhansl & Kessler, 1982. Copyright © 1982 by the American Psychological Association. Reprinted by permission.)

together and joining the left and right edges together. If you actually try this with a piece of paper, it will either wrinkle or rip, which is why an additional dimension is needed.[13]

Tonal hierarchies usually, but not always, reflect the frequency of occurrence of tones just heard: tones heard more often are judged to be more stable. When American college students were tested with samples of North Indian music, for example, their profiles were very similar to those of Indian students (Castellano, Bharucha, & Krumhansl, 1984). The profiles of both groups of listeners matched the hierarchies described by theorists of Indian music (Jairazbhoy, 1971), but they also reflected the frequency of occurrence of tones in the samples. This should not be surprising: Tones that are heard as stable have typically occurred more often in the preceding sample. Numerous studies of note counts (summarized extensively by Krumhansl, 1990) show this to be true. In tonal music of the common practice period, tonics tend to occur most often, followed by the other tones of the tonic triad, and then the remaining diatonic tones. Tonal pieces tend to reveal their tonality in the selection of pitch classes and their relative priority. Tonal hierarchies obtained in these experiments thus show, at the very least, that listeners have a memory system that can integrate the pitch classes heard in the immediately preceding sample (called the *proximal context*). This integrated representation then leads them to hear pitch classes that immediately follow as being differentiated on the basis of stability.

The distribution of pitch classes in the proximal context is not the sole determinant of the tonal hierarchy. The profiles of the Indian students in the study by Castellano, Bharucha, and Krumhansl (1984) were found to be influenced by an additional factor: past exposure (called the *distal context*) to these musical forms. This determination was made by a regression analysis. A regression analysis enables one to determine the extent to which different factors contribute individually to an outcome. After determining that frequency of occurrence of pitch classes in the proximal context was the strongest determinant of the profiles for both American and Indian listeners, frequency of occurrence was factored out, and the residual portions of the profiles were analyzed for the influence of additional factors. The residuals of the Indian listeners correlated with profiles based on music theory (Jairazbhoy), whereas the residuals of the American listeners did not. Since the essential difference between the two groups of listeners was their background, it can be concluded that the ratings given by the Indian listeners were based in part on their familiarity with that genre and not just on the information contained in the proximal context.

It is this residual effect of the distal context—that is, prior exposure—that justifies the postulation of a schema, a mental structure that encodes the regularities of a genre as opposed to the specifics of individual pieces. There must nevertheless be enough information in the proximal context to engage the appropriate schema; after all, we have schemas for many things, possibly even many different musical genres. The information in the proximal context (such as relative occurrence of different pitch classes) serves to activate the appropriate schema, which then generates expectancies that may compensate for the absence of tones that typically occur in those contexts.

There may be other determinants of tonality besides the distribution of pitch classes in either the proximal or distal context. Among them are the rareness of the intervals (see Chapter 8 by Butler and Brown in this volume).

Can Schematic Expectation Be Explained by the Structure of Sound and the Physiology of the Ear?

Consider two tones an octave apart, each containing eight harmonics. Every harmonic of the higher tone is present in the lower tone, and every second harmonic of the lower tone is present in the higher tone. This can be represented by the ratio 1:2, which, for convenience, we shall call the *overlap ratio*. Now consider two tones a perfect fifth apart. Every second harmonic of the higher tone is present in the lower tone, and every third harmonic of the lower tone is present in the higher tone. This interval has an overlap ratio of 2:3. For two tones a perfect fourth apart, every third harmonic in the higher tone is present in the lower tone, and every fourth harmonic in the lower tone is present in the higher tone. This interval has an overlap ratio of 3:4. If you are familiar with how these intervals sound, you know that an octave is the most consonant interval, followed by the perfect fifth, followed by the perfect fourth. As the overlap ratio gets more complex, the intervals sound more dissonant.

Pythagoras, the ancient Greek mathematician and philosopher, arrived at the same ratios more than 2,000 years ago on the basis of the lengths of stretched strings. A string player produces an octave above an open string by stopping the string at half its length, and produces a perfect fifth by stopping the string at two-thirds of its length, and so on. Since Pythagoras couldn't have known much about harmonics, and even less about the workings of the ear, he concluded that there was something inherently special about simple ratios. Today the most compelling account of why consonance is related to ratio simplicity is in terms of how the harmonics affect the inner ear.

The inner ear serves as a prism for sound: it separates sound into its various frequency (pure tone) components. For example, a tone with eight harmonics will cause the basilar membrane in the inner ear to vibrate at eight different places along its length. The vibration of the basilar membrane causes hair cells that are lined up against it to respond. The response of these hair cells thus constitutes a (spatial) representation of the sound spectrum.

Two frequencies that are very close together cause the basilar membrane to vibrate at two points that are close together. Under these circumstances, the membrane's response to one interferes with its response to the other. This produces a sensation of roughness that is typically heard as dissonant. Thus the more complex the overlap ratio between two tones, the greater is the extent to which the vibrations of the basilar membrane caused by one will interfere with those caused by the other, and the more dissonant the tones will sound together.

If the consonance of intervals can be explained by spectral overlap, can other relationships in musical harmony be explained in a similar way? At first glance, this approach might seem promising. Chords that are considered most closely related tend to have tones in common—e.g., tonic-dominant, parallel major and minor, and relative major and minor relationships. In contrast, chords that are considered most unrelated have no tones in common, C and F-sharp major. Could it be that schematic expectations are simply driven by common tones?

To answer this question, the priming paradigm mentioned earlier was employed. In the original priming experiments, the expected target chord was one step away from the prime chord along the circle of fifths; for example, if the prime was C major, the target was G major. Notice that these two chords share a component tone (as well as all the harmonics of this shared tone). In contrast, the unexpected target was diametrically opposite the prime chord on the circle, and these two chords share no component tones. Thus the faster and more accurate responses to the expected chord could possibly be due simply to the fact that some of its tone components had just been heard. To eliminate this problem, it was necessary for the expected target to have no shared tones with the prime. This condition is easily met by selecting a target two steps away from the prime along the circle of fifths. For example, a C major prime leads to a greater expectation for D major than for F-sharp major, yet shares tones with neither. To strengthen the case, all harmonics that were common to the prime and target were removed, thereby ensuring that the expected target wasn't favored because of its physical similarity to the prime. In spite of this, the expected chord was processed faster and more accurately and was more likely to be judged in-tune than the unexpected chord (Bharucha & Stoeckig, 1987).

There are purely theoretical reasons to reject spectral overlap as the sole determinant of schematic expectations. Consider the following pairs of major triads: C-D versus C-A. C and D do not share any tones, whereas C and A share one tone (E). Thus C and D have less spectral overlap than do C and A. Yet C and D are considered to be more closely related to each other than are C and A, because they are closer along the circle of fifths of chords (see Figure 9.3).

Before rejecting spectral overlap as the basis for harmony, however, perhaps we should question the validity of the circle of fifths for chords. The circle of fifths is typically used to describe the relationship between keys (of the same mode). The (shortest) number of steps from one key to another along the perimeter of the circle represents exactly the number of tones present in the diatonic set of one key but not in the diatonic set of the other. For keys (of the same mode), then, spectral overlap (i.e., the intersection of the diatonic sets of different keys) exactly mirrors the circle of fifths. For chords, however, it does not. Yet the circle of fifths accurately describes the harmonic distances between chords, because chords closer on the circle are more likely to occur in the same tonal piece (they have more parent keys in common).

Since we cannot rest our case on the mere use of the circle of chords as a descriptive device, a test is needed. The appropriate test is to see whether a chord generates stronger expectations for a chord that is closer on the circle of fifths but doesn't share a tone than for a chord that is further but does share a tone. This experimental design pits convention against acoustics in determining expectations. If schematic expectations are acoustically driven, C major would generate stronger expectations for E major (with which it shares a tone) than for D major (with which it shares no tones).[14] If, on the other hand, schematic expectations are driven by a schema that has encoded the chord relationships on the basis of their conventional typicality, C major should generate stronger expectations for D major than for E major. Recent results support the latter outcome (Tekman & Bharucha, 1991).

If schematic expectations are driven by spectral overlap, then any impairment of one's ability to process auditory spectra ought to be accompanied by a corresponding diminution of schematic expectations while listening to music. A man suffered a stroke that destroyed much of the auditory cortex of his brain. Although he could detect the presence of sounds at almost normal levels, he simply could not tell the difference between the in-tune and out-of-tune chords used in the priming experiments. He was unable to detect a mistuning so severe that people with normal hearing cringe almost without exception. In the priming task, his performance was never much above 50%, which would be expected from sheer guessing. What is remarkable is that he tended to judge expected targets to be in-tune and unexpected targets to be out-of-tune (Tramo, Bharucha, & Musiek, 1990). In other words, his sense of schematic expectation was intact even though his ability to process fine-grained spectral information was severely impaired. It seems that as long as some auditory information get through, the relevant schema can be activated, thereby generating schematic expectations. This is good news for people who experience a diminished ability to process the full range of the audible spectrum, as is typical with age.[15]

Even the relative consonance of simultaneously sounded tones cannot entirely be explained by the structure of sound and the mechanical characteristics of the ear. For otherwise one should be able to synthesize artificial sounds that have very different spectra, as Pierce (1969, 1983) has done, and predict the relative consonance of intervals formed with these tones. Although there is evidence for this using tones with nonharmonic partials that are so discrepant from harmonics that the tone has no clear pitch (Geary, 1980), cases in which the tones have clear pitch reveal an overwhelming tendency to hear the intervals as we are accustomed to.

Consider a clarinet tone, which has very little energy at the even-numbered harmonics. If the fundamental frequency is 440 Hz, the next harmonic would be $440 \times 3 = 1320$ Hz. The tone that should sound most consonant with the 440-

Hz tone is one whose fundamental frequency is 1320. All the harmonics present in the higher tone would also be present in the lower tone, and every third harmonic in the lower tone would also be present in the higher tone, yielding a 1:3 ratio of spectral overlap. This yields an interval of an octave and a fifth. Two clarinet tones an octave apart have no spectral overlap at all. If spectral overlap is the sole determinant of consonance, two clarinet tones should sound more consonant when they are an octave and a fifth apart than when they are an octave apart. Indeed, many other intervals should sound more consonant than an octave. Although this has not been tested with a careful laboratory experiment, the clear sense from hearing clarinet tones is that the intervals that are the most consonant (the octave, for example) are the same as with other instruments. Once again, this must be because of the effect of prior exposure to other instruments and human speech, which do contain even-numbered harmonics. One can only speculate about how the various intervals would sound if our only auditory exposure was to clarinet-like timbres.

One is compelled to conclude that there is much more to the perception of harmony, and the schematic expectations that are such a salient part of it, than is determined by the structure of sound and the mechanical properties of the ear. But it is a mistake to discount these factors completely. Since the time of Helmholtz (1885/1954), the notion that relationships in harmony can be explained by aspects of the structure of sound and processes in early audition has been a leading hypothesis and remains so today (see Parncutt, 1989). It would be surprising if the conventions that have been established were chosen arbitrarily. Factors such as spectral overlap and the consonance and dissonance it engenders may have played a role in the early establishment of the conventions that today drive our perception. One can imagine musicians in ancient and medieval times experimenting with combinations of tones and finding certain combinations to be more consonant than others, based entirely on spectral overlap. The ensuing choices then became convention, and today we are so inundated with music that adheres to those conventions that our internalization of those conventions can compensate to some extent when spectral overlap fails.

How Expectations May Be Learned:
Neural Net Modeling

The above evidence forces us to conclude that tonal expectations must be either innate or learned. There are obvious problems with the innateness hypothesis. First, although it is axiomatic that we must be innately endowed with a mechanism capable of supporting schematic expectations, it is difficult to think of the evolutionary pressures that would have given rise to the specific schematic expectations that occur in the perception of Western tonal music by Western listeners.

Cross-cultural studies would, of course, shed some light on how different or similar schematic expectations are around the world.[16] It is important to note, however, that universality does not imply innateness (see Bharucha & Olney, 1989). Studies with infants can only be suggestive because perceptual learning can occur very early, possibly even in utero.

Perhaps the most compelling argument against the innateness hypothesis is the existence of a plausible learning hypothesis. If schematic expectancies can be easily learned by mere exposure, there is no reason for them to have been wired innately. Much of the work in music cognition (as well as work on artificially intelligent musical systems) consists of postulating rules. This approach is most pronounced in the case of grammars. This work is invaluable because the rules serve as crystallizations of the constraints on the system. In particular, they characterize the knowledge that a musical schema must exhibit. Psychologists are often interested in also understanding the mechanisms that underlie the encoding of this knowledge. From this point of view, it is interesting to ask how the properties that are captured by rules are learned by passive exposure.

Recent advances in our understanding of how brainlike systems might learn provide an opportunity to explore how musical schemas might be learned (Rumelhart & McClelland, 1986). Models of brainlike systems are broadly referred to as neural nets, connectionist models, or parallel distributed models. These are, in turn, a special subset of a larger class of models that may simply be called associative networks.

In associative models, objects or features in the world are represented by units (or nodes). Representational units are linked together to form a network. The network as a whole represents the complex array of relationships between the objects represented by the units. The state of activation of a unit represents the degree to which the represented object is attended (suggested, implied, or expected).

If a network contains units that represent musical objects such as tones and chords, the connections between these units collectively encode the relationships that hold between these tones and chords as they are typically used. The state of activation of a unit represents the degree to which that tone or chord is currently being attended. A unit may be activated directly by a stimulus in the environment, such as a tone or chord, or indirectly through an associative network of such units. When a unit is indirectly activated, that tone or chord is suggested, implied, or expected. [17]

There are many arguments in favor of understanding music cognition in terms of associative networks. First, they easily accommodate ambiguities, with which music is rife. Many units can be active simultaneously to varying degrees, representing varying degrees to which different tones, chords, or keys are suggested. Second, they fill in missing pieces that are parts of typical patterns. For example, if the root and fifth of a triad are played, a network will suggest the major and minor third in proportion to their association with the prior context. Or if an F major chord is followed by a G major chord, the representational unit for C major will be strongly activated, representing a strong expectation for C major.

There are at least two additional arguments in favor of neural net models specifically. First, they are based on fundamental principles of neural organization in the brain. Second, and most important, they can learn.

Learning in a neural net model occurs by changing the strength of the connections between representational units. Consider a neural net that receives its input via units that represent octave-equivalent pitch classes (shown at the bottom of Figure 9.6a). Each such unit is said to be tuned to a particular pitch class. This is a valid assumption given that there are neurons in the auditory system that are tuned to specific frequency ranges and are laid out spatially according to frequency.[18]

Now suppose that this set of units is connected to another set of units that initially do not have any specialization (labeled "unspecialized" in Figure 9.6a). Each pitch class unit is connected to each unspecialized unit (the connections are not shown in the figure), such that the strengths of the connections are initially random. When a combination of tones is sounded, say an F-sharp major chord, the units representing the tones F-sharp, A-sharp, and C-sharp are activated (as shown by filled circles in Figure 9.6b). They in turn activate the unspecialized units. Since the connection strengths are initially random, the activations of the activation levels of the unspecialized units will be random.

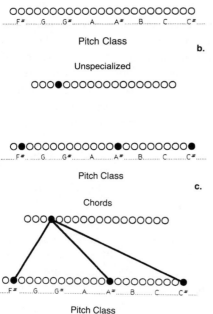

FIGURE 9.6. A neural network learning to represent typical combinations of tones. (a) Pitch class units in the bottom layer are connected to unspecialized units in the top layer via connections with random strengths. (b) In response to a combination of tones (F-sharp, A-sharp, C-sharp), the corresponding pitch class units are activated, and in turn activate the specialized units, one of which wins over the others. (c) The connections between the activated pitch class units and the winning unspecialized unit are strengthened, producing a unit that is now specialized for that combination of pitch classes.

A principle found in many parts of the brain is that units within a layer inhibit each other in proportion to their activation. The consequence of this is that only the most highly activated unspecialized unit remains active, and the others are shut down. So in response to the F-sharp major chord, some arbitrary unspecialized unit (the filled circle in Figure 9.6b) is going to win over the others in that set.

At this point, learning occurs by changing the strengths of the connections between the pitch class units and the winning unspecialized unit. The strengths are changed according to Hebb's (1949) rule: A connection becomes stronger in proportion to the product of the activations of the two units it connects. Since the F-sharp, A-sharp, and C-sharp pitch class units are the only pitch class units activated, their connections to the winning unit become strengthened (indicated by bold lines in Figure 9.6c) and the other connections to the winning unit become weakened. This winning unit has now become specialized to respond to F-sharp major chords. It will be even more likely to win the next time an F-sharp major chord occurs and will be even less likely to win in response to some other chord.

In this way, specialized representational units can form for all combinations of musical events that occur with great regularity. This process can be continued to yet another set of units to which the newly formed chord units are connected. This third set can become specialized to respond to typical combinations of chords, such as tonic, dominant, and subdominant.

Consider an idealized end-product of this learning scheme. It consists of pitch class units connected to units representing their parent chords, and chord units connected to units representing their parent keys, as shown in Figure 9.7 (see Bharucha, 1987a, 1987b, for details). The minor chord units are shown below the pitch class units for convenience only. Furthermore, the chords are shown in a systematic order for illustrative convenience only. What's important is the pattern of connectivity between units, not the layout of the units themselves.

After learning, the network can be tested to see if it has any interesting properties. When presented with the tones C, E, and G, units representing the chords that contain any of these tones are activated. These chord units in turn activate all units representing tones that are contained in these chords and keys that contain these chords. The activated key units in turn activate all units representing chords that are contained in these keys, and so on. The activation process eventually dissipates, and the network reaches an equilibrium state.

At this point, the activations of the chord and key units represent the degree to which chords and keys are suggested or expected. In response to three tones comprising a major triad, the expectations generated by the network are exactly in accord with the circle of fifths: chords and keys closest around the circle are most highly expected. In response to two major chords in succession whose roots are a whole tone apart (e.g., F major followed by G major), the network most strongly activates the key (C major) of which these chords are subdominant and

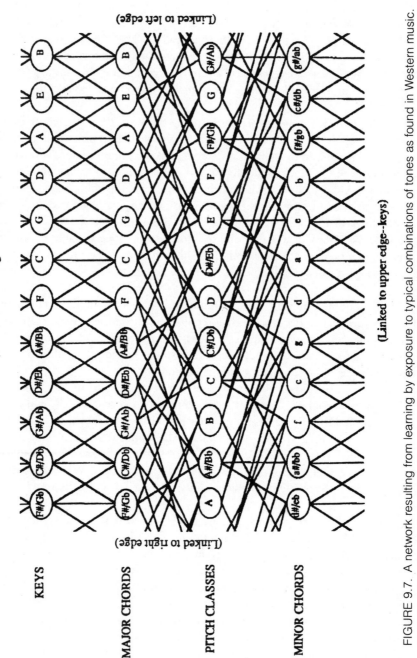

FIGURE 9.7. A network resulting from learning by exposure to typical combinations of tones as found in Western music. (Adapted from Bharucha, 1987a. Copyright by the Cognitive Science Society.)

dominant, and generates a strong expectation for the tonic chord. Finally, in response to a key-establishing context such as a major chord or a final cadence, the network generates expectations for the diatonic tones in that key. To this extent, the network can be seen to generate tonal hierarchies.

The network exhibits the patterns of expectation found in experiments on chord priming. The indirect activation of a chord unit represents an anticipatory processing of the represented object, resulting in faster and more accurate judgments about that chord, as observed in priming.

These complex behaviors of the network cannot be seen immediately by simply examining a diagram of the network such as Figure 9.7. They emerge from computer simulations of the activation process operating on the network. The network thus has emergent properties—that is, properties that are not directly evident from the initial assumptions but emerge from the way in which these assumptions interact. Emergent properties that are in accord with experimental data and music theory, as they are in this case, constitute strong support for a theory. Most theories that consist of rules (such as Lerdahl and Jackendoff's theory) postulate those rules explicitly and do not provide an account of how those rules are acquired. In a neural net, in contrast, the system behaves in accord with rules that weren't postulated explicitly but instead emerge from the complex interactions of more elementary processes that are themselves learned.

Neural nets thus offer the potential to understand how tonal schemata may be learned by passive perceptual learning, thereby giving rise to the schematic expectations that form such an integral part of our musical experience.

NOTES

1. These include (but are by no means limited to) Zarlino (1558/1968), Fux (1725/1943), Schenker (1935/1979), Schoenberg (1954/1969), Meyer (1956), Lerdahl and Jackendoff (1983), Narmour (1990), and Butler and Brown (Chapter 8 in this volume).

2. As opposed to rhythmic or melodic expectations.

3. In keeping with the goals of this book, I shall attempt to avoid detail and excursions in favor of elucidating a clear line of reasoning. The reader is directed to other sources for details, for additional work, and for alternative explanations that bear on the question of harmonic expectation. These include Deutsch and Feroe (1981), Sloboda (1985), Dowling and Harwood (1986), Handel (1989), and, most relevant to some of the material covered in this chapter, Krumhansl (1990). For details about the work of the author, see Bharucha (1987, 1991; Bharucha & Todd, 1989).

4. It should be noted that there is some debate about whether "emotion" is the appropriate term to describe the often subtle and ineffable experiences induced by the fulfillment and violation of tonal expectations. Whether one is willing to call these experiences emotions, however, they are clearly affective.

5. There is no known reason to suppose that one cannot have more than one musical culture.

6. Many cognitive psychologists would consider a schema to be a memory system,

too. For the sake of simplicity, however, we shall restrict the term "memory" to memory for pieces of music.

It may be possible for the schematic expectations to emerge from the memory instead of requiring a completely distinct structure. One way in which this might occur has been explored by Bharucha and Todd (1989). Other methods might generate the schema by an average or composite (e.g., Metcalfe, 1982) of all individual memory traces. Whether the schema and the memory are part of the same physical structure or separate structures is still an open research question. In this chapter it will be assumed that they are separate.

7. This conclusion must await further research, however, since the empirical determination of this issue is very tricky. When a piece of music is recalled from memory in order to perform or imagine it, the schema is activated just as it would be by the sound itself, thereby generating the event hierarchy. It therefore seems redundant to store the elaboration in memory, since it is generated automatically every time the piece is recalled. This is what makes an empirical answer to the question so difficult.

8. This is based on the probability with which chords follow each other in the musical genre to which the subjects have been most extensively exposed (Western tonal music for the subjects in these experiments). C major is most often followed by G major or F major and least often by F-sharp major. Hence, for these subjects, G and F are objectively more highly expected than is F-sharp, following C.

9. The figure shows root position triads in close position as an example only. Although the original experiments employed "Shepard" tones (Shepard, 1964), which render tones more ambiguous with respect to their particular octave, subsequent experiments (Stoeckig, 1990) have shown that the results from this priming experiment are quite robust for different inversions, positions, and voice leading. Thus the effect seems to truly capture the perceptual properties of the triads as wholes.

10. In the case of the linear spatial representation of pitch height this is true! Such a *tonotopic* representation of pitch height is found not just in the inner ear, but even in the cerebral cortex.

11. The information contained in a circle can be encoded by a computer in many possible ways, including a string of symbols specifying the mathematical equation of the circle. Similarly, the brain might encode this information in terms of a particular arrangement of neurons, even though this arrangement may not itself be circular. Cognitive psychologists explore mental representations at different levels of information abstraction, spatial representations being some of the most abstract and neural representations some of the least abstract. The advantage of abstract representations is that the essence of the information can be captured without worrying about the representational medium. The advantage of less abstract representations is that the causal mechanisms involved in encoding the information can be addressed.

12. The strength of a correlation of two profiles is given by a single number, the correlation coefficient, r, that ranges between -1 and 1. A correlation coefficient of zero signifies no correlation.

13. There is nothing mystical about a four-dimensional space. Mathematically, to say that more than three dimensions are required to capture all the relationships between major and minor keys simply means that more than three factors are needed for a complete description of these relationships. The difficulty of depicting the four-dimensional key space stems only from an attempt to illustrate the space in terms of a model that can be visualized.

14. Parncutt's (1989) theory of the psychoacoustic foundations of harmony predicts this outcome.

15. This is not the same as being able to imagine music after becoming completely deaf, which only requires auditory imagery. The familiar account of Beethoven continuing to compose while deaf doesn't in and of itself discount the spectral overlap hypothesis. If sounds are stored in memory in terms of their spectra, then, while imagining music, the imagined spectra would overlap or not, just as would real spectra.

16. See Bharucha (1987b) for a report of a preliminary priming experiment using Indian music and Indian subjects.

17. See Deutsch (1969) for an early model of this kind. Unlike more recent models, it couldn't learn, since the mechanisms by which neural nets might learn were not then well understood.

18. This is called a tonotopic mapping, and can be found all the way from the inner ear to the auditory cortex.

REFERENCES

Anderson, J. R. (1990). *Cognitive psychology and its implications.* New York: Freeman.

Bharucha, J. J. (1984). Event hierarchies, tonal hierarchies, and assimilation: A reply to Deutsch and Dowling. *Journal of Experimental Psychology: General, 113,* 421–25.

Bharucha, J. J. (1987a). MUSACT: A connectionist model of musical harmony. In *Proceedings of the Cognitive Science Society.* Hillsdale, NJ: Erlbaum.

Bharucha, J. J. (1987b). Music cognition and perceptual facilitation: A connectionist framework. *Music Perception 5,* 1–30.

Bharucha, J. J. (1991). Pitch, harmony, and neural nets: A psychological perspective. In P. Todd & D. G. Loy (Eds.), *Music and connectionism.* Cambridge: MIT Press.

Bharucha, J. J., & Olney, K. L. (1989). Tonal cognition, artificial intelligence and neural nets. *Contemporary Music Review, 4,* 341–56.

Bharucha, J. J., & Stoeckig, K. (1986). Reaction time and musical expectancy: Priming of chords. *Journal of Experimental Psychology: Human Perception and Performance, 12,* 403–10.

Bharucha, J. J., & Stoeckig, K. (1987). Priming of chords: Spreading activation or overlapping frequency spectra? *Perception and Psychophysics, 41,* 519–24.

Bharucha, J. J., & Stoeckig, K. (1989). *Chord priming: The automaticity of schematic expectancies.* Paper presented at the meeting of the Psychonomic Society, Atlanta, GA.

Bharucha, J. J., & Todd, P. (1989). Modeling the perception of tonal structure with neural nets. *Computer Music Journal, 13*(4), 44–53.

Carlsen, J. C. (1981). Some factors which influence melodic expectancy. *Psychomusicology, 1,* 12–29.

Carlsen, J. C., Divenyi, P. L., & Taylor, J. A. (1970). A preliminary study of perceptual expectancy in melodic configurations. *Council of Research in Music Education, 22,* 4–12.

Castellano, M. A., Bharucha, J. J., & Krumhansl, C. L. (1984). Tonal hierarchies in the music of North India. *Journal of Experimental Psychology; General, 113,* 394–412.

Deutsch, D. (1969). Music recognition. *Psychological Review, 76,* 300–7.

Deutsch, D., & Feroe, J. (1981). The internal representation of pitch sequences in tonal music. *Psychological Review, 88,* 503–22.

Dowling, W. J., & Harwood, D. L. (1986). *Music cognition*. San Diego: Academic Press.

Fux, J. J. (1943). *Steps to Parnassus* (A. Mann, Ed. and Trans.). New York: Norton. (Original work published 1725)

Geary, J. M. (1980). Consonance and dissonance of pairs of inharmonic sounds. *Journal of the Acoustical Society of America, 67*, 1785–89.

Handel, S. (1989). *Listening*. Cambridge: MIT Press.

Hebb, D. O. (1949). *The organization of behavior,* New York: Wiley.

Helmholtz, H. (1954). *On the sensation of tone.* New York: Dover. (Original work published 1885)

Jairazbhoy, N. (1971). *The rags of North Indian music: Their structure and evolution.* London: Faber & Faber.

Jones, M. R. (1981a). Music as a stimulus for psychological motion. Part I. Some determinates of expectancies. *Psychomusicology, 2*, 34–51.

Jones, M. R. (1981b). Music as a stimulus for psychological motion. Part II. An expectancy model. *Psychomusicology, 2*, 1–13.

Krumhansl, C. L. (1979). The psychological representation of musical pitch in a tonal context. *Cognitive Psychology, 11*, 346–74.

Krumhansl, C. L. (1990). *Cognitive foundations of musical pitch.* Oxford: Oxford University Press.

Krumhansl, C. L., & Kessler, E. J. (1982). Tracing the dynamic changes in perceived tonal organization in a spatial representation of musical keys. *Psychological Review, 89*, 334–68.

Krumhansl, C. L., & Schmuckler, M. A. (1986). The *Petroushka* chord: A perceptual investigation. *Music Perception, 4*, 153–84.

Krumhansl, C. L., & Shepard, R. N. (1979). Quantification of the hierarchy of tonal functions within a diatonic context. *Journal of Experimental Psychology: Human Perception and Performance, 5*, 579–94.

Lerdahl, F., & Jackendoff, R. (1983). *A generative theory of tonal music.* Cambridge: MIT Press.

Mandler, G. (1984). *Mind and body.* New York: Norton.

Metcalfe Eich, J. (1982). A composite holographic associative recall model. *Psychological Review, 89*, 627–61.

Meyer, L. (1956). *Emotion and meaning in music.* Chicago: University of Chicago Press.

Narmour, E. (1977). *Beyond Schenkerism: The need for alternatives in music analysis.* Chicago: University of Chicago Press.

Narmour, E. (1990). *The analysis and cognition of basic melodic structures.* Chicago: University of Chicago Press.

Parncutt, R. (1989). *Harmony: A psychoacoustic approach.* Berlin: Springer-Verlag.

Pierce, J. R. (1969). Attaining consonance in arbitrary scales. *Journal of the Acoustical Society of America, 40*, 249.

Pierce, J. R. (1983). *The science of musical sound.* Scientific American Books.

Rumelhart, D. E., & McClelland, J. L. (1986). *Parallel distributed processing: Explorations in the microstructure of cognition* (Vols. 1 & 2). Cambridge: MIT Press.

Schenker, H. (1979). *Free composition* (E. Oster, Ed. and Trans.). New York: Longman. (Original work published 1935)

Schmuckler, M. A. (1989). Expectation in music: Investigation of melodic and harmonic processes. *Music Perception, 7*, 109–50.

Schoenberg, A. (1969). *Structural functions of harmony* (L. Stein, Ed.). New York: Norton. (Original work published 1954)

Shepard, R. N. (1964). Circularity in judgments of relative pitch. *Journal of the Acoustical Society of America, 36,* 2346–53.

Sloboda, J. A. (1985). *The music mind.* Oxford: Oxford University Press.

Stoeckig, K. (1990). *The effects of octave transformations: Evidence from harmonic priming concerning the functional equivalence of chords and their inversions.* Unpublished doctoral dissertation, Department of Psychology, Dartmouth College, Hanover, NH.

Tekman, H., & Bharucha, J. J. (1991). *Dynamics of the development of harmonic priming: From tones to keys and back.* Paper presented at the meeting of the Eastern Psychological Association, New York.

Tramo, M. J., Bharucha, J. J., & Musiek, F. E. (1990). Music perception and cognition following bilateral lesions of auditory cortex. *Journal of Cognitive Neuroscience, 2,* 195–212.

Zarlino, G. (1968). *The art of counterpoint* (G. A. Marco & C. V. Palisca, Trans.). New Haven, CT: Yale University Press. (Original work published 1558)

10

Perception, Production, and Imitation of Time Ratios by Skilled Musicians

SAUL STERNBERG AND RONALD L. KNOLL

Introduction

The rhythmic element of music has always been a central topic for musicians (Cooper & Meyer, 1960; Yeston, 1976; Kramer, 1988; see Jaques-Dalcroze, 1972, for applications of rhythm to theories of music pedagogy). Psychologists, however, have shown increased interest in this area only in the last few years. Early research in the perception of rhythm was based more on the research in the perception of motor control and time (Lashley, 1951; Fraisse, 1963) than on rhythm within a musical context (reviewed in Fraisse, 1987).

A number of psychological studies have investigated the perception of polyrhythms, namely: sequences of rhythmic patterns occurring simultaneously (see Handel, 1984, for an overview). These experiments did not utilize musical stimuli, but rather sequences of tapping played at different pitches. They evaluated the listeners' ability to describe verbally what they heard, or to demonstrate by tapping one rhythmic pattern selected from several rhythms heard simultaneously.

Researchers have provided models of how listeners perceive rhythm, meter, and time. Steedman (1977) proposed a computer model of how listeners perceive musical rhythm and meter that utilized the occurrence of relatively long notes and the repetition of melodic phrases as cues to infer the meter of unaccompanied melodies. Steedman applied this model to analyze the metric structure of the 48 fugue subjects of *The Well-Tempered Clavier* by J. S. Bach.

Longuet-Higgins and Lee (1982) set forth a model that explained how listeners perceive the rhythms of note sequences based on the relative length

From J. Gibbon & Lorraine Allan (Eds.), *Timing and Time Perception*, Annals of the New York Academy of Sciences, vol. 423, copyright © 1984. Reprinted by permission.

of the notes. According to this model, after hearing the first two notes of a sequence, listeners already have in mind some hypothetical grouping, which they revise or confirm as they continue hearing the sequence of notes. The influential research of Mari Riess Jones has dealt with models of time perception and attention within music (Jones, 1987a, 1987b, 1992; Jones & Boltz, 1989).

The two chapters that follow illustrate how musicians perceive aspects of rhythm and timing. In "Perception, Production, and Imitation of Time Ratios by Skilled Musicians," by Sternberg and Knoll, the research is carried out in a laboratory setting, while in "The Interpretive Component in Musical Performance," by Shaffer and Todd, it is evaluated within musical performances.

"Perception, Production, and Imitation of Time Ratios by Skilled Musicians" summarizes a series of experiments that measured the abilities of musicians to reproduce, judge, and imitate (by tapping or by reproducing a note on the violin) a brief fraction of time corresponding to a nonstandard subdivision of the beat. The data showed that the subjects were inaccurate in reproducing, judging, and imitating the small fraction of time required by the experimental task.

The results demonstrate how tasks on the perception of timing that are psychologically very pertinent do not necessarily translate into tasks that are musically as pertinent. Subjects who are experts in responding to rhythm and timing within a musical framework cannot necessarily transfer their skills when making judgments or providing tapping responses to fractions of time in a context devoid of musical significance (vitality).

Regardless of their inability to be on target with the required experimental tasks, these expert musicians will nevertheless perform as skilled soloists and/or as a fine ensemble in a musical setting. In other words, they will all come in slightly early or slightly late, but they will all make their musical entrances *together,* as a group. In listening to music, listeners are not sensitive to how performers respond to a fraction of a second, but rather to their ability to *synchronize* their performances (Rasch, 1988).

REFERENCES

Cooper, G., & Meyer, L. (1960). *The rhythmic structure of music.* Chicago: University of Chicago Press.

Fraisse, P. (1963). *Psychology of time.* New York: Harper.

Fraisse, P. (1987). A historical approach to rhythm as perception. In A. Gabrielsson (Ed.) *Action and perception in rhythm and music,* volume 55. Stockholm: The Royal Swedish Academy of Music.

Handel, S. (1984). Using polyrhythms to study rhythm. *Music Perception, 1,* 465–84.

Jaques-Dalcroze, E. (1972). *Rhythm, music and education* (H. Rubenstein, Trans.). New York: B. Blom. (Original work published 1921)

Jones, M. R. (1987a). Perspectives on musical time. In A. Gabrielsson (Ed.), *Action and perception in rhythm and music* (Vol. 55). Stockholm: Royal Swedish Academy of Music.

Jones, M. R. (1987b). Dynamic pattern structure in music: Recent theory and research. *Perception and Psychophysics, 41*(6), 621–34.

Jones, M. R. (1992). Attending to musical events. In M. R. Jones & S. Holleran (Eds.), *Cognitive bases of musical communication.* Washington, DC: American Psychological Association.

Jones, M. R., & Boltz, M. (1989). Dynamic attending and responses to time. *Psychological Review, 96* (3), 459–91.

Kramer, J. D. (1988). *The time of music.* New York: Schirmer Books.

Lashley, K. S. (1951). The problem of serial order in behavior. In L. P. Jeffress (Ed.), *Cerebral mechanisms in behavior: The Hixon Symposium.* New York: Wiley.

Longuet-Higgins, H. C., & Lee, C. S. (1982). The perception of musical rhythms. *Perception, 11,* 115–28.

Rasch, R. A. (1988). Timing and synchronization in ensemble performance. In J. A. Sloboda (Ed.), *Generative processes in music: The psychology of performance, improvisation, and composition.* Oxford: Oxford University Press.

Steedman, M. J. (1977). The perception of musical rhythm and metre. *Perception, 6,* 555–69.

Yeston, M. (1976). *The stratification of musical rhythm.* New Haven, CT: Yale University Press.

Among the human skills in which timing and time perception are critical, musical skill is distinctive: for most players a notation specifies temporal pattern explicitly and provides a criterion to which performance can be compared. Because of their years of practice in the use of this notation, the behavior of professional musicians can plausibly reveal some of the ultimate capacities and constraints of human timing mechanisms. We have examined the performance of skilled musicians in three laboratory tasks designed to capture temporal aspects of music. We focused on the short time intervals—fractions of a second—that are among the shortest durations specified by musical notation. As in Western music, these intervals occurred in the context of a train of periodic beats and were defined as fractions of the beat interval. Our three tasks—perception, production, and imitation—all appear to be required of musicians during ensemble rehearsal and performance, for example. It is plausible that because players try to "keep together," ensemble experience would cause performance in the three tasks to become at least consistent and probably correct as well (that is, consistent with the notation). Neither of these expectations was borne out by our experiments; instead, we observed surprisingly large systematic errors and inconsistencies.

The principal subjects were three professional musicians: a flutist, a cellist, and Paul Zukofsky (PZ), violinist and conductor. We also obtained a small amount of corroborative data from Pierre Boulez, composer and conductor. A detailed report of our results is available, based on group data.[1] In the present chapter we describe only our more interesting findings, illustrated with data from PZ, who is the most musically experienced of our principal subjects, whose performance we examined in a wider variety of procedures than the other subjects, and whose data are more consistent than theirs, both within and across experiments. The picture generated by the group data is somewhat less clear, but leads to the same conclusions.

Three Tasks of Temporal Psychophysics

We used two kinds of stimuli, shown on the left of Figure 10.1. A *time pattern stimulus* contained two or more *beat clicks* separated by a *beat interval*. The beat interval was usually 1 sec. One or more of the beat clicks was followed by a *marker click* after a *fractional interval, f*, that defined a fraction of the beat. A *fraction-name stimulus, n*, was presented both as a numerical fraction and in musical notation, where a quarter note was defined as one beat. On the right of the figure are shown the two kinds of response. In making a *fraction-name response, N*, the subject would select a category such as "less than ¹/₈ beat" or "between ¹/₈ and ¹/₇ beat." In making a *timed response,* the subject tapped his finger after a beat click, thereby producing a fractional interval, *F* between beat click and tap.

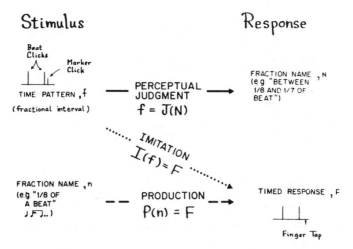

FIGURE 10.1. Stimuli, tasks, and responses.

Stimuli and responses were linked by three different tasks, as shown in the center of the figure. In *perceptual judgment* the subject assigned fraction names to time patterns. He thereby generated a *judgment function, f* = J(N), that maps fraction names onto their subjectively equivalent fractional intervals. In *production* the subject made a timed response to produce a fractional interval associated with a specified fraction name. He thereby generated a production function, P(n) = F. In *imitation* (sometimes called the "method of reproduction") a time-pattern stimulus elicited a subjectively equivalent timed response. We thereby obtained an imitation function, I(f) = F. To permit performance to stabilize, conditions in all experiments remained constant for at least 25 trials.

Perceptual Judgment of Beat Fractions

The stimulus pattern in our first perception experiment is shown in Figure 10.2. Two pairs of beat clicks separated by two beat intervals (a *rest*) were followed by a single marker click. For each of a set of fraction names we used an adaptive psychophysical procedure to determine the fractional interval that is subjectively equivalent to it. The resulting judgment function is labeled J, in Figure 10.3. The fractional interval, *f*. is plotted as a function of fraction name, N. Both scales are logarithmic.[1] If stimulus and response agreed, data would fall on the straight line with unit slope. Instead, our subject radically overestimated fractions less than $\frac{1}{4}$ beat (or 250 msec). Consider the case of $\frac{1}{8}$ beat, for example. Accurate performance would assign this fraction name to a fractional interval of 125 msec; instead, it is assigned to an interval of about 67 msec, or $\frac{1}{16}$ beat. Thus, for small fractions, the assigned fraction name is larger than the fractional

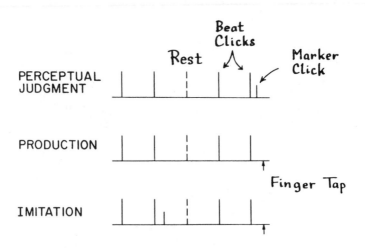

FIGURE 10.2. Sequences of beat clicks, marker clicks, and finger taps in experiments J_1, P_3, and I_5.

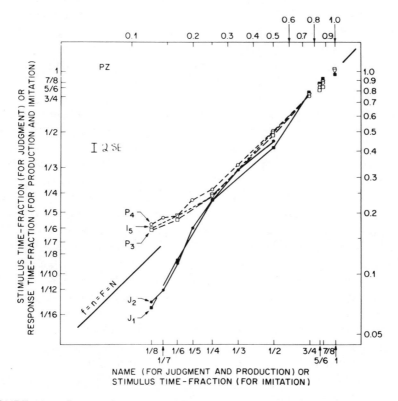

FIGURE 10.3. Results for subject PZ from five experiments: judgment (J), production (P), and imitation (I). Ordinate (*abscissa*) values are given as fractions on a logarithmic scale on the left (bottom) and as decimal values on the right (top). Error bar indicates approximately 2 S.E. based on between-session variability. If the ordinate value is regarded as a function of the abscissa value, the functions shown are estimates of $f = J^{-1}(N)$, $F = P(n)$, and $F = I(f)$.

interval.[2] The N-value grows more slowly than the f-value, however, coming into approximate agreement at about ¼ beat. Despite the poor *accuracy* for small fractions, judgment *precision* is high: the difference threshold at ⅛ beat was only 4.3 msec (about 6%), for example.

Production of Beat Fractions

The large errors in the *perception* of small fractions make it particularly interesting to examine musicians' accuracy in *producing* such fractions. One appealing possibility is that production is mediated by a simple feedback process in which the subject judges the fraction he produces with respect to the fraction name he is trying to produce, and adjusts later productions accordingly. Suppose also that produced fractions are judged by means of the same perceptual mechanism used in the judgment task. The production function should then approximate the judgment function: $P(n) = J(N)$ when $n - N$. Thus, overestimation of small fractions (assigning fraction names that are too large) would lead to underproduction (producing fractional intervals that are too small).

The events on each trial in our first production experiment are shown in Figure 10.2. They are the same as in the perception experiment, except for replacement of the marker-click stimulus by a finger-tap response.[3] With each tap the subject heard the thump of his finger striking a hard surface. The production function we obtained is labeled P_3 in Figure 10.3. The expectation from a feedback mechanism is violated dramatically. For small fractions the intervals produced are too large rather than too small. That is, we have over-production rather than underproduction. Whereas the subject *judged* 67 msec to be $1/8$ of a 1-sec beat, for example, he *produced* a mean fractional interval of 164 msec for the same fraction name. Furthermore, he seemed satisfied with his responses, and did not experience his taps as being late.[4] For small fractions in the perception task we have seen that the fraction stimulus, f, that is subjectively equivalent to a fraction name, N, changes more rapidly than the N-value. In contrast, the fraction, F, produced changes more slowly than the n-value.

Several analyses and experimental variants were directed at understanding the large systematic errors we had found in judgment and production, as well as their inconsistency. In the present report we consider nine of these. Others, together with these, are considered in greater detail in the full report (Sternberg, Knoll, & Zukovsky, 1982).

Further Analysis of Perceptual Judgment

Psychophysical Procedure

One concern is whether aspects of the judgment data may depend on special features of our psychophysical procedure. In any block of trials in the adaptive procedure, subjects judged time fractions with respect to just one fraction name, and the fractional intervals were concentrated in the range where judgments were the most difficult. In a second experiment we used a method more akin to traditional psychophysical scaling in which both these features were altered. The subject categorized a wide range of time-pattern fractions into one of eight categories of fraction names, ranging from "less than $1/8$ beat" to "greater than $1/2$ beat," in each trial block. Also in contrast to the first experiment, two beat clicks rather than only one were followed by marker clicks, providing two observations of the fractional interval on each trial. Results are labeled J_2 in Figure 10.3. The two judgment functions are almost identical, despite the differences between procedures.[5]

Fractional Interval Defined by Subjective
Onset Versus Offset of Marker

A second attempt to discover a source of the judgment errors was based on the possibility that the internal representation of a brief click may have a longer duration than the click itself. Suppose that when beat and marker clicks are close together, the subjective duration of the fractional interval is defined by the *onset* of the internal representation of the beat and the *offset* of the internal representation of the marker. Such a mechanism could then produce overestimation of the kind we observed. To test this possibility we compared judgments of our normal stimuli, in which clicks were 5-msec tone bursts, with stimuli in which the marker duration was prolonged by about 60 msec. Contrary to the idea that offset time is important, this variation produced no change in the judgments, for either small or large fractions.[6]

Further Analysis of Production

We next turn to five of our efforts to understand the systematic errors in the production task and the inconsistency between production and judgment performances for small fractions.

Opportunity for Adjustment to Feedback

As mentioned above, our subject did not report experiencing his finger tap responses as being late for either small fractions or large. Nonetheless there may have been discrepant feedback from the perception mechanism, but too little opportunity to adjust to it, given only one production per trial. On each trial in a second production experiment the subject produced timed responses after each of 10 successive beat clicks. We found no tendency for the error to be reduced over the 10 successive responses. Mean produced fractions based on all the responses are labeled P_4 in Figure 10.3. Performance agrees closely with the first production experiment. If anything, the tendency toward overproduction is slightly greater.

Subjective Delay of Tap versus Click

A second potential source of inaccuracies in production might be a difference between two critical subjective delays. One is the interval between the occurrence of a click and its perceptual registration. The second is the interval (possibly negative) between our measurement of a tap and when the subject perceives it to have occurred. If these two delays differed, then direct comparison of the intervals between beat click and marker click in perception and between beat click and tap in production would be inappropriate. To estimate the difference between the two subjective delays we asked subjects to tap in synchrony with one or more beat clicks. The difference can be estimated by the mean asynchrony between tap and click; the asynchrony was small—about 10 or 20 msec, depending on the procedure—clearly too small to explain the observed effects. On the assumption that the difference between subjective delays does not depend on the beat fraction, the production data in Figure 10.3 have been corrected by these small amounts.

Improved Feedback from Finger Tap

The disparity between performances in perception and production led us to question a feedback model of production, which suggested in turn that we scrutinize the feedback itself. The feedback from tapping the finger included tactile, proprioceptive, and auditory cues, but not the marker click used in the perception task. In additional production experiments with both single- and multiple-tap procedures, but limited to the fraction ⅛ beat, each finger tap generated a marker click. The sequence of clicks in judgment and production thereby became identical. The production performance was virtually unchanged, however; we found only a 10-msec change in the mean interval produced.

Musical Instrument Response

Another potential source of the production error might have been our choice of finger-tapping as a response. (The subject was a skilled violinist but not a skilled finger-tapper, at least at the start of these experiments.) We ran the single-response production experiment again, but now the response was to play a single note on the violin after the final beat click. We measured the onset time of the note as the subject attempted to produce the fractions ⅛, ½, and 1 beat. The amount of overproduction of the small fraction did not decrease. (In fact, it was nonsignificantly greater by 12 ± 11 msec for PZ.)

Minimum Reaction Time

The potential sources discussed above of the production error and the production-perception disparity had to be considered. However, we had little *a priori* reason to expect that even if they had been important, their effects would have depended on fraction size. One constraint that might have such differential effects is the existence of a minimum reaction time (RT). The minimum RT to auditory stimuli is between 100 and 150 msec. Furthermore, there are delays between excitation of a musical instrument and its acoustic response. The combination of these two effects makes it virtually impossible to produce a note 125 msec after a signal to respond (such as a beat click) when the signal is the event that initiates the response timing process. If we assume that the timing of an offbeat response starts with the immediately preceding beat, it follows that the notation often calls for production of discriminably different response delays, some of which are less than the minimum RT. One solution would be to bias productions just as we have observed, so that for different small fractions the mean intervals produced are greater than the minimum RT, but still distinct.

A test of this explanation is provided by variances of the finger-tap delays, $Var(F)$, together with an argument suggested by Snodgrass, Luce, and Galanter (1967). We assume that as its mean increases, the variance of a response delay also increases, where the delay is measured from the event that initiates the timing process. If the responses for all fractions were timed from the final beat click, we would therefore expect $Var(F)$ to increase with fraction size. Instead, we found it to vary as a U-shaped function of fraction size, with a minimum between $n = 1/4$ and $n = 1/2$.[7] This pattern of variability would be expected if small fractions, but not large ones, were timed from the penultimate beat; if so, overproduction cannot be explained as compensation for a limited speed of response.

Production of Multiple Subdivisions of the Beat

How can the existence of large production errors for small fractions be reconciled with our belief that musicians are able to fill a beat interval accurately with a sequence of equally spaced actions? Could the production error depend on our use of a single, isolated response?[8] To address this question we studied the three conditions shown in Figure 10.4 in a new production experiment. The beat interval here was $1/2$ sec instead of 1 sec, incidentally testing the generality of our effects. One of the conditions required an isolated offbeat response, with a target fraction of $1/4$ beat, equivalent to a fractional interval of 125 msec. There were two multiple-response conditions. In one the subject started with a tap on the beat, and alternated between index fingers to fill the beat interval with quarter-beat taps. An unusual interval between the first two taps here would reveal any general distortion of subjective time near the beat. In another condition the initial on-beat tap was withheld. If overproduction depends on response isolation, then the presence of later taps within the same beat interval should eliminate it, especially since the final tap was supposed to be made on the next beat.[9]

Consider first the results from the 5-tap condition. All tap delays, and in particular the delay of the second tap, fall close to the fitted line. There appears to be no general distortion of subjective time near the beat. Furthermore, the slope of the linear function is less than unity, giving a value of 435 rather than 500 msec for position 5. (Since the subject felt satisfied with his productions, we

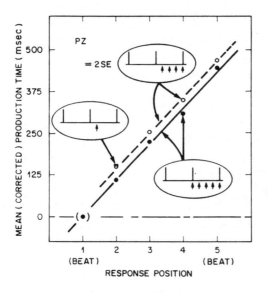

FIGURE 10.4. Stimulus and response patterns in three conditions in an experiment on multiple subdivisions of the beat, together with results. Mean response delays have all been corrected by the mean delay (-34.7 msec) between the second beat click and the first tap in the 5-response condition. Data from the two multiple-response conditions have been fitted by parallel lines. The displayed $\pm$ S.E. bar is appropriate for assessing adequacy of the fitted lines.

must assume that the subjective beat interval was shorter than the actual beat interval by about 13%.) In other words, with multiple subdivisions starting on the beat there is no evidence for overproduction of the small fraction. Consider next the 1-tap condition. Just as in our other experiments the response is delayed relative to the correct response time of 125 msec. Because of the shortening of the subjective beat interval, the amount of overproduction is even greater when referred to the second tap in the 5-tap condition. Consider finally the 4-tap condition. The first response—the tap in position 2—is delayed here as much as in the 1-tap condition. The overproduction effect therefore does not depend on the offbeat response being isolated. Instead, it appears to result from an onbeat response being withheld.

The displaced parallel lines provide a good description of performance in the two multiple-response conditions, indicating that every tap in the 4-tap condition is delayed relative to the 5-tap condition, and by about the same amount. This phenomenon seems best described as *displacement of the subjective beat*. As in some circadian phenomena, the phase of a periodic process has been changed with no alteration in its period. We find it especially remarkable that the delay of the first tap is propagated all the way through the last tap, despite the presence of a final beat click.

Conjectures About Failure of the Feedback Model of Production

The beat-displacement effect suggests one possible source of failure of the feedback model. It is plausible that subjects judge their response delays relative to the *subjective* train of beats. If so, the beat displacement associated with the delayed offbeat response would reduce the apparent delay of this response. Such an effect might explain a subject's inability to recognize and correct his overproduction. It would be too small an effect, however, to explain the major part of the discrepancy between overproduction and the underestimation we observed in the judgment task, which would require that the magnitude of beat displacement *exceed* the delay of the offbeat response, rather than merely equaling it.

The expectations from the feedback model of production that were violated depend on the assumption that the time-perception processes that accompany production are the same as those used in the judgment task. The beat-displacement effect leads us to question this assumption. The existence of the effect reminds us that in production the fractional interval terminated by the finger tap must not only be timed, but must also be placed in proper phase relation to the train of beats. Performance of small fractions in the production task therefore requires the timing of both a beat interval and a beat fraction within the same sequence. In contrast, there is no reason to believe that *judgment* of a beat fraction depends on concurrent judgment of a full beat interval.[10] It is possible that this difference between tasks contributes to the failure of the feedback model.

Results from a final judgment experiment provide weak evidence that favors this possibility, indicating that if successive long and short intervals must both be judged, the perception of at least one of them may be dramatically altered. We used click patterns like those shown in Figure 10.5, with a 1-sec beat interval, and asked whether judgment of the large interval between the final beat click and the pair of marker clicks would be influenced by the requirement also to judge the small interval between markers. On each trial the subject had to judge whether the interval between markers was large or small relative to $1/8$ beat, and then also to judge whether the interval between the final beat click and the markers was large or small relative to a full beat. Judgments of the small beat

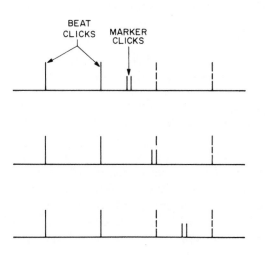

FIGURE 10.5. Examples of sequences of beat clicks and marker clicks in a dual-judgment experiment. Broken lines represent beats for which no beat click was presented.

fraction were very similar to performance in a single-judgment control condition. Judgments of the larger interval were enormously more variable than in its control condition, however: The difference threshold was increased by a factor of 10, from about 4% of the beat interval to about 40%.[11]

Imitation of Beat Fractions

Imitation of beat fractions is of interest partly because it provides a further opportunity to determine the sources of error in perception and production. In judgment and production tasks, subjects must associate beat fractions with fraction names. In imitation (see Figure 10.1), the stimulus of the judgment task is mapped onto the response of the production task; fraction names are not explicitly involved. If the errors in judgment and production are due to the input or output of fraction names, it follows that imitation performance should be accurate.[12]

Such accurate imitation of time intervals is one possibility that has been considered in previous research (Carlson & Feinberg, 1968). A second possibility that has been advanced is that imitation is accomplished by concatenating two processes, a judgment process that covertly assigns a name to the time pattern, and a production process that converts this name into a timed response (Thomas & Brown, 1974). Given our findings of overestimation as well as overproduction of small fractions, this *full-concatenation model* implies that the response fraction in imitation will be too large by the sum of the errors in the other two tasks; we call such an outcome *strong overimitation*.

The imitation data are labeled I_5 in Figure 10.3. Results conform to *neither* possibility. Instead, responses to small fractional intervals in imitation were virtually identical to responses to the names of these fractions in production. The significance of this outcome is best explained in the context of the following model of performance in our three tasks.

An Information-Flow Model of the Perception, Production, and Imitation of Beat Fractions

In the skeleton model diagrammed in Figure 10.6 we limit ourselves to accounting for the relations among performances in our three tasks. Each task involves processes that perform input, output, and possibly translation functions. Parsimony leads us to postulate the minimum number of processes consistent with our data, and hence the maximum number of processes shared between tasks.

The processes underlying perceptual judgment are shown by the two upper boxes. A time-pattern stimulus generates an internal fraction representation. This representation is converted into a fraction name to generate the required response. The processes underlying production are shown by the two lower

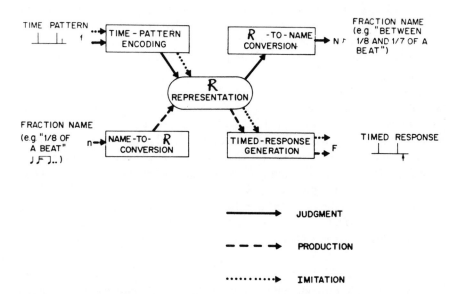

FIGURE 10.6 An information-flow model of perception, production, and imitation of beat fractions. The model incorporates four processes that convert time-pattern (f) or fraction-name (n) stimuli into time-pattern (F) or fraction-name (N) responses, and that make use of a common internal fraction-representation. Paths of information flow for the three tasks are represented by *arrows*.

boxes. A fraction name is converted into an internal representation of the same kind as in the judgment task. This representation is then used to produce the required timed response. A full-concatenation model of imitation would most naturally be represented by a mechanism in which the upper and lower pairs of processes made use of distinct internal representations. In such a mechanism information could not flow directly from time-pattern encoding to timed-response generation. Instead, to connect those two operations the covert output of the pair of processes used in judgment (a fraction name) would become the input for the pair of processes used in production. Because such a model can be rejected, we adopt a *partial-concatenation model* in which imitation makes use of a common internal representation, and shares only the encoding process with the judgment task and only the response-generation process with the production task.

Each of the four processes in the model can be thought of as a function or transformation that maps its input onto its output. Qualitative aspects of our data restrict the relations among these transformations. The most important of these relations is based on the close agreement of the data from production and imitation. When time-pattern and fraction-name correspond, they lead to the same timed response, so that $P \cong I$. This in turn means that they must have produced the same internal representation, thus the two input transformations are the same. The internal representation therefore creates a veridical mapping between the two kinds of stimuli.[13] By a complementary argument from the finding that responses to the same fractional interval in imitation and judgment are *not* the same ($J \neq I$) we conclude that the two output transformations are distinct.

Both the production and judgment tasks generate psychophysical scales that describe the subject's mapping of musical notation onto time fractions. As we have already seen, neither of these scales is veridical, and, moreover, they disagree with each other. Both scales are *explicit,* in that the subject's response is identified directly with one of the terms in the psychophysical function. By combining results from imitation, $F = I(f)$, and production, $F = P(n)$, which involves the same response, we generate an *implicit* psychophysical scale that relates musical notation, n, to time fractions, f, when both are presented as stimuli: $n = P^{-1}I(f)$. Our data indicate that this implicit scale is veridical, despite the systematic errors in each of the three explicit relations, J, P, and I.[14]

Summary

We have described our exploration of the judgment, production, and imitation of fractions of a beat by skilled musicians, illustrating our findings with data from violinist and conductor Paul Zukofsky. For small fractions we found systematic and substantial errors. In the judgment task small stimulus fractions are associ-

Summary of principal expectations and findings

For Small Fractions ($<\frac{1}{4}$ Beat)	
Perceptual Judgment	
Results: Overestimation	$f = J(N) < N$
Production	
Expectation:	
Underproduction	$F = P(n) < n$
(Feedback Model)	
Results: Overproduction	$F = P(n) > n$
Imitation	
Alternative Expectations:	
a) Veridical	$F = I(f) = f$
b) Strong Overimitation	$F = I(f) >> f$
(Full-Concatenation Model)	
Results: Overimitation	$F = I(f) > f,$
and, for $f = n.$	$I(f) = P(n)$

ated with names that are too large (overestimation). In both production and imitation tasks the fractions produced were too large (overproduction, overimitation). A summary of our findings and of the expectations they violate is provided in the table on page 254.

The temporal patterns we used are perhaps the simplest that qualify as rhythms, incorporating just a beat interval and a fraction. The phenomena we discovered in relation to these simple patterns, and their implications for underlying mechanisms, must be considered in attempts to understand the perception and production of more complex rhythms, as in actual music.

We explored and rejected several plausible explanations for the overestimation and overproduction of small fractions. Although we have as yet no satisfactory explanations of the errors themselves, relations among the errors have powerful implications for human timing mechanisms. The relation between the errors in judgment and production requires us to reject a feedback model of production, in which a subject uses the same processes as in the judgment task to evaluate and adjust his performance in the production task. An explanation of the inconsistency between judgment and production seems most likely to lie in a change in time perception induced by the production task. Together with the existence of systematic errors in judgment, the equality of the errors in production and imitation argues that imitation is not accomplished by concatenating all the processes used in judgment and production. Our results are instead consistent with a model containing four internal transformation processes, in which judgment and production share no process, but do involve the same internal-fraction representation, and in which imitation shares one process with judgment and another with production.

ACKNOWLEDGMENTS

We thank Paul Zukofsky, coauthor of the full report (Sternberg, Knoll, & Zukovsky, 1982) for significant contributions both as subject and collaborator. We are also grateful to Marilyn I. Shaw for helpful comments on the manuscript.

NOTES

1. Power functions appear as straight lines on such a plot.

2. Figure seven provides an outline of our principal findings.

3. Note that although infrequent in earlier music, the playing of a note after the beat without playing a note on the beat is not unusual in the music of the past 60 years.

4. This is an informal impression, not based on analysis of systematically collected data.

5. The procedural differences did influence judgment precision; however, difference thresholds were about twice as large in the second (multiple-fraction) experiment.

6. The measured mean change in $f = J(N)$, averaged over six fraction names, was 0.6 ± 1.9 msec. There was neither a mean effect of marker duration nor an interaction of marker duration with fraction size. This finding may reflect a general property of the perception of timing and rhythm in music, the dominance of the sequence of time intervals between successive *attacks*, and the relative unimportance of *release* times.

7. Because imitation performance is virtually identical to production, in variability as well as mean, a good estimate of the effect of fraction size on the variability of tap delay is provided by $Var(F)$ averaged over the two production experiments described above and the imitation experiment to be described [later]. Fractions that were examined in all three experiments include $^1/_8$, $^1/_6$, $^1/_4$, $^1/_2$, $^3/_4$, $^5/_6$, and $^7/_8$; for PZ the corresponding RMS values of the S.D. are 21.3, 20.3, 16.7, 25.2, 32.4, 42.2, and 42.4 msec, respectively.

8. Musicians could perhaps learn to fill an interval evenly, without accurate perception or production of isolated beat fractions, by employing judgments of evenness and synchrony, together with the ability to count actions.

9. The first tap in the 5-tap condition provided the synchronization correction that we used to adjust all taps in the three conditions. Application of the correction in this way requires us to assume that the location of the initial subjective beat as well as the subjective beat rate depend only on the beat clicks, and are influenced neither by whether there is a tap on the beat not by the number of taps that follow.

10. Judgment of a fractional interval could use a stored representation of the beat interval. Alternatively, the beat interval might not be directly represented at all, but would determine the calibration of a mechanism that assessed beat fractions.

11. In further work along these lines it will be important to force high accuracy in judgments of the large interval and to search for effects on both mean and variability of judgments of small fractions.

12. The converse does not follow: if imitation were accurate, we would know only that the function that relates stimulus fractions to their internal representations must be the inverse of the function that relates internal representations to produced fractions.

13. By a mapping of psychophysical scale that is veridical we mean one that associates the beat fraction $1/n$ with the fractional interval b/n, where b is the beat interval.

14. Given our model it is tempting to inquire whether "error" or "distortion" in any single constituent in the model can account for the performance errors in all three tasks, and their relations. Such an inquiry succeeds qualitatively: The only such single constituent that could be responsible is the internal representation, R, since this is the only constituent common to the three tasks. Suppose that for small fractions, R is "expanded" so as to correspond to a larger fraction. Examination of Figure 10.6 reveals that such an expansion, alone, would produce the three effects we observed: overestimation, overproduction, and overimitation. Quantitatively, however, this explanation fails, because it requires that $J^{-1} = I$, a relation we can reject reliably if we use the full range of data. The explanation might succeed, however, if we limited it to small fractions.

REFERENCES

Carlson, V. R., & Feinberg, I. (1968). Individual variations in time judgments and the concept of an internal clock. *Journal of Experimental Psychology, 77,* 631–40.

Sternberg, S., Knoll, R. I., & Zukofsky, P. (1982). Timing by skilled musicians. In D. Deutsch (Ed.), *The psychology of music* (pp. 181–239). New York: Academic Press.

Snodgrass, J., Luce, R. D. & Galanter, F. (1967). Some experiments on simple and choice reaction time. *Journal of Experimental Psychology, 75*, 1–17.

Thomas, F., & Brown, I, Jr. (1974). Time perception and the filled-duration-illusion. *Perceptual Psychophysiology, 16*, 449–58.

11

The Interpretive Component in Musical Performance

L. H. SHAFFER AND NEIL P. McANGUS TODD

Introduction

"The Interpretive Component in Musical Performance," by L. H. Shaffer and N. P. Todd, represents a line of studies that address the perception of rhythm and timing utilizing actual performances of music (see Gabrielsson, 1987a, for a review). With the aid of computerized equipment, this research analyzes the nuances in the rhythmic patterns that pianists display in repeated performances of a composition, and traces a profile of their rhythmic and expressive interpretations. Musical performance research is very valuable to psychologists and musicians alike (see Davidson's Chapter 4 and Sloboda's Chapter 6 in this volume for a discussion of musical skill and performance. See also Clarke, 1982, 1989; Gabrielsson, 1987b; Palmer, 1989; Shaffer, 1981, 1992; Shaffer, Clarke, & Todd, 1985; Sloboda, 1983; Repp, 1990).

Todd (1985) has suggested that pianists reflect the hierarchical structure of a piece by slowing down at points of stability in the piece. In the research described in this chapter, Shaffer and Todd used repeated performances of works by Chopin, J. S. Bach, and Satie to demonstrate that pianists are consistent in reproducing the musical expressions they wish to convey. The performers repeatedly utilize timing to convey and emphasize the structure of the compositions. Psychologically, the performers' overall consistencies indicate that their motor system has a definite representation of the timing parameters. Musically, this research illustrates that nuances such as *rubato* and deviations in tempo reflect a clear musical plan on the part of the performing artists.

From A. Gabrielsson (Ed.), *Action and Perception in Rhythm and Music*. Publications issued by the Royal Swedish Academy of Music No. 55, 1987. Reprinted by permission of the Royal Swedish Academy of Music.

REFERENCES

Clarke, E. F. (1982). Timing in the performance of Erik Satie's "Vexations." *Acta Psychologica, 50,* 1–19.

Clarke, E. F. (1989). The perception of expressive timing in music. *Psychological Review, 5,* 2–9.

Gabrielsson, A. (1987a). *Action and perception in rhythm and music* (Vol. 55). Stockholm: Royal Swedish Academy of Music.

Gabrielsson, A. (1987b). Once again: The theme from Mozart's piano sonata in A major (K.331). In A. Gabrielsson (Ed.), *Action and perception in rhythm and music* (Vol. 55). Stockholm: Royal Swedish Academy of Music.

Palmer, C. (1989). Mapping musical thought to musical performance. *Journal of Experimental Psychology: Human Perception and Performance, 15*(12), 331–46.

Repp, B. (1990). Patterns of expressive timing in performances of a Beethoven minuet by nineteen famous pianists. *Journal of the Acoustical Society of America, 88,* 622–41.

Shaffer, L. H. (1981). Performances of Chopin, Bach and Bartok: Studies in motor programming. *Cognitive Psychology, 13,* 326–76.

Shaffer, L. H. (1992). How to interpret music. In M. R. Jones & S. Holleran (Eds.), *Cognitive bases of musical communication.* Washington, DC: American Psychological Association.

Shaffer, L. H., Clarke, E. F., & Todd, N. P. (1985). Metre and rhythm in piano playing. *Cognition, 20*(1), 61–77.

Sloboda, J. A. (1983). The communication of musical metre in piano performance. *Quarterly Journal of Experimental Psychology, 35*(A), 377–90.

Todd, N. P. (1985). A model of expressive timing in tonal music. *Music Perception, 3,* 33–58.

Musical performance can be creative in a variety of ways. A jazz or classical musician can improvise on a tune, theme, or chord sequence, to embellish it, provide a set of variations, or construct a fugue. With a little less freedom, a player can extemporize on the harmonic skeleton of a figured bass. These feats may appear to be in contrast with that of a musician playing from a score, but the freedom to improvise is different in kind rather than in degree. Scores vary in explicitness and often do little more than adumbrate a musical form, stating a metre and giving pitch and time values for a sequence of notes. Parameters of tempo, intensity, and articulation of notes—the manner of their sounding and the extent to which they are connected or detached—are usually left to the discretion of the player, and it is implicitly understood that even the written pitch and time values of notes may be deformed in order to convey or enhance aspects of musical meaning. Thus the emphasis on creativity shifts from musical invention to the subtle shaping of sound.

There are, to be sure, differences of opinion among both composers and players, on the interpretive license given to the player. At one extreme a score is viewed as a text to be transcribed as accurately as possible. On this view there is an authentic interpretation and only this fully realizes the composer's intention. At the other extreme a score is seen as providing a series of basic forms the musical meaning of which can be re-created each time by the player. The sparse notation of a Bach or Scarlatti score suggests that these composers encouraged more license in interpreting their music than, say, Beethoven.

Interpreting a piece of music, then, requires a good working knowledge of the musical intentions of the composer in relation to the conventions and styles of his period, but it is an axiom of performance that it should clearly convey the meaning of the music. A pleasant feature of the world of music is that players are happy to take this axiom as a working brief when the concept of musical meaning is poorly defined. There is no paradox in this, since a player can have a tacit concept that is more definite than the public version. The corollary, however, is that different players can have different concepts. This raises the empirical questions of what players contribute in interpreting a piece of music, whether there is significant agreement in the interpretations of a piece by different players, and what consistent principles may players bring to playing different pieces. Some of these questions are taken up here. They are of interest, though perhaps in different ways, to students of cognitive science and music theory.

Though the concept of musical meaning is inexplicit, we can at least agree with Meyer (1956) that it is a manifold concept having major components that relate to formal structure, emotion, and physical movement. We shall not consider music such as song, theatre music, and tone poem, that is literary in origin or descriptive of the external world. In these it is the programmatic origin rather than the music itself that is likely to govern the use of expression. Putting them aside, what remains is a vast repertoire of absolute music, mainly concerned with developing musical ideas. Such music can convey nuances of mood through choices of tempo, key, modality, pitch register, and pitch contour. It can also suggest kinds of physical movement or gesture by abstractly imitating the rhythms of dancing, walking, speaking, and so on (Gabrielsson, Bengtsson, & Gabrielsson, 1983). Indeed the titles or Italian markings in a score often indicate these nonmusical references, allowing a three-beat measure to be differentiated into the swirl of a Viennese waltz or the more stately stepping of a minuet. It is further claimed that some kinds of ethnic music are based on the motor gestures that are formally required in playing them on a particular instrument (Bailey, 1985). Similar claims may be made for some of the Etudes of Chopin and Debussy, written as virtuoso pieces to capture complex patterns of movement on the keyboard.

Thus even absolute music makes reference to external states and events in conveying mood or physical movement. In these referential functions it acts as an alternative to natural language. Perhaps the major sense of musical meaning, however, lies in the structure of the music itself, and in this sense music is a closed system making reference only to its own sonic domain (Lerdahl & Jackendoff, 1983). The structures have their own meaning, and this autoreferential function of music is in contrast to natural language, in which syntax provides only a key to a more abstract semantics (Lyons, 1981). The structures of music are contained in its metre, rhythm, melody, and harmony and they can act both independently and together in patterning the music.

The different aspects of meaning must all enter into the planning of a performance. There is scope for giving prominence to one or other of these but ignoring or misjudging any of them carries the risk of leaving the musical listener baffled or unsatisfied. Altering the mood of a piece or giving a dance a song-like character (these are not independent factors) may give the music an arbitrary flavor. Failure to convey its structure may leave it without shape, a directionless concatenation of sounds. Simple monodic pieces can look after themselves, as long as they are accurately transcribed, but the more complex the texture of the music the more relevant this last point becomes.

This chapter looks at some of the ways in which concert pianists make expressive use of timing to convey musical structure. The exercise requires two things, the ability to capture sensitively the pianist's use of timing and the ability to describe musical structure in a way that is informative and relatively unequivocal. Difficulties arise on both points. Objective timing is easily measured, but subjective timing for both player and listener may depend on a subtle blend of real time, intensity, tone quality, and the articulation of successive sounds. Also, although there has been progress in the description of musical structure (Lerdahl & Jackendoff, 1983; Schenker, 1969) the methods of description still require a degree of musical intuition in their application and there are not yet accepted canons for describing even relatively conventional tonal music. Nor can it be claimed that the current alternatives are variants that can be generated by a common abstract formalism. Thus lowering our sights a little we shall concentrate on a particular expressive device, the use of slowing to indicate the boundary of a musical group. This device is ubiquitous in music (Seashore, 1938; Shaffer, 1980) and speech (Klatt, 1976), but it gains its effect by being used with discretion. Some of the factors that govern its use are examined here.

The Data

The performances were given on a Bechstein grand piano modified to obtain computer recordings without affecting the sound or touch of the instrument (Shaffer, 1981). Photocells placed in vertical pairs opposite each of the hammers in the action provide recordings of both the timing and intensity of every key-press. The timing gives information about note duration and the legato/staccato articulation of its succession.

Chopin: Prelude in F-Sharp Minor

The pianist, PB, had recently practiced this piece for a recital. She gave two performances of the Prelude in a single recording session. The first few measures of the piece are shown in Figure 11.1. It is a four-beat measure and there is a fixed rhythmic pattern at each beat that recurs throughout the piece. This allows us to consider the performances in a hierarchy of musical units and we have chosen the beat as the basic unit of timing. The graph in Figure 11.1 shows played duration on the ordinate for each beat on the axis, for all but the last measure. Note that if there were no expressive timing the graph of a performance would be a horizontal line.

The departure from metrical timing is immediately apparent in the graph and its magnitude is quite large. The median beat duration is about 800 ms, and the duration ranges between 600 and 1600 ms, excluding the final rallentando. What is impressive, and important for a cognitive theory, is the very high agreement of timing between the two performances. The shapes of the two curves are almost identical. They differ occasionally in the degree of speeding or slowing but are almost unanimous in where these occur. Such precision has been repeatedly found in studies of concert musicians since the work of Seashore (1938). What it demonstrates is that an expressive form can have a precise mental representation and can be precisely executed. This in turn implies the presence in the brain of an excellent timekeeper and a very good way of coding expression. The musical interest lies more perhaps in the shape of the curves. This reveals a patterning of timing that is responsive to a hierarchy of musical units. There is a typical gesture of acceleration and slowing that can be seen in the beats in a measure, the measures in a four- or two-measure phrase, the phrases in a section and indeed the sections in the piece. Thus the gesture has been used recursively in each level of the hierarchy. Furthermore, there is the stronger result that at each level, the amount of slowing at a boundary tends to reflect the depth of that boundary in the hierarchy. This last result becomes clearer when assigning the parameters to a mathematical model in order to simulate the expressive form, the result of which is shown in Figure 11.2.

The model takes a structural description of the music as its input and gener-ates an expressive form from this. Its success in simulating the data rests on the validity of two factors, the choice of a parabola to represent a basic timing gesture, and the choice of a structural description setting the parameters and hence the shape of each parabola. The assignment of structure makes use of the idea of time-span reduction discussed by Lerdahl and Jackendoff (1983), but with a piece as harmonically complex as the Chopin Prelude some intuition is in-

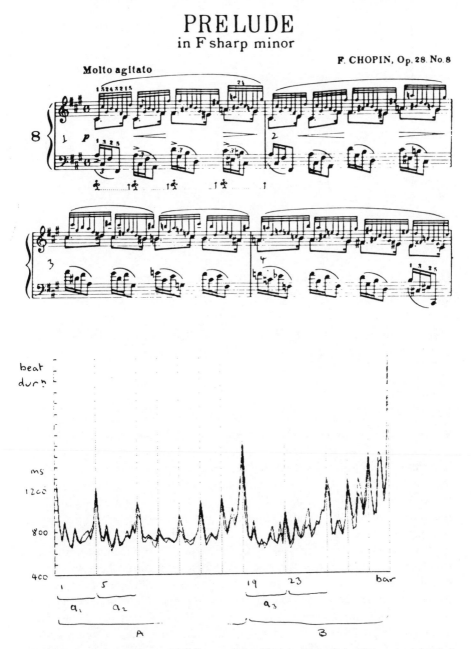

FIGURE 11.1 The first four measures of the Chopin Prelude in F sharp minor and a graph of played beat duration in two performances of the whole piece by PB. The bar, section, and phrase boundaries of the piece are indicated. (The score reproduced by permission of The Associated Board of the Royal Schools of Music, Publishing Limited.)

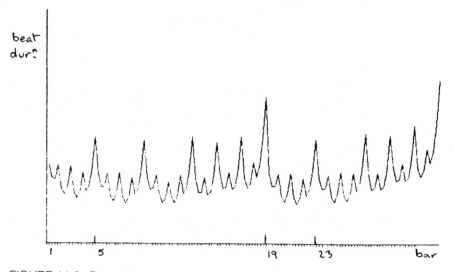

beat
dur.?

i   5   19   23   bar

FIGURE 11.2. Beat duration for the Chopin Prelude, generated by a mathematical model.

volved in using evidence of cadence and parallel structure to assign the hierarchy.

Bach: Prelude in C

The first Prelude in the first book of Bach's *Well-Tempered Clavier* is familiar to any pianist and it was given two performances here by the pianist RH with little prior practice. Like the Chopin Prelude the piece has a fixed rhythmic pattern recurring (almost) throughout. Again there is a hierarchy that contains repeating eight-note patterns within four-beat measures, and four-measure phrases, except for an elision at the beginning that makes the last measure of the first phrase also the first measure of the second. Thus there is some reason to expect that expressive patterns should be similar in performances of the two pieces. The timing of the performances of the Bach, taking the measure as the timing unit, is shown in Figure 11.3. There is less agreement of tempo and rubato between the two performances than in the Chopin. This may reflect a willingness to experiment with tempo and rubato in a piece that the pianist plays seldom, and it will later be shown that in more practiced pieces his timing is much more consistent. There is an additional factor obscured by the different timescales of the graphs in Figures 11.1 and 11.3: all the time differences shown in Figure 11.3 are small and of a lower order than in Figure 11.1. Bar duration in the second, faster, performance had a median of about 2500 ms and ranged between 2400 and 2600 ms, excluding the final rallentando. Hence in the Bach there was relatively little departure from metrical timing, apart from the final rallentando, the last measure of which is omitted from the graph.

ERSTER TEIL
Praeludium I

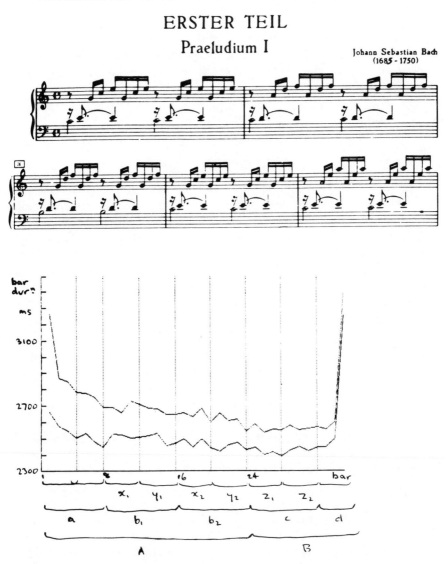

FIGURE 11.3. The first five measures of the Bach Prelude in C and a graph of played measure duration in two performances of the whole piece by RH. The boundaries of bars and phrases, and a hierarchic grouping for these are indicated.

The musically relevant result is that contrary to what was expected the timing gesture of acceleration and slowing was not used to convey hierarchy in the musical structure. Instead there was a single parabolic gesture embracing the whole piece. Yet there are cadences at the phrase boundaries marking intermediate points of rest in the music, which are not always present in the Chopin

Prelude. Unlike that piece, however, the Bach Prelude never properly leaves its home key and it has only a rudimentary melodic line. It can be interpreted, then, as a didactic exercise in exploring the varieties of sonority and progression made possible by inverting and chromatically altering chords, sometimes thereby creating secondary dominants, of the key of C. This didactic function can be underlined by playing the piece as a single tonic to dominant to tonic trajectory (cf. Schenker, 1969).

Satie: Gnossienne No. 5

The pianist JM has recorded the piano music of Satie, including this piece, for the gramophone. He gave three performances here of the Gnossienne among other pieces recorded during the session (Shaffer, Clarke, & Todd, 1985).

In contrast to the other pieces described so far, the Gnossienne has a simple periodic rhythm in the left hand but the right hand has a melodic rhythm that changes continually, embracing a wide variety of rhythmic figures and note durations. Also, whereas the Bach has a clear tonal center throughout and the Chopin much of the time, the Satie appears to vacillate between G and its relative, E minor, without establishing either and so remaining tonally ambiguous, except in a brief bridging passage that is clearly in C. Nor is there a simple relationship between melodic grouping and metre. Hierarchic structure can be discerned only in terms of the recurrence of melodic groups (see Shaffer et al., 1985).

The timing in the three performances, taking the beat as the unit, is shown in Figure 11.4. Again we see the precisely reproducible timing that a concert musician brings to a practiced piece. As in the performances of Bach, there is little use of rubato, the beat duration ranging between 2000 and 2400 ms, nearly half of which is accounted for by a tempo drift described below. However, there is almost an inversion of expressive gesture: the underlining of grouping is now reserved for the lowest level of unit, motivic groups of notes, marked in the score by slurs; there is also a rallentando at the end and, tentatively, before the recapitulation. The other notable feature of timing is that the performances drift throughout to a progressively slower tempo, as if to emphasize the essential lack of harmonic direction of the music. Thus the player appears to have interpreted the piece as a concatenation of musical fragments, an interpretation consistent with a melodic rhythm that alternates groups of short notes with long notes, acting as pauses.

Chopin: Mazurka in A Minor

In order to establish a more direct comparability between players and pieces, we turn to performances of the same piece by the pianists PB and RH, who played the Chopin and Bach preludes, respectively. PB gave one performance of the Mazurka and RH gave two.

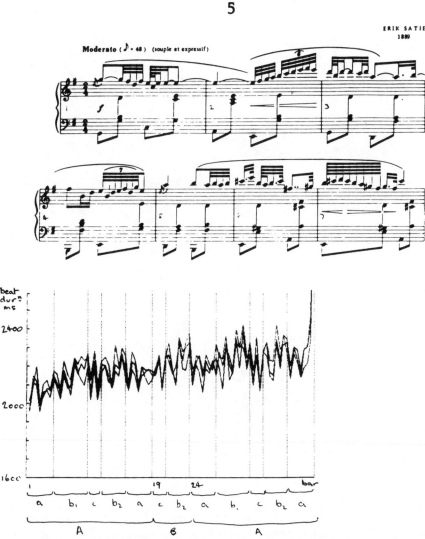

FIGURE 11.4. The opening measures of Satie's Gnossienne No. 5, together with a graph of played beat duration in three performances of the whole piece by JM. Boundaries of the melodic groupings are indicated. (The score reproduced by permission of Editions Salabert, Paris/UMP.)

The graphs in Figure 11.5 show timing based on the unit of a measure. The opening and closing phrases are omitted, because the use of rests in the music makes it difficult to estimate measure duration. Several points can be made from the graph. The first is that, in contrast to his Bach performances, RH demonstrates a very high order of timing consistency in the repeat performances of the more often practiced Mazurka, and he also shows a greater freedom in using

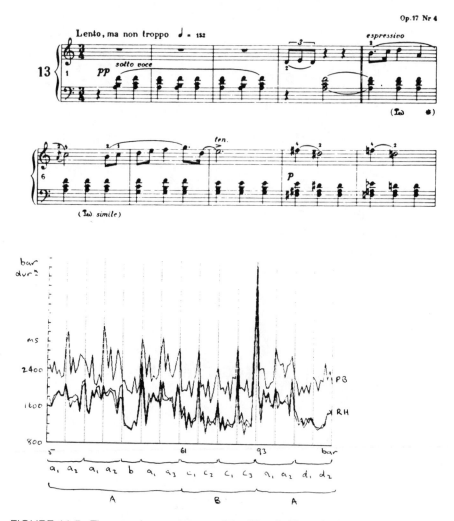

FIGURE 11.5. The opening measures of the Chopin Mazurka in A minor, together with a graph of played measure duration in two performances of the whole piece by RH and one by PB (shown as the uppermost curve). The boundaries of bars, phrases and their hierarchic groupings are indicated (excluding the opening and closing phrases). (The score reproduced by permission of PWM Editions (Alfred A. Kalmus Ltd.))

rubato, though still more restrained than PB. The two players choose different tempi, reflected in measure durations around 2300 ms for PB and 1600 ms for RH. The range of variation in using rubato is about 1200 ms for both players, excluding the rallentandi at the recapitulation and end. Yet RH reserves rubato more to mark phrase boundaries. The effect of these and other timing differences is that RH plays the piece more consistently as a dance. Despite such differences in interpretation they agree in marking the boundaries of the eight-measure phrases and, at the sectional level, the imminence of the recapitulation. If anything it is RH who more punctiliously observes the hierarchy in the musical structure. The players also agree in playing the themes (marked b, c, and d in Figure 11.5) that alternate with the major theme (marked a) at a faster tempo. Note that in the b theme the music modulates from the minor to the major mode, and in the c and d themes there is a higher degree of restlessness in the music produced by harmonic dissonance.

Discussion

It would be preferable to have data of each pianist playing all pieces to enable direct comparisons of players and pieces, but the elegance of experimental design is not easily arranged with concert pianists having different repertoires. Luckily PB and RH both have a special interest in the music of Chopin.

A result reiterated in this study and confirming the findings in earlier studies is that a concert musician has a very precise means of reproducing tempo and its variation in playing a practiced piece of music. At the cognitive level, this implies that the motor system has access to a stable and accurate timekeeper together with a fairly definite representation of the relevant timing parameters. At the musical level it demonstrates that tempo and rubato are not matters of current whim but are the outcome of coded decisions of interpretation. The timing profile in playing a piece typically has a complex pattern, and so we can suppose that it stands in some definite relation to properties implicit in the musical notation. The alternative would be that the player has to memorize a large number of arbitrary parameters.

We have concentrated on the way in which timing is used expressively to convey, or emphasize, musical structure. It has long been known that slowing is used to convey the boundaries of musical units, and the present results extend the picture of this, showing it to depend on a number of factors. It is too early yet to say whether there may be systematic principles governing its use, but the results suggest where to look for these.

Most music can be shown by analysis to contain hierarchic structures, and the results demonstrate that the player can convey one or more of these hierarchies by a recursive and hence graded use of slowing at a boundary. Rather than make this an invariant principle of performance, which would turn this form of expression into a somewhat pedantic exercise, the player may choose which aspects of hierarchy to reveal so as best to characterize the music. This character may in turn relate to a structural or referential component of musical meaning. Fortuitously, the Bach Prelude and the Satie Gnossienne provide almost a polar contrast in musical purpose, the one developing a linear thesis that invites a single trajectory of musical tension in its performance, the other dissipating its trajectory in a series of tonally ambiguous gestures, encouraging an interpretation in terms of overall stasis. It is also worth noting that in these performances, in contrast to the Chopin, the selective use of boundary slowing is associated with an overall limited compass of rubato. One may argue that a decision to restrict the compass limits the scope for discriminating hierarchy, or conversely that a decision to ignore hierarchy allows a smaller use of rubato, but it is also possible that the association is accidental and neither variable constrains the other. We shall require many more performances of different pieces before we can settle on the rules that best describe, or generate, these results. What is clear from the performances of the Mazurka by different players is that the use of structural information is not arbitrary.

ACKNOWLEDGMENTS

This research is supported by a grant, No. C00232213, from the Economic and Social Research Council.

REFERENCES

Bailey, J. (1985). Musical structure and human movement. In P. Howell, I. Cross, & R. West (Eds.), *Musical structure and cognition.* London: Academic Press.

Gabrielsson, A., Bengtsson, I., & Gabrielsson, B. (1983). Performance of musical rhythm in ³/₄ and ⁶/₈ meter. *Scandinavian Journal of Psychology, 24,* 193–213.

Klatt, D. H. (1976). Linguistic uses of segmental durations in English. *Journal of the Acoustical Society of America, 59,* 1208–21.

Lerdahl, F., & Jackendoff, R. (1983). *A generative theory of tonal music.* Cambridge, MA: MIT Press.

Lyons, J. (1981). *Language, meaning and context.* Bungay, Suffolk: Fontana.

Meyer, L. B. (1956). *Emotion and meaning in music.* Chicago: University of Chicago Press.

Schenker, H. (1969). *Five graphic music analyses.* New York: Dover Publications.

Seashore, C. E. (1938). *Psychology of music.* New York: McGraw-Hill.

Shaffer, L. H. (1980). Analysing piano performance. In G. Stelmach & J. Requin (Eds.), *Tutorials in motor behaviour.* Amsterdam: North-Holland.

Shaffer, L. H. (1981). Performances of Chopin, Bach and Bartok: Studies in motor programming. *Cognitive Psychology, 13,* 327–76.

Shaffer, L. H., Clarke, E. F., & Todd, N. P. (1985). Metre and rhythm in piano playing. *Cognition, 20,* 61–77.

Todd, N. P. (1985). A model of expressive timing in tonal music. *Music Perception, 3,* 33–58.

The Perception
of Musical Compositions

12

Can Listening to Music Be Experimentally Studied?

RITA AIELLO

Introduction

Research in the perception of music has been influenced by research in psychoacoustics and psycholinguistics (see Chapter 2 in this volume; for reviews see Deutsch, 1982; Dowling & Harwood, 1986; and Sloboda, 1985). This led to many experiments that focused on the perception of isolated musical variables and used very brief, computerized musical stimuli. In most cases, to control the variables, the musical stimuli were extremely impoverished, and therefore they did not represent the richness of music as we all experience it.

This chapter discusses some of the valid methodological reasons that originally favored the reductionistic approach to the research in the perception of music. Furthermore, it addresses some of the difficulties that must be considered if we investigate listening to actual performances from the repertoire, and reviews some recent experiments that used recorded performances of musical works as stimuli. Finally, it argues that research in the perception of music cannot remain research in the perception of isolated musical variables couched within very brief stimuli because music is more than the sum of its parts and is experienced over a temporal continuum. The perception of actual musical compositions or excerpts ought to become a priority for the research in the psychology of music.

REFERENCES

Deutsch, D. (Ed.) (1982). *The psychology of music.* New York: Academic Press.
Dowling, J. W., & Harwood, D. (1986). *Music cognition.* New York: Academic Press.
Sloboda, J. A. (1985). *The musical mind.* Oxford: Oxford University Press.

Interested readers may ask: Does the research in the psychology of music explain how the listener perceives an actual musical composition? Which experiments describe this process, and how? Such questions are valid indeed. Musicians, musicologists, and music educators have always emphasized the value of listening and describing music (Corredor, 1956; Meyer, 1956, 1967; Copland, 1957; Sessions, 1970; Brendel, 1976; see also the first six chapters in this volume). But despite the major advances in the psychology of music in the last two decades, music psychologists have been reluctant to investigate how listeners perceive actual pieces of the repertoire. Therefore, little is known about the processes that take place while listening to a composition.

By and large, psychologists have addressed music listening theoretically. Several authors have proposed models of how a listener may listen to tonal music in general, or to certain tonal compositions specifically (Deutsch & Feroe, 1981; Lerdahl & Jackendoff, 1983; Marsden, 1987; Jackendoff, 1991). These models have been based on the hierarchical or perceptual processes that the authors theorize to be inherent in music compositions or fragments of music, and not on empirical data gathered from the listeners' experiences.

There are several reasons why researchers have not conducted in-depth investigations of listeners' perceptions of musical compositions. Let us examine some of them.

The Influence of Psychoacoustics

First, speaking from a historical perspective, research in the psychology of music developed mainly from the research in psychoacoustics. Therefore, early studies in music psychology addressed mainly the psychoacoustical attributes of isolated pitches. Although psychoacoustical studies have proven to be most valuable for our understanding of isolated sounds, they aimed to describe exclusively the parameters of single pitches or of a few pitches heard together.

The psychoacoustical influence favored the construction of brief musical stimuli that have been used in the experiments, and allowed sound variables to be clearly manipulated. But this has happened too often at the expense of the aesthetic qualities of the musical stimuli themselves. Referring to the tradition to use brief and artificial sequences as stimuli, Clarke and Krumhansl (1990) pointed out:

> There are certain obvious advantages in this very controlled kind of approach, and it has proved extremely powerful and productive for advancing our understanding of tonal and metric hierarchies. However, it has left untouched a range of issues concerned with listeners' understanding of more extended and elaborate structures in which a considerable degree of interaction between different parameters can be expected. (p. 214)

In the past, to suit experimental goals, stimuli were often designed at the expense of musical aesthetics. Deliège and El Ahmadi (1990) write:

> The usual practice, in our field, as in any scientific discipline, is to isolate the variable that one wishes to study and to incorporate it in a series of brief and repetitive sound sequences (that are called musical), constructed by the psychologist for the needs of the experiment, in order to be able to identify it afterward, in appropriate manner, in the statistical analysis of the data. . . . Unfortunately, many studies in the field of psychology of music scarcely achieve their aims because a musical objective is being sought through the use of material that is both too simple and too trivial. (p. 22)

The Influence of Psycholinguistics

The psychology of music has also been influenced by developments in psycholinguistics. As in psycholinguistic research, the emphasis in the psychology of music has been on investigating the phonetic and the grammatical levels of brief strings of words without an in-depth look at the perception of entire discourses, so research in the cognitive psychology of music has examined the perception of brief melodies or sequences of musical stimuli, and has not thoroughly investigated the perceptual processes that take place when listening to longer musical excerpts. The psychology of language emphasizes research on the perception of isolated sentences. Similarly, the psychology of music, for the most part, has looked at the perception of single musical phrases not occurring within a full musical context. Generally, the length of the experimental stimuli has ranged from a few notes to one or two phrases. This limitation does not replicate the actual musical experience.

Perhaps it was premature to expect that we could have built a house without foundations. Therefore, the reader who sincerely asks about the perception of genuine musical compositions can consider the last two decades of the research in the psychology of music as a foundation on which to build better investigations. Notwithstanding music psychology's good intentions, however, questions regarding how listeners perceive actual musical compositions still remain to be answered and it becomes much more pressing to ask them now. We must face that to do full justice to the laboratory, the psychology of music has not yet done justice to the concert hall or the cassette player.

Several researchers have already voiced concerns along these same lines (Sloboda, 1985; Deliège, 1989; Clarke & Krumhansl, 1990; Deliège & El Ahmadi, 1990; Butler, 1992; see also Nicholas Cook's chapter in this volume). But in order to research how one listens to a composition there are methodological difficulties to address. It is very difficult for the psychologist to design an experiment that investigates what may occur while listening to an actual musical composition. Performing, composing, and writing about music produce palpable results: a composition, an interpretation, an article, or a book—all evidence of what has actually happened between the individual and the music. But listening to music, *per se* does not yield such evidence, does not lay bare the intellectual and emotional responses of the listener, gives us no product to manipulate and analyze. Therefore, it is much more difficult to research music listening adequately (Sloboda, 1985: 151–54). Sloboda writes: "when I go to a symphony concert or listen to a gramophone record there may well be a lot of 'mental' activity, but there is not necessarily any observable physical activity. The principal end-product of my listening activity is a series of fleeting, largely incommunicable mental images, feelings, memories and anticipations" (p. 151). Nevertheless, can we say anything about how we perceive music? How can we research and measure what occurs when we listen to a musical piece?

When we listen to a composition, we hear an array of very complex temporal stimuli. Many musical variables occur simultaneously. It is a difficult task for the listeners themselves to listen attentively to a music performance. But unless there is control of variables, to what could we ultimately attribute the experimental results? "Musical material . . . cannot offer dimensions that are in all points controllable and systematically repeatable" (Deliège & El Ahmadi, 1990: 23). On the other hand, listening to an actual piece, *not* to artificially controlled laboratory stimuli, is what has provided us with the knowledge and the richness of our musical heritage.

I believe that when we listen, consciously or subconsciously, we *choose* what to focus on. This may be because of outstanding features of the music itself, certain features that are emphasized in the particular performance we are hearing, or because we just choose to focus on this or that element during that particular hearing. A piece of classical music is filled with more information than a listener can process in a single hearing. Music has a temporal, horizontal dimension (melody and rhythm), a vertical dimension (harmony), and a depth dimension (including combinations of dynamics, timbre, orchestration, and interpretation). Which among these dimensions does the listener choose to attend to from time to time? In designing an experiment, how can the freedom on the part of the subjects and the complexity on the part of the temporal stimulus be accounted for properly? How can they be tested and analyzed? If the psychologist asks the subjects to focus on this or that detail, already the task does not resemble listening as it occurs when we listen at our own discretion.

Given the complexity and the richness of the musical stimulus, listening implies choosing which elements to attend to. The artificial musical stimuli used in experiments limit the choices that a listener can make. For the reasons stated above, experimentally, the musical possibilities have been greatly impoverished in favor of reliable, controllable results. Clearly, many methodological difficulties must be considered in addressing listening to actual music, but shouldn't the music listening experience be at the very heart of the psychology of music?

In summary, listening to music in a laboratory condition does not duplicate listening to music outside of the laboratory. The experimental experience and the actual experience may differ in the complexity of the stimuli, their lack of aesthetic value, their brevity, and the very validity of the task. The research of the last decades has provided a valuable foundation for understanding how we perceive controlled, brief, auditory sequences. What are needed are ways to develop a more sensitive understanding of the music listening experience and the mental representation of listening. The psychology of music must strive toward these goals.

Recently, there has been a growing interest in using excerpts or entire musical compositions as stimuli (Cook, 1987; Ruggieri & Sebastiani, 1987; Smith & Witt, 1989; Asada & Ohgushi, 1991). A number of studies have focused on examining some properties of live piano performances. With the help of computerized equipment, these studies investigate the similarities between the patterns of expressive characteristics that pianists display during repeated performances of a piece (Shaffer, 1981; Clarke, 1982; Gabrielsson, 1987).

In the remainder of this chapter I will review five recent studies that investigated aspects of music listening using recorded performances from the musical repertoire, all of which are approximately the same duration. All these studies investigated how listeners listen to music *as the music unfolded*. They did not ask the subjects only to respond post facto. By the nature of the required tasks, all these studies aimed to look at the subjects' perception of music as they heard the music.

Pollard-Gott (1983) researched whether repeated listening changes a listener's perception of a piece by focusing on the perception of musical themes. She asked musically trained and musically naïve subjects to rate the similarity of pairs of brief passages from the Franz Liszt Piano Sonata in B minor. This piece is in a single movement, structured around two principal themes and three minor themes. The standard division of a sonata in exposition, development, and recapitulation are all combined into a single, closely structured movement. In this study, the subjects heard the first 12 minutes (ending on measure 328) of a recording by Vladimir Horowitz.

The piece begins with the presentation of theme A (measures 8–13), a gap-filled melody, which is immediately followed by a contrasting, staccato theme B (measures 13–17). The piece continues with three variations of theme A and theme B in the following order: theme A, theme B, first variation on a2, a3, b2, b3, a4, and b4. The experimenter selected four examples of each of the two principal themes and recorded them separately.

The subjects were asked to write observations while listening, and, after listening to the first 12 minutes of the piece, they were asked to compare pairs of passages from the sonata judging their similarity on an 11-point scale (1 extremely dissimilar, 11 extremely similar). The listeners were also asked to decide whether each passage was best described as an example of theme A or theme B. It was found that, with repeated listenings, subjects improved in rating the similarity between the themes and also became more able to apply their understanding of the piece to passages that occurred much later in the same composition. Subjects with some musical background seemed to perceive the importance of the thematic material more quickly than the musically naïve subjects.

Clarke and Krumhansl (1990) have investigated how musically experienced subjects segment music, focusing on how they identify boundaries, locate excerpts within the overall piece, and estimate their duration. The researchers used performances of two stylistically different compositions as the stimuli: Karlheinz Stockhausen's *Klavierstücke IX*, and W. A. Mozart's Fantasie in C minor, K. 475. Both pieces are for solo piano, in a single movement, and contain a variety of different musical ideas. Each piece lasts approximately 10 minutes. Stockhausen's *Klavierstücke IX*, composed in 1961, is an atonal piece organized according to the principles of 12-note serialism. It is broadly divided in three regions, with the middle region being the most developed. Rhythmically and dynamically it is highly varied, alternating sections at different tempi. Mozart's Fantasie in C minor, K. 475 is also extremely varied rhythmically. There is tonal diversity and a multiplicity of different musical ideas. It may be divided in five sections, each one marked by different tempi and meter. The piece reflects the improvisatory style suggested by its title and displays many contrasts and sharply demarcated transitions from one section to the other.

To investigate the identification of boundaries, the subjects, after hearing each piece in its entirety, were asked to indicate where segmentation occurred in the music by pressing a foot pedal immediately after hearing a boundary. In later trials, they were asked to mark in the score the location where they perceived that segmentation had occurred, and were asked to describe briefly the features of the music that helped them form the boundaries. In general, the listeners agreed on the relative strength of the boundaries in both pieces, and reported this task to be quite easy. They cited similar criteria for making their judgments of where boundaries occurred in both compositions.

To investigate how listeners located brief excerpts in relation to the entire piece, the researchers first presented the piece in its entirety to the subjects, and then followed it with the presentation of brief segments. The subjects were asked to mark on a horizontal line on a piece of paper where they thought each segment occurred in the piece considering the left of the line to represent the beginning of the piece and the right of the line to represent the end.

The segments that occurred toward the beginning and toward the end of the piece appeared to be located closer to the center of the piece than was actually the case. This finding was true for both the atonal and the tonal composition. Clarke and Krumhansl propose that these results may be due to systematic changes in attention in the course of listening to music. In subsequent experiments, the subjects were asked to estimate the approximate duration of brief excerpts, being told that on average they lasted 30 seconds. The listeners were quite accurate in judging the relative duration of the excerpts in both pieces.

Deliège and El Ahmadi (1990; see also Deliège, 1989) have addressed listening and the perception of musical form. Specifically, these researchers investigated how musical cues help the listeners perceive boundaries in a musical composition, and whether there may be perceptual differences between musically trained and musically naïve subjects. The piece chosen as the stimulus was a recorded performance by Walter Trampler of *Sequenza IV*, a composition for solo viola by the contemporary composer Luciano Berio. This work is in six main sections and is characterized by contrasting structures. It fully exploits the timbre of the viola. The experiments presented the composition to the subjects three times. The first hearing was meant for the subjects to familiarize themselves with the piece, the second and third hearings were intended for the collection of the experimental data. The playing of the piece was synchronized with a timing mechanism on a microcomputer, and the subjects were asked to indicate where they perceived segmentation by depressing a key on the computer console.

The data revealed that the listeners utilized two organizing principles in their analytical hearings of this piece: "sameness" and "difference." The principle of sameness helped them constitute groups out of what they heard, while the principle of difference helped them differentiate what they listened to. Both musicians and nonmusicians showed important similarities in their perception of the composition.

Deliège also investigated how these same subjects located excerpts within this piece (reported in Deliège, 1989). In a subsequent experiment, first she explained to them that the piece was in six main sections, and then played for them 47 brief excerpts from the piece, ranging from 5 to 10 seconds. The subjects were asked to indicate after each excerpt in which of the six main sections of the piece each excerpt occurred. Significant differences were found in the accuracy with which some excerpts were localized. In general, the results were quite uniform for all subjects, regardless of their musical training. However, nonmusicians localized excerpts that occurred in the opening and the closing sections of the work better than they localized excerpts from the middle of the piece.

I am particularly interested in understanding how musicians with extensive training perceive music. Given the complexity of music, musicians are the ones who, potentially, have at their disposal the vocabulary necessary to describe what is occurring in the music. I am also interested in the perceptual freedom that one exercises when listening to music, and in understanding the differences among listeners. How do musicians capture what is happening in the music *as* the music unfolds? Given the scarcity of literature on this topic, this is a question that is as fascinating as is it difficult.

In a recent experiment (Aiello, Tanaka, & Winborne, 1990) we began to address what information musicians select from the music as it unfolds over time. Specifically, this experiment looked at which musical elements musicians report focusing on when listening to a complex musical work if they were free to report any of the elements present in the music. Graduate music students from the Juilliard School served as subjects in this study. They were asked to name on a sheet of plain notebook paper (not music paper) which musical elements they heard as they listened to a recording of the first movement of W. A. Mozart's

Symphony in G minor, K. 550, a work well known to all of them to eliminate any potential familiarity bias. The performance was by the London Symphony Orchestra, Carlo Maria Giulini conducting.

The subjects were asked to listen to this performance twice: during the first hearing, they were asked only to listen attentively. During the second hearing, *as the music unfolded*, they were to write down what they heard using any musical term that they wished. It was emphasized that they could write down any musical element that they wanted, and that this investigation addressed only the analytical aspect of listening to music.

The data were analyzed by grouping the musical elements listed by the subjects into categories. Strong individual differences emerged: some musicians' data reflected a gestalt holistic mode of perception, while the responses of other subjects showed an analytical, more segmented approach. These latter subjects focused on smaller details of the musical work. Regardless of the quantity of elements that the subjects reported listening to, they all reported attending most often to musical elements that are very salient in this movement: tonality, rhythm, and the use of specific chords. In addition, the data indicate that the listening strategies of each subject were not related to his or her major performance instrument or training in composition.

In a series of subsequent experiments (Aiello, Palij, and Gerstman, manuscript in preparation) we addressed whether the perceptual strategies of musicians remain consistent over repeated hearings of a piece, and evaluated their responses to compositions of different musical styles. The overall procedure was the same as that of our previous experiment, except that now subjects repeated the experiment listening to the very same pieces after approximately six weeks. In addition, we evaluated the subjects' responses to compositions of different musical styles presenting Mozart, Beethoven, Chopin, and a jazz improvisation by Miles Davis.

Generally, the data indicate that the subjects seem to write down less during the second experimental session. We think that this finding may be attributable to the nature of the experimental task. Perhaps, when the subjects repeat the experiment, they may wonder what they should write during the second time that is different from what they wrote during the first experimental session. In general, these subjects seem to list more elements when listening to Mozart than when listening to the other composers.

In my experiments, as well as in the other ones that I have reviewed here, the subjects listen to "real" musical stimuli, but their responses may or may not duplicate their actual experience when listening to music in a nonexperimental situation. But I look at all these data as steps being taken toward a direction, toward a kind of research in the psychology of music that addresses the ecological validity of listening to performances of the repertoire, and considers the processes that occur while listening to music.

In summary, I believe that listening to performances from the repertoire is what shapes our sensitivity to music. Many methodological difficulties must be solved to investigate thoroughly how we perceive actual performances rather than controlled laboratory stimuli. But, unless we address these methodological difficulties we will never find potential solutions to them. Research in the psychology of music has begun to consider the importance of listening to musical performances, and there is much to discover.

REFERENCES

Aiello, R., Palij, M., & Gerstman, L. Manuscript in preparation.

Aiello, R., Tanaka, J., & Winborne, W. (1990). Listening to Mozart: Perceptual differences among musicians. *Journal of Music Theory Pedagogy*, 4(2), 269–93.

Asada, M., & Ohgushi, K. 1991. Perceptual analyses of Ravel's *Bolero*. *Music Perception*, 8(3), 241–50.

Brendel, A. (1976). *Musical thoughts and afterthoughts*. Princeton, NJ: Princeton University Press.

Butler, D. (1992). *The musician's guide to perception and cognition*. New York: Schirmer Books.

Clarke, E. F. (1982). Timing in the performance of Erik Satie's *Vexations*. *Acta Psychologica*, 50, 1–19.

Clarke, E. F., & Krumhansl, C. (1990). Perceiving musical time. *Music Perception*, 7, 213–51.

Cook, N. (1987). The perception of large-scale tonal closure. *Music Perception*, 5(2), 197–206.

Cook, N. (1990). *Music, imagination and culture*. Oxford: Oxford University Press.

Copland, A. (1957). *What to listen for in music*. New York: McGraw-Hill.

Corredor, J. M. (1956). *Conversations with Casals* (A. Mangeot, Trans.). New York: Dutton.

Deliège, I. (1989). A perceptual approach to contemporary musical forms. *Contemporary Music Review*, 4, 213–30.

Deliège, I., & El Ahmadi, A. (1990). Mechanisms of cue extraction in musical groupings: A study of perception of *Sequenza IV* for solo viola by Luciano Berio. *Psychology of Music*, 18(1), 18–44.

Deutsch, D., & Feroe, J. (1981). The internal representation of pitch sequences in tonal music. *Psychological Review*, 88, 503–22.

Gabrielsson, A. (1987). Once again: The theme from Mozart's *Piano Sonata in A major* (*K. 331*): A comparison of five performances. In A. Gabrielsson (Ed.), *Action and perception in rhythm and music* (Publication No. 55). Stockholm: Royal Swedish Academy of Music.

Jackendoff, R. (1991). Musical parsing and musical affect. *Music Perception*, 9(2), 199–230.

Lerdahl, F., & Jackendoff, R. (1983). *A generative theory of tonal music*. Cambridge, MA: MIT Press.

Marsden, A. (1987). A study of cognitive demands in listening to Mozart's Quintet for Piano and Wind Instruments, K. 452. *Psychology of Music*, 15(1), 30–57.

Meyer, L. B. (1956). *Emotion and meaning in music*. Chicago: University of Chicago Press.

Meyer, L. B. (1967). *Music, the arts, and ideas*. Chicago: University of Chicago Press.

Pollard-Gott, L. (1983). Emergence of thematic concepts in repeated listening to music. *Cognitive Psychology, 15,* 66–94.

Ruggieri, V., & Sebastiani, M. P. (1987). New approaches to musical interpretations from a psychophysiological point of view: Analysis of some instrumental interpretations. *Musik Psychologie, 4,* 65–89.

Sessions, R. (1970). *Questions about music.* New York: Norton.

Shaffer, L. H. (1981). Performances of Chopin, Bach, and Bartok: Studies in motor programming. *Cognitive Psychology, 13,* 326–76.

Sloboda, J. A. (1985). *The musical mind: The cognitive psychology of music.* Oxford: Oxford University Press.

Smith, D., & Witt, J. (1989). Spun steel and stardust: The rejection of contemporary compositions. *Music Perception, 7*(2), 169–86.

AUTHOR INDEX

283

SUBJECT INDEX

287